# MESSAGE
# FROM NAM

*Leonard Bailey*

# DANIELLE STEEL

# MESSAGE FROM NAM

Delacorte
Press

Published by
Delacorte Press
Bantam Doubleday Dell Publishing Group, Inc.
666 Fifth Avenue
New York, New York 10103

Library of Congress Cataloging in Publication Data

Steel, Danielle.
  Message from Nam / by Danielle Steel.
    p.  cm.
  ISBN 0-385-29907-9
  ISBN 0-385-30137-5 (lim. ed.)
  ISBN 0-385-30136-7 (lg. print)
  I. Title.
PS3569.T33828M4    1990
813'.54—dc20                                        89-39230
                                                        CIP

Manufactured in the United States of America

Published simultaneously in Canada

June 1990

10 9 8 7 6 5 4 3 2 1

BVG

To the love of my life,
John,
who makes every moment
worth living.

And to our beloved boys,
Trevor, Todd,
Nicholas, Maxx,
may you never, ever
have to fight a war,
like this one.

With all my heart
and love,

d.s.

*"The torch has been passed
to a new generation."*

From John Fitzgerald Kennedy's
inaugural address.

## The Boys Who Fought in Nam

Passed hand to hand,
    the wishes,
        the dreams,
the hopes
    of an entire generation,
      an entire nation
        sent to war,
    a score
      of old men
leading all our boys
    to die,
    while we watched
      in horror,
      in pain,
        in grief,
    the disbelief
that we had to lose
    so many of our boys,
    their toys
      barely left behind,
their eyes
    so young,
      so bright,
so full of hope,
    the fight
      so long,
        so sad,
    the pain
      so bad,
    the wounds
      so deep
until at last
    our young men sleep
in their maker's arms again,

their names carved
in stone,
never to come home,
never to touch our tears
again. . . .
lest we forget,
lest we grow old,
our hearts must never
be so cold,
we must not run and hide,
we must remember them,
the boys who
died . . .
let it not be in vain,
let us not forget,
the pain,
the cries,
the agonies,
the braveries,
the heroes,
and the smiles,
the time that was
so long ago,
across so many miles
in a land so bright
so green
caught in a place
just in between
hope and lies,
we must remember still,
must promise that
we always will
touch their hearts
while still
we can,
remember, friends. . . .
remember. . . .

the boys who died,
        who lived,
            who cried,
        the boys
            who fought
    in Nam.

# MESSAGE
# FROM NAM

# PART I

⌄

# United States:
## SAVANNAH...
## BERKELEY...

*November 1963–June 1968*

# CHAPTER 1

∨

It was a chill gray day in Savannah, and there was a brisk breeze blowing in from the ocean. There were leaves on the ground in Forsyth Park and a few couples were wandering hand in hand, some women were chatting and smoking a last cigarette before they went back to work. And in Savannah High School, the hallways were deserted. The bell had rung at one o'clock, and the students were all in their classrooms. There was laughter coming from one room, and silence from several others. The squeak of chalk, the looks of bored despair on the faces of sophomores ill prepared for a surprise quiz in civics. The senior class was being talked to about College Boards they were going to take the following week, just before Thanksgiving. And as they listened, far away, in Dallas, gunfire erupted. A man in a motorcade catapulted into his wife's arms, his head exploding horrifyingly behind him. No one understood what had happened yet, and as the voice in Savannah droned on about the College Boards, Paxton Andrews tried to fight the sleepy waves of warm boredom. And all of a sudden in the still room, she felt as though she couldn't keep her eyes open a moment longer.

Mercifully, at one-fifty the bell rang, all doors opened and waves of high school students poured into the halls, freed from quizzes, lectures, French literature, and the pharaohs of Egypt.

Everyone moved on to their next rooms, with an occasional stop at a locker for a change of books, a quick joke, a burst of laughter. And then suddenly, a scream. A long anguished wail, a sound that pierced the air like an arrow shot from a great distance. A thundering of footsteps, a rush toward a corner room normally used only by teachers, the television set flicked on, and hundreds of young worried faces pressing through the doorway, and people saying "No!" and shouting and calling and talking, and no one could hear what was being said on the television, as still others shouted at them to be quiet.

"Hush up, you guys! We can't hear what they're saying!"

"Is he hurt? . . . is he . . ." No one dared to say the words, and through the crowd again and again, the same words . . . "What's happening? . . . what happened? . . . President Kennedy's been shot . . . the President . . . I don't know . . . in Dallas . . . what happened? . . . President Kennedy . . . he isn't . . ." No one quite believing it at first. Everyone wanting to think it was a bad joke. "Did you hear that President Kennedy's been shot?" "Yeah . . . *then what*? What's the rest of the joke, man?" There was no rest of the joke. There was only frantic talking, and endless questions, and no answers.

There were confused images on the screen with replays of the motorcade breaking up and speeding away. Walter Cronkite was on the air, looking ashen. "The President has been seriously wounded." A murmur went through the Savannah crowd, and it seemed as though every student and teacher at Savannah High School were pressed into that one tiny room, and crowding in from the hallways.

"What'd he say? . . . what did he *say*?" a voice from the distance asked.

"He said the President is seriously wounded," a voice from the front started back to the others, and three freshmen girls started to cry, as Paxton stood somberly in a corner in the press of bodies around her, and watched them. There was suddenly

4

an eerie stillness in the room, as though no one wanted to move, as though they were afraid to disturb some delicate balance in the air, as though even the tiniest motion might change the course his life would take . . . and Paxton found herself thinking back to another day, six years before, when she was only eleven. . . . Daddy's been hurt, Pax. . . . Her brother George had told her the news. Her mother had been at the hospital with her father. He liked to fly his own plane to go to meetings around the state, and he'd had to bring it down in a sudden thunderstorm near Atlanta.

"Is he? . . . will he be okay? . . ."

"I . . ." There had been a strange catch in George's voice, a terrible truth in his eyes that she had wanted to run and hide from. She had been eleven then, and George was twenty-five. They were fourteen years apart and several lifetimes. Paxton had been an "accident," her mother still whispered to friends, an accident that Carlton Andrews had never ceased to be grateful for, and which still seemed to startle Paxton's mother. Beatrice Andrews had been twenty-seven years old when their son George was born. It had taken her five years to get pregnant with him, and as far as she was concerned, her pregnancy was a nightmare. She was sick every day for nine months, and the delivery was a horror she knew she would always remember. George was born by cesarean section, finally, after forty-two hours of hard labor, and although he was a big beautiful ten-pound baby boy, Beatrice Andrews promised herself that she would never have another baby. It was an experience she wouldn't have repeated for anything, and she saw to it with great care that she wouldn't have to. Carlton was, as always, patient with her, and he was crazy about his boy. George was the kind of boy any father would have loved. He was a happy, easygoing, reasonably athletic boy, with a serious penchant for his studies which also pleased his mother. Theirs was a quiet, happy life. Carlton had a healthy law practice, Beatrice had an important role with the Historical Society, the Junior League, and the Daughters of the Civil War. Her life was fulfilled. And she played bridge every Tuesday. It was there that she felt the first twinge, that for the first time she felt suddenly violently nauseous. She assumed she had eaten something off at the League breakfast that day, and went home to lie down right after her bridge game. And three weeks later she knew. At the age of forty-one, with a fourteen-year-old son about to enter high school, and a husband who wasn't even gracious enough to hide his delight, she was pregnant. This pregnancy was easier for her than the first, but she didn't even seem to care. She was so outraged by the indignity of it, the embarrassment of being pregnant again when other women were thinking about grand-children. She didn't want another baby, she had never wanted another child, and nothing her husband said seemed to appease her. Even the tiny, perfect, angelic-looking little blond baby girl they put in her arms when she awoke barely seemed to console her. All she could talk about for months was how foolish she felt, and she left the child constantly with the huge, purring black baby-nurse she had hired when she was pregnant. Eliza-beth McQueen was her name, but everyone called her Queenie. And she wasn't really a nurse by trade. She had borne eleven children of her own, only seven of whom lived, and she was that rarest of rare gifts of the South, the old beloved black mammy. She was filled with love for everyone, but most especially for children and babies, and she loved Paxton with a passion and a warmth that no mother could have surpassed had she given birth to her, and certainly, Beatrice Andrews didn't. She re-mained uncomfortable around the little girl, and for reasons she herself couldn't really explain, she always kept her distance. The child always seemed to have sticky hands, or she wanted to touch the delicate bottles of perfume on Beatrice's table and she invariably spilled them, and somehow mother and child always seemed to make each other nervous. It was Queenie who comforted her when she cried, whose arms she ran to when she was hurt or afraid, Queenie who never left her, even for a moment.

There were no days off in Queenie's life. There was nowhere she really wanted to go on a day off, her children had their own lives now, and she couldn't imagine what would happen to Paxxie if she wasn't there to help her. Her father was always good to her, and he loved that child so, but her mother was a different story. As Paxton grew older, the difference between them grew, and by the time she was ten, Paxton had already guessed that they had almost nothing in common. It was difficult to believe that they were even related. To her mother, her clubs were everything, her women friends, her auxiliaries, her bridge days, and benefits for the Daughters of the Civil War, her life with those women were what she lived for. She almost seemed uninterested when her husband came home, and she listened politely to what he said at the dinner table at night, but even Paxton noticed that her mother seemed almost bored by her husband. And Carlton noticed it too. Although he would never have admitted it to anyone, he felt the same chill emanating from his wife as Paxton had for years. Beatrice Andrews was dutiful, loyal, organized, well-dressed, pleasant, polite, perfectly bred, and she had never felt a single emotion for anyone in her entire lifetime. She simply didn't have it in her. Queenie knew it, too, although she expressed it differently than Carlton would have, she'd long since said of her to her daughters that Beatrice Andrews's heart was colder and smaller than peach pits in winter. The closest she ever came to loving anyone was what she felt for her son, George. They had a kind of rapport that she had never been able to allow herself with Paxton. She admired him, respected him, and he had long since affected a kind of cool, aloof, clinical way of looking at things that eventually led him into medicine, and she was impressed by that too. She liked the fact that her son was a doctor. He was even brighter than his father, she secretly told her friends, in fact, he reminded her

7

a great deal of her own father who had been on the Georgia Supreme Court, and she felt certain that one day George would do great things. But what would Paxton ever do? She would go to school and graduate, and eventually get married and have children. It hardly seemed an impressive path to Beatrice, and yet it was the one that she herself had followed. At her father's insistence, she had gone to Sweet Briar. And married Carlton two weeks after graduation. But in truth, although she enjoyed their company, and sought it out at every opportunity, she had no great respect for women. It was men who impressed her, who accomplished the great things. And there was no doubt in her mind that the pretty blond child who put her sticky little hands everywhere at every opportunity was certainly not destined for greatness.

Walter Cronkite's voice droned on, as Paxton and the others stared silently at the television screen at school. The few people who were still talking were doing so in whispers. And every few minutes, Cronkite was switching over to the reporters now standing in the lobby of Parkland Memorial Hospital in Dallas, where the President had been taken.

"We don't have any real answers for you yet," the face on the screen said, "all we know is that the President's condition is critical, but there haven't been any new bulletins in the last few minutes." With that, a teacher's hand reached out and switched the dial, just in time to hear Chet Huntley say almost exactly the same thing on another network. The students were looking at each other, with terror clearly etched on their faces. And again, Paxton could remember George coming to pick her up at school to tell her about their father. The accident, the plane coming down . . . and George's face as he told her. He had just finished medical school then, and he was waiting to start his residency at Grady Memorial Hospital in Atlanta. He had managed to stay in the South for his entire education, although their father was a Harvard graduate and had encouraged him to go north. But Beatrice felt that it was important to stay close to their roots, and support the educational institutions of the South, and she frequently said so.

It was two o'clock, and Paxton stood breathlessly in the corner of the room trying to believe that he would be all right, fighting back tears, and not sure if she was crying for their President, or her father. Her father had died the day after his plane crashed, his injuries too great, his wife and son at his side, while Paxton waited at home with Queenie. At eleven, they thought she was too young to see him at the hospital, and he had never regained consciousness anyway. She had never seen him again. He was gone, with all his warmth and his love and his broad wisdom about the world, his fascination with people and history and things far, far from Savannah. He was a southern gentleman of the old school, and yet in some secret ways he didn't fit into the mold he had been born to, and it was that that Paxton loved about him. That and everything else in fact, the way he hugged her tight when she ran to him, the way he sounded when they went for long walks and talked about things she wondered about, like the war, and Europe, and what it had been like to go to Harvard. She loved the way he sounded and the way he smelled, the spice of his after-shave would leave a fresh smell in the room after he'd walked through it . . . and the way his eyes crinkled when he smiled, and the things he said about how proud he was of her . . . she felt as though she had died when they played "Amazing Grace" at his funeral, and Queenie sat in the back row and cried so loud, Paxton could hear her from where she sat between George and her mother.

Her life had never been the same again since her father died. It was as though he had taken a piece of her with him, the piece that used to smell wild flowers with him, and go to his office to visit him when he had to work on Saturday mornings, the piece that could talk to him as though she really understood the world, and ask him all kinds of questions. She had an uncanny sense about people, and she had once said to him that she didn't think her mother really loved her. It didn't really bother Paxton anymore. It just was. And she had Queenie and her father.

"I think . . . I think she needs someone like George. . . . He doesn't make her nervous, and he talks about the things she cares about. He kind of *is* like her, don't you think, Daddy? Sometimes when I say I really *love* something, I think it scares her." She was more perceptive than she knew, and Carlton Andrews knew it too, but he never admitted it to his only daughter.

"She doesn't express her feelings the way you and I do," he said honestly, sitting back in the comfortable old leather chair that she liked to swivel in until it threatened to fall off its moorings. "But that doesn't mean she doesn't have them." He felt an obligation to protect his wife, even from Paxton, although he knew that what Paxxie said was true. Beatrice was as cold as ice. Dutiful and loyal and a "good wife" in her own eyes. She kept a nice home, was always polite and kind to him, she would never cheat on him, or be rude to him, or betray him. She was a lady to her very core, but like Paxxie he wondered if she had ever loved anyone or anything, except George, but even there she kept a cool, comfortable distance. It was just that their son was so much like her, he didn't expect more than that. But Carlton did, and so did Paxxie, and they both knew that, from Beatrice, they would never get it. "She loves you, Pax." But even as he said it, Paxton thought he was lying. She didn't totally understand the subtle shadings of just how much the woman was capable of, or wasn't. Carlton had a much clearer picture.

"I love you, Daddy." She had thrown her arms around him then, without hesitation or reserve. She never held back anything from him, and he laughed as she almost knocked him off the ancient swivel chair.

"Hey, you . . . you're goin' to have me on the floor here in a minute." He dreamed about her going to Radcliffe one day, and as he held her close to him, he could imagine her grown and beautiful, and the pride of his sunset years. She was everything he had ever dreamed of, warm and loving and giving and caring. She was everything he himself was, although he didn't know it.

And then, he was gone, and Paxton was alone with them, except for Queenie. She studied hard, and she read all the time. She wrote letters to her father, as though he were away on a trip, and she could mail the letters to him, except that she couldn't. Sometimes she put the letters away, and sometimes she just tore them up. But it helped her to write them. It was a way of still "talking" to him, since she couldn't talk to "them." Her mother seemed to jump at everything she said, she disagreed with everything Paxton said, and sometimes Paxxie almost felt as though she'd come from another planet. They were so different in every way. And George was just like her. He would urge Paxton to "behave" and try to see things her mother's way, to be "reasonable," and remember who she was, which only confused her further. Who was she? Her father's daughter, or theirs? Who was right? But in her heart of hearts, there was no confusion. She knew that his broader love of the world was the only way for her, and by the time George finished his residency at Grady Memorial, and she turned sixteen, she knew without a moment's doubt that she wanted to get out of the South and go to Radcliffe. Her mother wanted her to go to Agnes Scott or Mary Baldwin, or Sweet Briar where she had gone herself, or even Bryn Mawr, but she thought it a ridiculous idea for Paxton to go to Radcliffe.

"You don't need to go to a northern school. We have everything you need right here. Look at your brother. He had every opportunity to go anywhere in the country, and he stayed right here in Georgia." The very idea of it made Paxton feel claustrophobic. She wanted to get away from their narrow ideas, from her mother's friends, from the things she heard about the "horrors of integration." Civil rights were something she discussed with her friends, or with Queenie, sotto voce in the kitchen. But even Queenie clung to the old views and thought that black folks should stay where black folks belonged, and that ain't the same place as white folks. The thought of mixing the two frightened her, and it was only her children and her grandchildren who wanted the same changes as Paxton. But Paxton thought the things she had grown up with were wrong, and she wasn't afraid to say so, or write papers about it for school. She knew her father would have agreed with her too, he always had, and that added fuel to her fervor. It was a subject she had learned not to discuss with her mother and brother. But that fall, she had applied to half a dozen northern schools, and two in California. She had applied to Vassar, Wellesley, Radcliffe, Smith, and in the West, Stanford, and UC Berkeley. She didn't really want to go to a girls' school, and Radcliffe was the only one she really wanted. She had applied to the two western schools because her adviser thought she should, and she had finally applied halfheartedly to Sweet Briar, to appease her mother. And her mother's friends kept telling her how happy she was going to be there, as though her going to Sweet Briar was a foregone conclusion.

It was something she couldn't even think of now, as her eyes clung to the clock. It was only two o'clock, half an hour after the President had been shot, ten minutes since they had been watching the television for news of him, as the entire nation prayed, and his family knew what Paxton had learned six years before when her father died . . . that it was over.

At 2:01, Walter Cronkite looked into the camera with a defeated look and told the American people that their President was dead, and in the tiny room at Savannah High, there was a murmur of grief that became a wail, and the room was suddenly filled with the sound of sobbing. People were crying everywhere and teachers and students embraced, muttering incoherently about how could a thing like that happen. Walter Cronkite went on, two doctors were interviewed, and Paxton felt as though she were moving underwater. Everything seemed to have slowed down, and everything seemed to be happening at a great distance. People were crying everywhere, and Paxton could barely see as the tears coursed down her cheeks and she felt a breathlessness she had felt once before, as though someone had squeezed all the air out of her and she would never catch her breath again. It was a pain and a grief almost beyond bearing. And in an odd way, this was like losing him all over again. Her father had been fifty-seven years old when he died, and John Kennedy was only forty-six, and yet both had been cut down in the prime of their lives, filled with fire and ideas and excitement about living, both had families, both had children who loved them dearly. And Jack Kennedy would be mourned by an entire world, Carlton Andrews was only mourned by those who knew him. But it felt the same to Paxton now, and she could feel what his children must feel, the terrible grief, the loss, the sorrow, the anger. This was so terrible, so wrong, how could anyone do it? She walked blindly down the halls as she left the school, without saying a word to anyone, and she ran the half-dozen blocks to their home on Habersham, and the door to their house slammed as she flew into the front hall, still crying, her white-blond mane still flying behind her. She looked like her father, too, or as he had as a boy, with shining blond hair, and big green eyes that always seemed to be searching for answers. And she looked frighteningly pale now as she dropped her books and her bag, and hurried to the kitchen to find Queenie.

Queenie was humming to herself as she hustled around the kitchen she loved. The copper pots shone to perfection as they hung on the racks above her head, and there was the fragrant smell of her baking. And she turned in surprise to see Paxton standing staring at her with a wild-eyed look and her lovely young face frightened and tear-stained. At that moment, Paxton was the symbol of an entire nation.

"What happen', child?" Queenie looked frightened as she moved her enormous bulk toward the girl she had raised and loved like no other.

"I . . ." For a moment, Paxxie didn't know what to say. She couldn't find the words, didn't know what to tell her. "Haven't you watched TV today?" Queenie was addicted to the soaps, but she only shook her head and stared at Paxton.

"No, your mom took the kitchen set to be fixed yesterday. It's broke. And I never watch the big set in the living room." She looked hurt at the suggestion. "Why?" She wondered if something terrible had happened in downtown Savannah . . . maybe Dr. George . . . or Mrs. Andrews . . . or even her own children might be affected . . . maybe one of those terrible civil rights demonstrations . . . maybe . . . But she was in no way prepared for what Paxton told her.

"President Kennedy was shot."

"Oh, my land . . ." Queenie sank her enormous bulk into the nearest chair with a look of shocked horror. Her eyes moved to Paxton's then with an unspoken question.

"He's dead." Paxxie began to cry again, and then knelt next to Queenie and put her arms around her. It was like losing her father all over again. That terrible feeling of loss and despair and grief and betrayal. And Queenie held her as they both cried for a man they had never known and who had been felled so young, and for what? Why? Why had they done it? How angry could anyone be? What purpose would it serve? And why him as an example? Why a man with two small children and a young wife? Why anyone? And why someone so alive and so full of hope and promise for so many? Paxxie mourned him in Queenie's arms, and the old black woman held her and rocked her as she had as a child, as she herself cried for a man she had never known, but believed to be a good person.

"Lawd, child . . . I can't hardly believe it. Why would anyone do such a thing? Do they know who did it?"

"I don't think so." But when they went to the living room and turned on the TV, there was fresh news, a man named Lee Harvey Oswald had shot and killed a Dallas policeman who tried to question him, and had been traced to the Book Depository where the fatal shots had been fired into the motorcade at one-thirty. And he was believed to be President Kennedy's killer. Oswald had been apprehended, the policeman and the President were dead, a secret service agent too, Texas governor John Connally had been severely wounded, but was doing well, and the President's body was on its way to Washington on Air Force One, with his wife beside him. President and Mrs. Johnson were on board, too, and there had been earlier reports that he had been wounded slightly, which were later proven to be only rumors. An entire nation was in shock, and Paxton and Queenie stood there mutely, still unable to believe what they were hearing and seeing. They were still standing there, watching silently, tears streaming down their faces, when Paxton's mother walked in a few minutes later. She went to the hairdresser every Friday afternoon and was just returning from her weekly appointment. She had heard the news there, and she looked grim as she silently joined them. Several of the women had gone home with wet hair, and most of the hairdressers didn't have the heart to finish what they had started. Everyone was in tears, and Beatrice Andrews had been having her hair rinsed when they first heard the news. But she had stayed to have everything done, and even convinced one of the girls to finish her manicure. She hated to let it all go for a few more days. She had a lot to do that weekend before Thanksgiving, and her bridge club was giving a dinner. It never dawned on her that no one would be giving anything. Every festivity imaginable would be canceled, as people sat glued to their TVs and an entire nation went into mourning. But that hadn't occurred to her, and she had come home, feeling subdued, but not hysterical by any means. She thought some of the women got a little too carried away. She knew what real grief was, she had lost her own husband, after all, hadn't she, and it was impossible to feel the same emotion for a public figure. And yet people did feel that for him, that intense kind of personal grieving as though they had known and loved him. He had brought new hope to everyone, the promise of youth brought to ancient tasks, the magic of a world they would never know and could only dream of. And his beautiful wife reminded everyone of a fairy princess.

Beatrice Andrews stood solemnly beside her daughter and the woman who had raised her, and then sat down to watch Lyndon Johnson take the oath of office on Air Force One, but she did not invite Queenie to join her. The cameras showed Judge Sarah Hughes administering the oath to Lyndon Johnson, as Jacqueline Kennedy stood beside him, and everyone watching suddenly realized that she was wearing the same pink suit, the suit she had worn when he was killed, the suit that was still covered with his blood. And her face showed the ravages of grief, as Lyndon Johnson became President, and Paxton sank slowly into a chair beside her mother. The tears were pouring down her cheeks, and she stared at the screen in disbelief, unable to absorb what had happened.

"How could anyone do such a thing?" She sobbed as Queenie shook her head, and still crying herself, went back to the kitchen.

"I don't know, Paxton. They're talking about a conspiracy. But I don't think anyone knows yet why it happened. I feel sorry for Mrs. Kennedy and the children. What a terrible thing for them."

It made Paxton think again about her father. Although he hadn't been assassinated, he had died unexpectedly, and his absence still hurt her. Maybe it always would. And surely the President's children would always feel his absence too. Why did it have to happen?

"These are times of terrible turmoil," her mother went on, "all the racial disturbances . . . the changes he tried to make . . . perhaps this is the price he paid for it in the end. . . ." Beatrice Andrews looked prim as she turned off the TV, and Paxton stared at her, wondering if she would ever understand her.

"You think this is because of civil rights? You think that's why it happened?" Paxton sounded suddenly angry. Why did she think that way? Why did she want to keep everything back in the Dark Ages? Why did they have to live in the South? Why had she been born in Savannah?

"I'm not saying that's why it happened, Paxton. I'm saying it's possible. You can't turn an entire country around, and change traditions that people have felt comfortable with for hundreds of years and not pay a price for it. Perhaps this was the price to be paid. A terrible one, to be sure."

Paxton stared at her in disbelief. But the argument between them was not a new one. "Mother, how can you say people are 'comfortable with' segregation? How can you say that? Do you think the slaves were 'comfortable' too?"

"Some of them were. Some of them had much better lives than they do now, when they belonged to responsible people."

"Oh, my God." But she believed it. And Paxton knew it. "Look what happens to the blacks today. They can't read, they can't write, they work like dogs, they're abused, separated, seg-regated, they don't have any of the privileges that you and I do, Mama." It was rare that she called her mother that, only when she was desperate or very involved, or upset as she was now, but Beatrice Andrews seemed not to notice.

"Maybe they wouldn't be able to handle those privileges, Paxton. I don't know. I'm just saying you can't change the world overnight and not have some terrible repercussions. And that is just what has happened."

Paxton didn't say another word. She went to her room and lay on her bed and cried until dinnertime, when her brother arrived, and she emerged pale-faced and swollen-eyed for their regular Friday night dinner. He came for dinner every Tuesday and Friday night, unless his work interfered or he had an important social engagement, which seemed to be very seldom. And like his mother, he was at opposite poles from his much younger sister. But he only smiled when she expressed her views, or pooh-poohed what she said and told her she'd feel differently when she was older. It was why she seldom expressed her views to either of them, and she lived in relative silence and kept a respectful distance. She had nothing to say to them, and trying to have philosophical or political discussions with them only drove her crazy. She saved her views for her friends at school, or her more liberal teachers, or the essays she wrote, and when she thought Queenie would understand it, she talked to her, and the old woman had a wisdom that belied her very sketchy education. But she was wise in the ways of the world, and often a good person for Paxton to talk to. Paxton had even talked to her about the colleges she had applied to, and what she thought of them. And Paxton was adamant when she explained to her that she didn't want to stay in the South, and Queenie understood that. It made her sad to think of Paxie going away, but she knew it would do her good. She was too much like her father not to.

"I think it's a Cuban conspiracy," George stated over dinner that night. "I think they're going to find there's a lot more to it than meets the eye, once they start digging below the surface." Paxton looked at him and wondered if there was any truth in that. He was an intelligent man, even if he wasn't an exciting person. Most of the time he was totally involved in his medicine, and nothing really interested him except that. He had extremely insular views, and the only time he ever got really excited was over some new research development in the fields which interested him, particularly adult onset diabetes, none of which seemed overly fascinating to Paxton. He was thirty-one years old, and he had almost gotten engaged the year before, but it had fallen through, and for some reason she had a feeling her mother was relieved, although the girl was from a family her mother knew, but Beatrice had said more than once that she thought George was too young to get married. He had to establish himself first before he got bogged down with a wife and children.

And Paxton never liked the girls he went out with anyway. They were always nice-looking, but silly and superficial. There was no substance to them, and you couldn't have a serious conversation with them. The last one he'd brought home to a dinner party their mother gave had been twenty-two years old and she had giggled all evening. She had explained that she hadn't gone to college because she had such terrible grades, but she loved doing work for the Junior League and she was going to be in their fashion show that week and she could hardly wait, and by the end of the evening, Paxton was ready to strangle her. She was so stupid and so irritating, she couldn't imagine how her brother could bear her, except that she seemed very coy and clingy when they left, and she was still giggling when they got into his car to go out for a nightcap. And Paxton had long since become resigned to the fact that she would probably hate the girl that George eventually married. She would be sweet, simple, undemanding, unthinking, unchallenging, and extremely southern. Paxton was southern, too, but in Paxton's case it referred to geography, not an excuse or an affliction. There still seemed to be so many girls who wanted to play "southern belle," and use it as an excuse for being uninformed, or just plain stupid. Paxton hated girls like that, but it was more than obvious that her brother didn't.

19

Paxton couldn't sleep all that night, and she was obsessed by the TV. She kept coming back to it, and finally at about three in the morning, she just sat there. She saw the casket carried into the White House at 4:34 A.M., with Mrs. Kennedy walking beside it. And for the next three days, Paxton felt as though she never left her television set at all. On Saturday, she watched members of the family and senior members of the government come to see the man they'd loved. And on Sunday she watched the coffin taken to the Capitol by horse-drawn caisson. She watched Jacqueline Kennedy and her daughter Caroline kneel beside the casket, and the little girl slipped her hand under the flag that draped it, their faces filled with grief. And then Paxton saw Lee Oswald shot by Jack Ruby as they transferred him to a different jail, as she watched in amazement, at first thinking it was a mistake, or some confusion. It seemed impossible that yet another person had been killed in this endless horror.

On Monday, she watched the funeral, and cried uncontrollably as she listened to the mournful sound of the endless drumbeat. And when she saw the riderless horse again, for some reason, she was reminded of her father. The grief seemed interminable, the pain one that would last forever, the sorrow bottomless, and even her mother looked shaken by Monday night, and she and Paxton barely spoke as they ate their dinner. Queenie was still wiping her eyes afterward when Paxton went out to the kitchen to talk to her, and she sat in a chair, mindlessly watching her clean up, and then helped her dry the dishes. Her mother had gone upstairs to call a friend. As always, they seemed to have nothing to say to each other, to offer each other encouragement or solace. They were too far apart, and always had been.

"I don't know why . . . but I keep feeling the same way I did when Daddy died . . . as though I'm expecting something different to happen. Like he's going to come home any minute and tell me it's not true, it's all a big joke . . . or Walter Cronkite is going to come on the news and say it was all a test, the President is really spending the weekend in Palm Beach with Jackie and the children, and they're really sorry they upset us . . . but it doesn't happen like that. It just keeps on . . . and it's real . . . it's a weird feeling."

Queenie nodded her old gray head so full of wisdom. She knew, as she always did, just what Paxton was feeling. "I know, child. It's like that when someone dies. You sit and wait for someone to tell you it didn't happen. I felt like that when I lost my babies. It takes a long time for that to go away." It was hard to think of Thanksgiving now. Hard to be thankful for a confused, angry world that stole people away before they were meant to leave it. It was hard to think of the holidays, and if Paxton felt that way now, she could imagine how the Kennedys felt. It must have been the worst possible nightmare for Jacqueline Kennedy and her children. She had done a beautiful job with the funeral, orchestrated everything to perfection, right down to the mass cards printed on White House stationery. She had handwritten herself the words "Dear God, please take care of your servant John Fitzgerald Kennedy" and had excerpts from his inaugural address printed as well. It was the end of an era . . . the end of a moment in time . . . of a time that had almost come . . . ephemeral, fleeting, gone. The torch had indeed been passed to a new generation who held it fast now, but were no longer sure where to take it.

And as Queenie turned off the lights in the kitchen that night, and kissed Paxton good night, they stood there for a moment in the dark, the old and the new, the white and the black, the sadness of everyone's loss enveloping them, and then Queenie went downstairs to her room, and Paxton went upstairs to hers, to think of what had been lost, and what lay ahead now. She felt as though she owed something to him, so he wouldn't have died in vain. Just as she owed something to her father . . . and to herself. She had to be someone for them . . . do something important with her life . . . something that mattered. But what? That was the question.

She lay in bed and thought about both of them, about what they had stood for, and what they had believed, the one man she had loved so much and known so well, the other she could only guess at. And suddenly, all she wanted was to start her life . . . to get on with it . . . and get going . . . all she could think of now was her dream of going to Harvard, just as they had. She lay in bed and closed her eyes, and silently promised both of them to make something of herself, to be someone they would be proud of. It was her gift to them, the legacy they had left her, and a promise she knew she would keep. All she had to do now was wait for the spring . . . and pray that she would be accepted at Radcliffe.

# CHAPTER 2

∨

The last envelopes arrived in the second week of April. Sweet Briar had sent its acceptance in March. And Vassar, Wellesley, and Smith all sent their acceptances in the first few days of April. None of which interested Paxton. She placed the letters neatly on her desk, and continued to wait for the one that really mattered. Radcliffe. And in her mind, the two California schools were backups. She was praying she would get in to her first choice, and in truth, the prospect of not getting in didn't seem very likely. Her father had gone to Harvard after all, and she had strong grades. Not perfect grades, but very good ones. The only thing that worried her was that she was not great in sports, and had never developed a lot of outside interests. She loved to write poetry and short stories, enjoyed the photography classes she took, had taken ballet as a child, and joined the drama club freshman year, but then dropped out because she thought it interfered with her studies. And she had heard more than once that Harvard wanted people who were good at everything, and had strong extracurricular interests. But still she was pretty sure she'd be accepted.

Her mother had been smug and pleased when the early acceptance to Sweet Briar came, and as far as she was concerned, Paxton had heard from the only school that mattered. It pleased her to be able to say that Paxxie had been accepted at the other Ivy League schools, but like Paxton, she was unenthused about them. And as far as Beatrice Andrews was concerned, the schools in California might as well have been on another planet. She urged Paxton to make the most "sensible" move, and accept Sweet Briar before even waiting to hear from any of the others.

"I can't do that, Mother," Paxton said quietly, her big green eyes searching the face that always seemed more like a stranger's. "I made myself a promise a long time ago." But it was more than just a promise to herself, it was something she felt she owed her Daddy.

"You'd never be happy in Boston, Paxton. The weather is appalling. And it's an enormous school. You'd be much better off closer to home, in familiar surroundings. You can always take some graduate classes at Harvard later."

"Why don't we just wait and see if I get in, that makes more sense." But what made sense to her made very little sense to her mother. It annoyed her no end that Paxton was holding out so stubbornly for a northern school when she could have gone to Sweet Briar and stayed so much closer to home. George turned up one Saturday afternoon to vent his views and Paxton smiled to herself while she listened to him. Talking to George was just like talking to her mother. They both believed that her life was destined to be close to them, and that it was foolish of her to try to spread her wings and expand her horizons.

"What about Daddy, George? He seemed to have come out okay, in spite of venturing up north to go to school with the Yankees." She was teasing him, which amused her if not him. Among his many other virtues, her brother George had not been blessed with their father's sense of humor.

"That's not the same thing, Pax. And you know I'm not fixated about the South. I just think that for a woman, Sweet

Briar is a better choice. Mother's right. And there's no reason for you to go all the way to Boston."

"With that kind of attitude, they might not even have discovered America, George. Imagine if Queen Isabella had told Columbus that there was no reason for him to go all the way to the New World. . . ." She was laughing at him and he was not amused by it.

"Mother's right. You're still a child, and it's ridiculous to do this just to prove a point. You're not a man, and there's no reason on earth for you to go to Harvard. You're not pursuing any career like medicine or law, there's just no reason for you to go anywhere. You should be close to home with us. What if Mama gets sick? She's not as young as she used to be, and she needs us here." He tried everything on her, including guilt, and it served only to enrage his sister. She couldn't understand why they wanted to clip her wings. But they seemed to feel they owned her.

"She is fifty-eight years old, not ninety-three, George! And I'm not going to sit here for the rest of my life, waiting to take care of her. And how the hell do you know what career goals I want to pursue? For all you know, I want to be a brain surgeon. Does that make it okay for me to go north to school, or do I have to stay here and bake cookies no matter what, just because I'm a woman?"

"That's not what we're suggesting." He looked pained by her bluntness.

"I know that." She tried to regain her cool. "And Sweet Briar is a wonderful school. But all my life I've dreamed of going to Radcliffe."

"And if you don't get in?" He looked at her pointedly.

"I will. I have to." She had promised her father's memory. She had promised him before that. She had sworn she would make him proud of her and follow in his footsteps.

25

"And if you don't get in?" her brother persisted cold-bloodedly. "Then will you agree to stay in the South?"

"Maybe . . . I don't know. . . ." The three Ivy League schools didn't appeal to her either, and she hadn't given any serious thought to Stanford or Berkeley. She couldn't begin to imagine going there, and she didn't know anyone in California. "I'll see."

"I think you'd better give it some serious thought, Paxton. And you'd better think twice about upsetting Mama." Why did he have to do this to her? It wasn't fair. Why did she have to sacrifice her life for them? What did they want from her, and why did they want her there in Savannah? It seemed so pointless. Just so she could go to luncheons and meetings of the Daughters of the Civil War with her mother, and eventually join a bridge club, so Beatrice wouldn't be "disgraced," so Paxton stayed within the mold. But she didn't want the mold. She wanted something more. She wanted to go to the School of Journalism at Radcliffe.

She had often told Queenie as much, and Queenie was the only one who encouraged her, who loved her enough to be willing to release her. She knew what Paxton needed, and she wanted to see her fly free of the two people who seemed to expect so much from her and had always given her so little. She had a right to more than that in her life, and her mind was so bright, so full of new ideas, she deserved something more than the life she would have if she stayed in Savannah. And if after she went away to school, she wanted to come back, then Queenie would be there to welcome her with open arms. But she wasn't going to beg her to stay, or nag her like the others.

The envelope arrived on a Tuesday afternoon, and it was sitting in the mailbox when she got home, along with one from Stanford. And Paxton held her breath the moment she saw them. It was a warm spring afternoon, and she had strolled slowly home, thinking of the boy who had asked her to the spring prom just that afternoon. He was tall and dark and hand-some, and she had admired him for the past year, but he had been going with someone else. And now suddenly he was free, and Paxton's head was full of dreams and wishes. She was going to tell Queenie all about him eventually, and now suddenly, there was the letter she'd been expecting. Her whole future on a sheet of clean white paper, folded and sealed into an envelope from Harvard. Dear Miss Andrews, we are pleased to inform you that you have been accepted to . . . Dear Miss Andrews, we are sorry to inform you that . . . which one was it?

Her hands shook as she took the envelopes out, trying to decide which one to open first, as she sat down on their front steps in front of the solid-looking brick house, and decided to open the one from Radcliffe first, because in truth it was the only one that mattered and she couldn't bear the suspense of waiting till she had opened the other. She flung her long blond mane over her shoulders and down her back, closed her eyes and leaned against the intricate wrought-iron railings, praying for her father's blessing on their answer . . . please . . . please . . . oh, please let me have gotten in . . . She opened her eyes and, as quickly as she could, ripped open the letter. And the opening line was not at all what she had expected. It gave nothing away at all, and droned on endlessly about what a fine institution Harvard was, and what a fine applicant she was, and it was only in the second paragraph that they said what she'd been looking for, and she could almost feel her heart stop as she read it.

"Although you have all the qualifications to make an excel-lent candidate for Radcliffe, we feel that . . . at this time . . . perhaps another institution . . . we regret . . . we are sure that you will do extremely well at any academic institution you choose . . . we wish you well. . . ." Tears filled her eyes and the words danced in a blur of grief as they cut through her heart. She had failed him. They had turned her down. All her dreams dashed in a single instant. Radcliffe had denied her. And what would she do now? Where would she go? Did she really have to stay in the South, with all its narrow thinking, familiar themes, and proximity to her mother and brother? Was that it? Had it come to that, then? Or would she go to Vassar? Smith? Wellesley? Somehow they seemed so boring.

Hesitantly, she tore open the second envelope, feeling nervous now. Maybe it was time to give some serious thought to Stanford. But not for long. They said it in the first paragraph instead of the second, and their answer was almost identical to Radcliffe's. They wished her well, but felt she would do better at another institution. Which left . . . nothing. The choices she already knew she had, and an unknown quantity at Berkeley. She could feel her spirits plummet as she stood, walked up the steps, and let herself into the house. She dreaded having to tell her mother.

She told Queenie first, of course, and the old woman was grief-stricken for her at first, and then, finally, philosophical.

"If they didn't accept you, then it wasn't meant to be. One day you'll look back at that, and know it." But in the meantime, the prospects it left her with were depressing. She didn't want to stay in the South, didn't want to go to a girls' school, and she couldn't even imagine going to Berkeley. Now what? But Queenie's thinking was more advanced than Paxton's. "What about California? It's a long way from here, but you might like it." One of her daughters had moved to Oakland several years before, and although she'd never been there, she had always heard that San Francisco was lovely. "I hear it's beautiful. You won't be cold like you will up north." She smiled gently at the child she had loved and comforted since she was born, and it hurt her now to see her so bitterly disappointed. "Your Mama would kill me if she could hear me suggesting it to you, but I think you ought to be thinkin' about California." Paxton grinned. Her mother would kill both of them if she could hear half of their conversations.

"It seems so far away . . . so . . . I don't know . . . so foreign. . . ."

"California?" Queenie grinned. "Don't be silly, it's only a few hours away by plane, leastways that's what my Rosie keeps tellin' me. So you think about that too. And you pray about it tonight. Maybe that school in Berkeley gonna be your solution."

But that night at dinner with her mother and George, they continued to believe that her solution lay a great deal closer to home, and as far as they were concerned, the answer from Radcliffe settled the question. They weren't even disappointed for her, they were relieved. And like Queenie, they said it was meant to be. But unlike the old black woman who had cared for her, they seemed almost pleased to see her dreams ended. And through it all, Paxton felt as though somehow she had disappointed her father, as though she had let him down, because she had been turned down by his alma mater. She wanted to say that to someone, to admit how terrible she felt, but for once she didn't think Queenie would understand, and it was obvious that her mother and brother wouldn't either. And her own friends were wrapped up in their own miseries and joys. Everyone was totally obsessed with the schools they were hearing from, and whether they were getting turned down or accepted.

The boy who'd invited her to the prom called that night, and she tried to share some of her feelings with him but all he could talk about was having just been accepted by Chapel Hill, and he seemed not even to hear her. It seemed to be a time for solitary grief or celebration. And that night when she went to bed, she lay there thinking of what Queenie had said that afternoon, and wondering if the idea was totally mad, or if it was worth thinking about. More importantly, if they'd even accept her. But by the end of the week, her mother and George had worn her down, and she agreed to enroll at Sweet Briar the following week, with a silent promise to herself to re-apply to Radcliffe the following year and keep on trying until she got in, no matter how hard she had to work to get in, or what it took to convince them. She felt a little better having established that plan, and knew it would be more bearable staying close to home as long as she knew it wasn't forever.

And then on Monday, the answer came from Berkeley. They were delighted to inform her that she'd been accepted. And although she wasn't even sure why, her heart skipped a beat, and suddenly she was excited. She hurried into the kitchen to show Queenie the letter they'd sent. The old woman beamed at her, as though it was the answer to everything, and she had known all along it would come.

"See that? That's yo' answer."

"What makes you so sure?" How could she know? How could she be certain? But the other options certainly didn't appeal to her.

"How do it make you feel?"

"Good. Actually. Kind of excited and scared . . . but happy."

"And the other schools you been talkin' about? How do they make you feel?"

"Depressed . . . bored . . . pretty awful."

"That don' sound like a happy solution to me. I'd say this be a better solution. But you think on it, honey. You pray. You listen to the lord, and listen to yo' stomach. Always listen to yo' gut . . . always listen to what you feel inside. *You know.* We all do. We know it right here." She pointed to her big belly with a serious air. "When you feel good, it's the right answer for sure, but you feel kinda sick, kinda squirmy, kinda miserable, then you done make a *big* mistake, or if you didn't yet, you going to!" Paxton laughed at the simple wisdom, but she knew Queenie was right, as usual. She always was. The old woman knew. She was a lot smarter than Paxton's mother, or George, or even Paxton.

"The crazy thing is I think you're right, Queenie." She sat down in a kitchen chair, nibbling on a carrot stick and looking pensive. She was young and beautiful, and there was something very peaceful about her face. She was someone who was at one with herself, and had been for a long time. She was quiet and strong, and whole, which was rare for a girl her age, but since her father's death almost seven years before, she had done a lot of thinking. "What am I going to say to them?"

"The truth, when you know what that truth is. And don't do something 'cause I tell you to. You too smart for that, girl. You do what *you* want to do, and what you know is right, when you know it. Think about it first. You'll know when it's right." She pointed to her stomach again and Paxxie laughed and stood up. She was tall and lean and lanky, like her father had been, and oddly graceful. She was taller than many of her friends, but she had never really minded. And much to Queenie's surprise, she had no particular interest in her looks. She was beautiful, but it was almost as though she didn't know or care. She was interested in other things, matters of the heart, the head, the soul. She was too much like her father to be aware of her looks, and her indifference to her blond good looks frequently irritated her mother. She wanted her to model in Junior League fashion shows, and events for the Daughters of the Civil War and Paxton wanted none of it. She was quiet and shy, and amused by all the pressure and politics that went with those events, but she had no interest in them whatsoever. She liked talking about serious things with the teachers at her school, the recent developments in Viet Nam, the ramifications of Kennedy's death, Johnson's stand on civil rights, Martin Luther King and his marches and sit-ins. She had a passion about the important events going on around the world, and their links and ties and

31

effect on each other. It was what she liked to write about, and think about, and be involved with.

And later that week, she sought out one of her favorite teachers and asked him what he thought about UC Berkeley.

"I think it's one of the best schools in the country. Why?" He looked directly at her and she hesitated, but only for a moment.

"I'm trying to decide if I should go there."

"The news from Radcliffe wasn't what you hoped?" He knew how badly she had wanted to go there, how much she had counted on it, and why, and he was prepared to be disappointed for her if she hadn't been accepted.

"They turned me down. Stanford too. Everyone else accepted." She told him what the other choices were and without hesitation he advised her to go to Berkeley. He was from the North himself and he strongly believed in diversifying one's experience. He thought kids from the West should go east, eastern kids should go out West for a year or two, and kids from the South should head north, to see something different.

"I wouldn't hesitate for a minute, Pax. Grab the chance while you can, and don't give Radcliffe another thought. You can always go there for graduate school. To hell with it for now, go west." He smiled at her. "You're gonna love it." And as she listened to him, she could feel her whole body fill with excitement. Maybe Queenie had been right after all. Maybe this was the answer.

She didn't say anything to her mother for several days, and at the end of the week, she sent her acceptance off, and on Friday night when she had dinner with them, she told them.

"I sent my acceptance off today," she said quietly, waiting for the storm she knew would come.

"Good girl." Her brother was quick to offer praise. She had done as they had told her to, finally. She wasn't as difficult as their mother said after all. "Are you proud of yourself, Pax?

You should be." She smiled at the lavish praise, knowing what was coming.

"Yes, I am, as a matter of fact. I thought about it a lot, and I think I made the right decision. I know I did, in fact."

Her mother looked at her cautiously, afraid to say too much. "I'm glad things worked out this way, Paxton," she said sparingly.

"So am I," Paxton answered.

"A lot of nice girls go to Sweet Briar, Paxton. It is a wonderful school," her brother said happily as Paxton looked quietly at both of them.

"Yes, it is," she agreed, "but I'm not going there." For a moment, everything stopped in the dining room. This was not what anyone had expected. "I'm going to the University of California at Berkeley."

For an instant, they were both stunned into silence and then her brother sat back in his chair and threw his napkin on the table. "Now what made you do a damn fool thing like that?" Queenie left the room with a smile, to replenish the platter of roast beef.

"I spoke to my senior adviser about it, and a couple of my teachers. They think it's an excellent school and a good choice for me, since I didn't get into Radcliffe."

"But California?" her mother said despairingly. "Why in God's name would anyone go there? Why would you want to go all the way out there?" But they all knew why, whether or not they wanted to admit it. Paxton wanted to get away from them. She had been unhappy at home since her father had died, and they had done very little to change that. Her mother and brother had pursued their own lives, with only occasional attempts to force her to join them, whether she enjoyed what they were doing or not. She was expected to "fit" into their lifestyle, whether it suited her or not. To them, that just wasn't important. And now she wanted her own life, she wanted to follow her own destiny. And for the moment that path was leading her to California.

"This is something I feel I have to do," she said quietly, the piercing green eyes looking deep into her mother's. She wasn't arguing with her, but she was absolutely definite about what she was doing. And her father had given her that luxury. He had left a small trust in her name, to pay for her education, which meant that her mother couldn't threaten not to pay for college if she didn't go where she was told to. She had the freedom of choice, and she had exercised that freedom when she accepted Berkeley.

"Your father would be very disappointed in you," her mother said coldly, which was a low blow, and Paxton felt it.

"I tried to get into Harvard, Mother," she said as calmly as she could. "I just didn't make it. I think maybe he'd understand that." She remembered his stories of trying to get into Princeton and Yale and being turned down, and having to "settle" for Harvard. So she had "settled" for UC Berkeley.

"I mean I think he'd be disappointed by your leaving home so abruptly, and going so far away from us."

"I'll be back," she said softly, but even as she said the words, she wondered if she really meant them. Would she be back? Would she want to? Would she be dying to come home once she got away, or would she fall in love with California and want to stay forever? In some ways, she was desperately anxious to leave, in others she was sorry to go. She was sad to leave her friends, and in some ways, she was relieved to be leaving home. She had always felt she didn't quite fit there. She never really did what her mother wanted. But she couldn't do what they wanted her to do. It was too much to ask. She couldn't stay in the South, couldn't stay with them, couldn't go on pretending to have something in common with them, when she didn't. She couldn't pretend to be one of them anymore. And suddenly she was ready to admit how different she was, and to start her own life, in Berkeley.

"And just how often do you think you'll come home?" her mother asked accusingly as Queenie watched from over her shoulder.

"I'll come home for Christmas, I guess, and in the summer, of course." It was all she had to offer them, all she could give, and all she wanted from them was her freedom. "I'll come home as often as I can." She smiled tentatively at them, wanting them to be happy for her, but they weren't. "And you can come visit me, if you like, in California."

"Your father and I went to Los Angeles once," her mother said with a look of stern disapproval. "It's an awful place. I'd never go back there."

"Berkeley is just outside San Francisco." But she might as well have said "just outside hell" from the look on her mother's face, and for the rest of the meal, they ate in silence.

# CHAPTER 3

Paxton stood in the cozy kitchen the morning she left, looking around her as though she were being forced to leave home, with tears bulging in her eyes, and her head resting on Queenie's soft, comfortable shoulder.

"How am I going to live without seeing you every day?" she whispered, feeling like a child again. Suddenly she had the same feeling of sadness and loss she had had when she'd lost her father. She knew she wouldn't be seeing her anymore, and although Queenie would still be there, she couldn't just reach out and touch her.

"You'll be fine," Queenie said, bravely fighting back her own tears. She was determined not to let Paxxie see what she was feeling. "You be a good girl in California now. Remember to eat yo' greens, get lots of sleep, and once a week rinse that pretty hair of yours with lemon." She had been doing that for her almost since she was a baby, and took full credit for the fact that Paxton was still as blond as she was eighteen years later. "Wear a hat in the sun, don't get burned . . ." There were a thousand things she wanted to say, but all she really wanted to tell her was how much she loved her. She pressed Paxton close to her then, and the warmth of heart and her body said it all, as Paxton hugged her back just as fiercely.

"I love you so much, Queenie . . . take care . . . promise me you'll take care of yourself. And if you get a bad cough this winter"—as she did every year—"this time you go to a doctor."

"Don't you worry about me, chile. I'm going to be just fine. You behave yourself out there in . . . California . . ." She hardly dared to say the word, and yet it was Queenie who had encouraged her to go, who had helped her to take her freedom. They pulled away from each other then, and Queenie's eyes were damp, but down Paxton's creamy face, there were two streams of tears, and her eyes looked greener than ever.

"I'm going to miss you so much."

"So am I." Queenie dabbed at her eyes with her apron as she smiled, and then patted the pretty young girl's shoulder. She had loved her as her own as a little child, and she loved her even more now as a young woman. They were bonded to each other for life, and no distance, no time, no place, could pull them apart now, and they both knew it. Paxxie squeezed her hand for a last time, kissed her soft black cheek, and then left the kitchen to go back to the others.

"I'll call you," she whispered as she left, and Queenie winked at her, and then after she was gone, she went downstairs to her room and sobbed into her apron. It broke her heart to see Paxton go, but she knew better than anyone that Paxton had to move on now. Her life hadn't been the same since her father's death, and she knew that they didn't mean to be unkind to her, they were just so different. She was full of fire and life and excitement about everything. And there was a warmth and love in her that she was aching to share with the people around her. But the love she had to give frightened her mother, and George had no idea what to do with it. George and his mother were two of a kind, and Paxton was too much like her father. Queenie felt as though she'd been caring for a rare tropical bird for eighteen years, keeping it warm and safe and alive and feeding it from her very soul, and now she'd set it free, to go to a more hospita-

37

ble climate. Paxton didn't belong there anymore, she hadn't for a long time, and young as she was to leave home at eighteen, Queenie knew she'd be better off without them. There was a whole new world waiting for her out there, and in some ways Queenie could hardly wait for her to find it. But deep in her own heart, she felt the pain of losing her, of not being able to stand right next to her anymore, or look into her eyes in the afternoon, or kiss the silky hair on the top of her head when she sat down to breakfast every morning. But it was a sacrifice she was willing to make because she loved her. And she ran to the windows as she heard them leave, just in time to wave at Paxton, hanging, blond mane and all, as far as she could out the car window.

Her mother was looking very solemn as they drove out of town, and George said not a word as they headed toward the airport.

"It's not too late to change your mind," her mother said quietly, which may have been her own way of saying she would miss her.

"I don't think I can," Paxton said just as quietly, still thinking of Queenie's face before she left, and the warmth of her shoulders, the safety of her arms when she hugged her.

"I'm sure the dean at Sweet Briar would be happy to arrange it," her mother said frigidly. She still took it as a personal affront that Paxton was leaving the South. It had been insult enough that she wanted to leave Savannah.

"Maybe if things don't work out in California," Paxton said politely, and started to reach out to touch her mother's hand, and then thought better of it and pulled her hand back. Her mother made no effort to move closer to her, and there was no further conversation on the way to the airport. Paxton knew she was supposed to be consumed with guilt, and she felt sad to leave, but she was also very excited. Lately, she had been hearing a lot of interesting things about UC, and she could hardly wait to see California.

She had sent a trunk and two duffel bags ahead, and her brother took her single valise out of the trunk and handed it to a skycap. He then handed Paxton the baggage check, and ushered the two women inside to find the right gate, and wait for Paxton's plane to Oakland.

"I suppose the weather will be pleasant there," her mother said in a strained voice, and Paxton nodded. She looked at her mother then, and tears filled her eyes. It had been a very emotional morning. Even leaving her room at home had brought tears to her eyes, and she had spent a few minutes in her father's old den at six o'clock that morning. She had sat across from his desk, still seeing him there, and told him what had happened in a low, audible whisper.

"I didn't get into Harvard, Dad . . ." It was a confession she somehow imagined he already knew. ". . . But I'm going to Berkeley." And she hoped he'd be pleased. She was sad to leave home in a way, sad to leave the people and places that were familiar. But she also knew that, unlike the others, she took her father with her everywhere. He was a part of her now, just as he was a part of the morning sky, and the sunsets she loved to watch when she borrowed the car and drove to the ocean. He was part of everything she did, and was. She would never lose him.

"Mom." She cleared her throat as they waited for the plane. "I'm sorry . . . about Sweet Briar, I mean. . . . I'm sorry if I hurt you." The directness of her words took her mother aback for a moment and it was obvious that she didn't know what to answer. She almost stepped back and recoiled from her daughter, but what she was really recoiling from was the sincerity of the emotion, the intimacy that had always threatened her, and which was so much a part of Paxton. "I'm sorry . . . I just wanted to tell you that before I left." She had learned something early in life, that you didn't leave things unsaid with people you cared about, because you never knew if you would ever have another chance to say them. It was a lesson she had learned too early and too dearly.

"I . . . uh . . ." Her mother spluttered on her own words. ". . . It's all right. Maybe this will work out for you, Paxton. You can always transfer next year, if it doesn't." It was an enormous concession for her, and Paxton was grateful that she had given in that much. She hated to leave them on bad terms, and even George didn't look quite as annoyed as he kissed her good-bye and warned her to behave herself in California, but he knew she would. She was a good girl basically, even if she was a little headstrong. And considering what other kids her age were up to these days, she hadn't really caused their mother too much trouble.

They both waved to her as she boarded the plane, and she left feeling relieved and free of them. It was only Queenie she missed as the plane took off and circled slowly over Savannah. It was a town she knew she wouldn't miss, and in any case, she knew she was coming back for Christmas. Many of her friends were going away too. They were going to universities all over the South, only two had chosen to go to college in the North, and she was the only one going to California. And she leaned back against the seat and closed her eyes as the plane flew west toward California.

It was only noon in California when they arrived, with the time change, and it was a gloriously sunny day as Paxton stepped off the plane and looked around her. The airport was small and most people seemed to be dressed in T-shirts and jeans, or flowered shirts, and a lot of the women were wearing miniskirts or cool-looking tie-dyed gauzy dresses. Everyone had long hair, and she felt instantly at home as she picked up her valise at the baggage claim and walked outside to hail a cab, feeling fiercely independent.

The driver told her everything he thought she should know, about the best restaurants near school, the hangouts where all the kids went, the action on Telegraph Avenue, and he commented more than once on her accent and said he liked it. When they reached the campus, he pointed to a collection of tables at the corner of Telegraph and Bancroft, and explained that they were organized to support various causes. There were signs everywhere for SNCC, for CORE, peace symbols, and there was a huge cardboard sign propped up heralding "Campus Women for Peace." And she was suddenly excited just being there. Just breathing the air there excited her, and reassured her that she had done the right thing in coming. She could hardly wait to get out and look around, start meeting people, and go to her classes.

She already knew the name of the hall where she would live, and the driver took her right there, and shook her hand and wished her luck before he left her. Everyone seemed to be friendly and open here. No one cared if you were black or white, rich or poor, Junior League or a bum, northern or southern, all the labels and distinctions she was so fed up with after growing up in Savannah among her mother's friends, to whom it meant everything if your grandfather or great-grandfather had fought in the Civil War, and whether or not you had owned a plantation and slaves. It was like living plunged in the past, a past she abhorred and wanted no part of.

The room she'd been assigned was on the second floor, way at the end of a long hall. In fact, it turned out to be the very last room, and it turned out to be a "quad," two bedrooms joined by a sitting room, with two girls assigned to each bedroom. There was a brown tweed couch in the middle of the sitting room, with multicolored patches sewn all over it to cover the abuses of earlier tenants. There were posters everywhere, a few battered pieces of furniture, and an orange rug, with an avocado-green vinyl armchair. For a moment, Paxton stopped as she surveyed the room. It was far from lovely, and a far cry from the quiet elegance of her mother's home in Savannah. But on the other hand, this was a small price to pay for freedom.

The bedroom she had been assigned to was smaller and more austere. It was a tiny room with two single metal cots, a desk, two chests of drawers and a straight-backed chair, and a closet barely big enough to put a broom in. They would have to be good friends to live in a room like that, but she hoped that she was about to meet three new people who would rapidly become soul mates. She had quickly glimpsed three suitcases stacked up in the other room, and a moment later, when she walked back into the sitting room again, wondering what they could do to it to make it a little less brutally ugly, she saw that one of her roommates was there. She was a beautiful girl with long legs, and creamy coffee-colored skin, and she was quick to tell Paxton that she was from Alabama, and her name was Yvonne Gilbert.

"Hi." Paxton smiled warmly at her. She was a striking-looking girl, and she had bright, alert, almost jet-black eyes, and she wore her hair in an impressive Afro. "I'm Paxton Andrews." But somehow she hesitated when it came to telling the girl where she was from. But the girl had heard it anyway.

"North Carolina?"

"Georgia. Savannah." Paxxie smiled easily, but Yvonne looked instantly wary.

"Great. Just what I needed. A cracker. What do they want us to do, re-fight the Civil War? Someone in central casting has a hell of a sense of humor." She looked deeply annoyed and Paxton continued to treat it lightly.

"Don't worry about it. I'm on your side."

"Yeah. I bet. I can hardly wait to see where the others are from. How about Mississippi and Tennessee? Maybe you can start up a chapter of the Daughters of the Civil War, this oughtta be real fun, honey. I'm just gonna love roomin' with y'all." She exaggerated her own drawl with a vicious glance at Paxxie, and then strode into her own room and slammed the door, as Paxton sat down on the couch with a look of dismay. It was going to be interesting anyway. And certainly different.

The next to arrive was a pale, ethereal-looking girl with a milk-white face, jet-black hair to her waist, china-blue eyes, and she appeared to be wearing an almost transparent white night-gown. "Hi," she whispered, "I'm Dawn." And she was from Des Moines. And her given name had actually been Gertrude. Dawn had come upon her more recently, with a little touch of LSD, during her senior year, and she had decided to continue to use it. Dawn Steinberg. She was also an honor student, and had played viola with the local orchestra, and she'd been offered a scholarship at Stanford. She had been assigned to the other room, and she opened the door Yvonne had slammed only moments before, and closed it gently again, and no one emerged. There were no screams. There were no sounds at all, and Paxton could only gather that Ms. Gilbert was satisfied with her new roommate. Des Moines did not have to live down the racist reputation Yvonne had accused Savannah of having.

And as Paxton pondered the two young women she had just met, she decided to unpack her bags. The two duffels and the trunk had been left in her room the day before, and she decided to make both beds. It would make the room look friendlier when her roommate arrived, and she found herself suddenly praying that she wouldn't be black, angry, and hate women from Georgia . . . please, God . . . she whispered to herself. . . . I know I may not deserve this, and you have better things to do today . . . but could you please make her like me?

Her roommate still hadn't arrived at four o'clock, and Paxton decided to stock their small fridge. Before she left for the nearest market, she stopped and knocked at the other girls' door, and it seemed to take a long time but finally Dawn came to the door and answered.

"Yes?" she whispered at Paxton, as though afraid someone would hear her. Although her hearing was good, Paxxie found it almost impossible to understand what Dawn was saying. And the temptation when talking to her was to whisper back. Even a normal tone of voice sounded too loud when trying to converse with this ethereal vision.

"Do you want something from the store?" Paxton whispered back to her. "I wanted to go out and get some food. I'm starving." Suddenly, she was missing Queenie's well-stocked kitchen. And for her, it was seven o'clock at night and she was ready for dinner.

"I'd love some herb tea and honey, and some lemons . . . and maybe some brown bread." None of it sounded appealing to Paxton, but she was willing to bring anything back in order to make friends, and she quickly jotted down Dawn's order.

"What about Yvonne?" she said carefully. "Would she like anything?" Paxton glanced into the room and saw that they'd been unpacking. Dawn had put up some posters, and Yvonne had clothes everywhere, and there were colorful blankets and a pair of pink satin bedspreads that looked more like Alabama than Des Moines, but it was a little hard to tell in the confusion. "Do you want anything from the store?" Paxton spoke directly to Yvonne as she approached the door with a hostile look at Paxton.

"Yeah. Martin Luther King. Think you can find him, sugar?"

"Don't give me that." Paxton looked annoyed. "You're making some pretty crummy assumptions, considering the fact that we only met two hours ago, and you don't know me." Paxton wasn't afraid of her, and the girl's prejudice made her angry.

"What assumptions should I make?" Yvonne stood almost nose to nose with her, but Paxton didn't back down. She knew she had to establish herself with the girl now, or forget it. And she didn't hesitate to stand her ground. Paxton was passionate and strong, and she had a quiet kind of courage. Living with her mother's constant chill had taught her to be strong a long time before, and she wasn't afraid of the angry black girl from Alabama. "You're from Georgia, aren't you?" Yvonne went on. "What am I supposed to think?"

"You're supposed to give me a chance. Just like I'm supposed to do for you. Isn't that what civil rights is all about? We judge each other on who we are, what we think, what we believe, what we stand for, what we *do,* not the color of each other's skin . . . or just because your skin is black and my license plate says Georgia. Maybe it's not even my car. Maybe you're dead wrong about me. Maybe there's a reason why I'm not sitting around smelling magnolia blossoms and drinking mint juleps in the Deep South. Did you ever think of that? I'll bet that never even occurred to you. Not everyone white in the South is related to George Wallace. Give me a chance, for chrissake. It might pay off." That was the whole point wasn't it? What Martin Luther King marched for.

"Yeah. Great. Bring me back a six-pack of Coke and a pack of Kools." No thank-you, no please. She just turned around and strutted back into her bedroom. And Paxton added her requests to the list without saying a word, and walked out of their quad to find the nearest food store off campus. It was going to be interesting dealing with Yvonne, she thought to herself. She was angry, and filled with hate, and Paxton wondered if they would ever make it. She had tried to make friends with the few black girls she met, at volunteer projects, and on a church camping trip, much to her mother *and* Queenie's dismay. Their generation was not ready for that, and it had upset Queenie even more than her mother. But it was something she felt differently about. Once, when she'd gone to lunch with a black girl she knew slightly, they hadn't been served and Paxton was livid. They'd gone to three restaurants, and finally given up, and shared a bag of potato chips on a bench in Forsyth Park. But the black girl understood. She was used to it, and she'd been touched by Paxton's caring and compassion.

And for a long time, Paxton had wanted to go on a march, but so far she hadn't dared, because she knew that if she got arrested, her mother would lock her in the house for a year. And more than that, it would have mortified Paxton's mother among her friends, and Paxton hadn't had the heart to put her through it. But one day, she knew she would. One day, she knew she would have to. And here she was, suddenly living with a black girl who hated her just because she was from Georgia. And suddenly she laughed as she crossed Telegraph. She laughed so hard that a couple of people turned around, because she suddenly realized what her mother would have said if she knew one of her roommates was black. And Queenie! Paxton was glad. And she was going to make friends with Yvonne, no matter what it took to do it.

She bought everything on their list, and then candy bars for all of them, a couple of Cokes for herself, and a few things to make sandwiches with, and a box of doughnuts. She carried the bag back to their room, and as she walked up the stairs, she saw a slightly overweight but attractive short redheaded girl trying to drag three suitcases up the stairs at once, while a very good-looking, tall young blond man wrestled with an enormous trunk that seemed to weigh a lot more than he did.

"What the hell did you put in this thing, Gab? Rocks? Or barbells?"

"Just a few books . . . there's nothing in it, really . . . I swear. . . ."

"Bullshit. You carry this thing. I'll be damned if I'll get a hernia hauling your goddamn luggage all over school." He looked wildly exasperated as Paxton attempted discreetly to get by them, and then decided to offer a hand, although the trunk didn't look too appealing.

"Maybe if the three of us carry it?" she said hesitantly, looking from one to the other as they stood on the stairs, and she juggled her groceries on one hip, and prayed she wouldn't blush while she could feel the good-looking boy look her over.

"Don't do her any favors," he growled, "she doesn't deserve it." And he looked so annoyed that for a moment Paxton wondered if they were married. But something about the similarity of their profiles suggested that they were either very narcissistic or related.

"I'll give you a hand with it, if you like," Paxton offered again, tossing her long blond hair away from her face, and looking at the smiling redhead.

"That's nice of you. My brother's being a big pain in the ass over carrying one small bag."

"One *small* bag!" he shrieked, as his words echoed down the stairs. "Do you have any idea what this thing weighs? It must weigh four hundred pounds if it weighs an ounce. And I'm not even sure the three of us could carry it."

"We could try," Paxton reassured him, and he looked her over again with warm appraisal.

"Why don't we just leave her with this mess of her own making, and you and I go have a beer at Kips? That sounds a lot better."

Paxton laughed, as his sister threatened him with a look that didn't begin to suggest amusement. "Peter Wilson, you go anywhere and I'll strangle you. Don't forget that *your* sheets are in my other bag, and if you don't carry this stuff for me, you can sleep on your mattress for the rest of the year for all I care."

"You're breaking my heart." He looked past her at Paxton again, smiling. "Come on, let's go have a beer and ditch her." Paxton was laughing, too, but she was gamely trying to lift the other end of the trunk with the redhead.

"Come on, asshole . . . pick up your end!" the girl was instructing him, and finally with a groan of complaint, he did and they made it up the stairs, but barely. He was right, Paxton realized. The thing weighed a ton, and she couldn't begin to imagine what the redhead had put in it.

"Where's your room?" He was looking annoyed again, and he glanced at his watch. He had better things to do on a Sunday afternoon than play porter for his sister.

"I don't know yet."

"Christ, are you even in the right building?" He looked like he was going to murder her again, but she nodded.

"Yes!" She fumbled in her handbag and found a piece of paper. She was wearing jeans and a flowered shirt, and what looked like a pair of very expensive loafers. But nothing else gave her away, except for the fact that she must have put gold bars in the trunk, and all of her luggage was leather. "Okay, here it is." She read off the number and Paxton stared at her in surprise and then smiled. She was lucky. It had turned out okay. She already liked her.

"You're my roommate," Paxton announced, and the tall young man groaned, and sat down on the trunk with a sympathetic look at Paxton.

"You poor thing. You have no idea what you're in for." And then he stuck out his hand and shook Paxton's. "I'm Peter Wilson, by the way."

"I'm Paxton Andrews."

"I'm Gabrielle. Gabby Wilson," she explained, and then smiled warmly at Paxton. "Where're you from? I love your accent."

"I'd never thought I had one till I came here." Paxxie laughed. "And I'm glad someone does. As you'll see in a few minutes, one of our roommates is not exactly crazy about it."

"Tell her to go screw herself," Gabby said chattily, as Peter stood up and began wrestling with the trunk again with a look of disapproval.

"That's my little sister, ever the lady. Come on, big mouth, if you can pack this stuff, you can carry it too. Help me get this to your room. I have a date at five-thirty."

"You're breaking my heart," she said unsympathetically as she picked up the other end, and Paxton helped her.

"You're breaking my back, which is worse," he complained, but a moment later they got the enormous trunk to the living room, and set it down on the orange carpet, and then the threesome went back for her valises. "Where are you going to put all this stuff?" he asked, knowing full well that there was nowhere to put it.

"I haven't figured that out yet." And then she glanced over at Paxxie. "Who decorated the living room? Dracula? My God, where did they get that stuff? The Salvation Army?"

"Probably the dump," Peter said cheerfully. "That's where we got our stuff."

Gabby looked at him and shook her head in despair, as Paxton smiled at him again, while carrying one of Gabby's enormous valises. Where *was* she going to put all her stuff, Paxton wondered too. Having seen the single tiny closet in their room, it was an interesting question.

"Are you a senior?" Paxxie asked him.

"I was. I graduated in June. I'm just starting law school. But I've been living off campus for the last two years. Thank God the brat didn't talk my parents into that, or she'd really have driven me crazy." They were back at the entrance to the living room again and he looked as though he was about to leave, and pleased to do it. "Well, she's all yours." He glanced at the mountain of bags they had dumped in the middle of the room, helped himself to a doughnut from Paxton's bag, and waved as he made an escape, and Gabby stood smiling at Paxton.

"Thank you for your help. And I apologize for him," she said as soon as her brother left. "He's a hopeless jerk. But the truth is, I love him. I wouldn't admit it to him, but I can to you. He's hopeless, and he used to beat me up . . . or try to." But it was

49

obvious that they were very fond of each other, and for a moment, Paxton envied them. She and George had never shared that kind of playful affection. But he was also ten years older than Peter, and had no sense of humor whatsoever.

Their conversation drew out the other two, and as Paxton and Gabby helped themselves to doughnuts and Cokes, Dawn and Yvonne emerged from their room, to stare at Gabby's mountain of valises.

"My God, where did all that come from?" Yvonne said with a look of immense irritation. "Did you get my Kools?" she asked Paxton.

"I did." Paxton handed them to her, and Yvonne handed her the correct change. She didn't want any gifts from Savannah. And Dawn went to unpack the rest of the groceries, after Paxton had introduced them to Gabby. Yvonne was looking suspiciously at her, smoking a cigarette, and she was quick to ask her where she came from.

"San Francisco. I haven't exactly ventured far from home," she apologized with a small shrug. "But I love it here. I've been visiting my brother here for four years, and all my friends are here, the ones who went to college anyway." She looked at the three of them enthusiastically. "You're gonna love it." Yvonne shot a quick glance at Paxton, indicating that she wasn't so sure, and even Dawn looked a little uncertain.

"I didn't really want to go to college at all, but my parents insisted I come here." Her father was a professor of English.

"Did you want to go to school back home?" Gabby was interested in all of them, and she looked like an open, easygoing, happy person.

"No." Dawn shook her head with a sad smile. "I wanted to get married. And we want to go to India to study Eastern religions."

"I want to go to law school," Yvonne confessed, smoking her cigarette and using an ancient, half-melted olive-green plastic ashtray. "But it's a long road from here. I'm here on a scholar-ship, and I've got to make the grades, or I'm gonna be out on my black ass and back in Alabama before I know it. And I'm not goin' back till I can do something to change it. What about you, Savannah?" Paxton didn't want her calling her that, but she decided not to antagonize her further.

"I want to be a journalism major." She smiled. "So I can write about you changing the South." Yvonne grinned in spite of herself, and lit another cigarette as soon as she put out the first one. She was nervous, but she was also very beautiful, and Paxton found herself wondering if the black girl had ever mod-eled.

"I don't know what I want to be," Gabby admitted to all of them. "I just want to have a good time and stay in school till I get married."

"Are you engaged?" Dawn looked at her hopefully, feeling she had found a kindred spirit, but Gabby shook her head sadly.

"Not yet. I haven't found anyone, but I'm looking." Paxton and Yvonne laughed, and Paxton couldn't help thinking that lots of boys would be running after Yvonne and Gabby.

"You should find plenty of what you're looking for here," Yvonne offered her encouragement. "I've seen a whole bunch of cute guys since I got here."

"Me too," Paxton confessed with a shy smile. She had seen several on her way to the store, and Gabby's brother was the best-looking of all, and he was even more attractive because he was a little older. But she suspected that most law school stu-dents probably wouldn't be caught dead with freshmen. Which made it all the more surprising when he turned up at their room again several hours later. Dawn had already gone to bed, and Yvonne was reading on the couch and wearing a very seductive dressing gown when Peter suddenly appeared with a friend car-rying a six-pack. He saw Paxton coming out of the other room, and held a beer out to her with a shy smile.

51

"We came back to see if you needed any help." She was surprised to see him, and Gabby was even more so.

"What are *you* doing here?" she asked suspiciously. "And no, I can't cash a check." She turned to Paxton with a conspiratorial air. "He passes bum checks on me all the time, don't ever cash one for him." And then she noticed his friend, standing in the doorway. "Hi, Sandy, come on in, no one's naked."

"Damn, how disappointing," he said, blushing nonetheless, but Peter looked more relaxed, as he glanced from Yvonne to Paxton.

"Actually, we were hoping that you were. Anyone want a beer?" Even Yvonne smiled at him, as she offered Sandy a cigarette, and the two boys made themselves at home on the floor and the chair, while Gabby and Paxton sat on Gabby's trunk, which they had decided to use as a coffee table. Sandy was at the law school, too, and he was one of Peter's seven roommates. They had a house on Ellsworth, and it was cozy and cute, and an utter shambles.

"We'll have you over to dinner sometime," Peter said cheerfully, "after we get a bulldozer in to clear out the kitchen. I think we still have pizza in the oven from last year but I'm afraid to look." He smiled happily as he finished his beer. "What about you?" He looked suddenly straight at Paxton, and the intensity of his blue eyes surprised her. "Can you cook?"

"I try," she said shyly.

"Can you make grits?" Yvonne asked with sudden interest, and Paxton wasn't sure if she was baiting her again. "Or ribs, or hogbacks?" But Paxton decided to tell the truth. Queenie could, but she couldn't.

"About the best I can do is a steak, or an omelet and hash browns."

"That'll do," Peter said quietly. "Maybe we'll find someplace to cook dinner one night. Or maybe we'll just have to go out and eat." He could think of worse fates and there was a mo-

ment's silence in the room as Yvonne watched them with interest. And Sandy was watching Yvonne too. He thought she was a
knockout, much to Gabby's chagrin. She had always liked him.
Things were definitely getting interesting very early, and very
quickly. They had all arrived only that day, but Paxton could
already see some good times on the horizon.

The boys hung around for a little while, and then went on
their way. They were meeting friends at Kips, and when they
left, Paxton admitted that she was tired. It was two o'clock in
the morning for her, and all of a sudden she could really feel it.

"You didn't look tired to me when Gabby's brother was
here," Yvonne teased. "You looked fine to me."

"And you looked pretty fine to Sandy." Paxton gave it right
back to her, and this time they both laughed. And Yvonne was
still sitting on the couch and reading when Gabby and Paxton
went to their room to change into their nightgowns.

"I can't believe it," Gabby said to her as she slipped her
nightgown over her head a few minutes later. "He *always* hates
my friends. I can't think of a single friend I've ever had that he's
liked . . . and suddenly, he's dropping by to make friendly
chitchat with a six-pack. I can't believe it." She looked at Paxton with absolute amazement. "It's you. It really is. You're the
first girl he's ever liked that he's met through me, or even with
me. I can't believe it."

"It's just curiosity. He won't be back. There are a lot more
interesting girls out there at the law school."

"I doubt it." Gabby had been impressed by her too. She was a
stunning-looking girl, and one of the nice things about her was
that she seemed not to know it. She was quiet, and smart, and
when you talked to her a little bit, she was really funny. And
Gabby still liked the sound of her accent. And there was a lot
more to Paxton than met the eye, more wisdom, more compassion, and more inner beauty. And Gabby knew from experience

53

that her brother was no fool. He had spotted a good one. Maybe even a great one.

"He'll be back. You'll see." And then Gabby groaned as she lay on the narrow, uncomfortable bed, and thought it over. "In fact, I may see more of him this year than I've ever seen before. I'm not so sure I like that."

"Believe me. He'll forget us all by next week, except maybe Yvonne . . ." And then in a whisper, she decided to say something to Gabby. "She's incredible-looking, isn't she? She's so beautiful!"

"But such a bitch!" Gabby whispered.

"I don't think she really is," Paxton defended her, "I think she's just uptight about me, because I'm from Georgia."

"I don't know." Gabby thought about it for a little bit. "She looks like a tough customer to me. I'm not sure I'd want to get on her bad side."

"Maybe life hasn't been easy for her. Blacks have it rough in Alabama. They have it rough everywhere, except maybe up here. Maybe she's got good reason to be the way she is." Gabby shrugged, not particularly worried about it as she glanced at Paxton.

"What do you think about Dawn?"

"I think she's scared, poor thing. I don't think she really wants to be here."

"She sleeps all the time." She had taken two naps that afternoon. "Maybe she's got a disease. You know, like narcolepsy or something really exotic." Gabby looked hopeful and Paxton laughed, she was so relieved to discover that she liked her roommate. And she really did. Gabby Wilson was zany and fun and Paxton couldn't think of a better person to room with.

"We'd better get some sleep," Paxton finally whispered to her. She was already half asleep, and it was long after midnight, and Gabby was still rattling on, and sounded as though she could go on for hours, but Paxton couldn't stay awake a moment longer. "We've got orientation tomorrow, and I have to see my adviser and try and pick my classes."

"Don't worry about a thing. Just pick the easy ones, the stuff you've already done in high school." Paxton laughed at the suggestion. "There's no point killing yourself while you're here, Paxton. We're here to have fun. Don't forget that." Gabby was serious. She had come to Berkeley to have a good time. And find a husband. "Remember, Pax, we're here to have fun."

"I'll remember that . . ." Paxton whispered as she drifted off to sleep. She was dreaming of Queenie, and a beautiful black girl, and a handsome prince who kept offering her a beer, while somewhere in the distance her brother danced with a crazy redhead. . . .

# CHAPTER 4

⋁

Paxton and Gabby both did exactly what they'd set out to do when they'd come to Berkeley. Gabby signed up for the easiest classes she could, and managed to go out almost every night. She was having the time of her life, although she had not yet found a husband. And Paxton, on the other hand, had signed up for the toughest classes open to her, particularly those involved with journalism or writing. She was also taking a political economics class that was so hard it terrified her, physics, math, and Spanish. Her adviser had fought her on everything except Spanish and math, but she seemed to be doing well in every class except physics, and that was a required class anyway, and she was taking it on a pass/fail basis. But she was exhilarated by everything she learned and did, and still managed to go out with Gabby and her friends sometimes, and she almost always enjoyed them. They were a fun-loving crowd, and they seemed to be involved in everything. Two of them were involved in CORE, several were trying to raise money for SNCC, which were causes that appealed to Paxxie, too, as they benefited southern blacks, and one evening she met Mario Savio, the leader of the Free Speech Movement. Gabby seemed to know everyone, and although she knew the cause people, she also knew the more social ones, too, and most of her friends were pretty tame, which was comfortable for Paxton.

By the second month of school, Paxton had had several run-ins with Yvonne Gilbert. The black girl seemed determined not to give Paxton a chance about anything, and she constantly assumed that if something was wrong, it was Paxton's fault, and it was beginning to seriously annoy Paxxie. It was prejudice in reverse, and it was getting to be a challenge to hold her temper.

Not surprisingly, given her extraordinary looks, Yvonne had found a boyfriend by the second week of school. He was the star running back on the football team, a huge, handsome black boy from Texas, and by association and because of her own personality, she was becoming quite a star on campus. All the boys were running after her, but she seemed to be serious about Deke, and she'd already made it clear to several of her admirers that she had no interest in white boys.

She was in Paxton's physics class, but she never talked to her, and they hardly ever spoke except when they ran into each other in their living room and really had to. But the exchanges were never really friendly.

And Dawn seemed to live her own life too. She still slept most of the time, and more than once Paxton had wondered if she ever even went to classes. "She's never going to make it, if she keeps it up like this," she'd said to Gabby several times, who seemed to feel it was not her problem. She had her own life to lead. And she was having a good time going out with two of her brother's friends from the law school. And her own prediction had proven true. She was seeing more of her brother than she had in years, and although she complained about it constantly, she really enjoyed it. He had started turning up every few days just to make sure she was "alright," or to bring her things, like a six-pack or a pizza or some pastry he'd just happened to pick up, or a bottle of cheap wine, but Gabby knew he wasn't worried about her, he was interested in Paxton. The two

57

would sit for hours sometimes, on the battered couch, or on the floor, talking long into the night, drinking coffee or beer, or just Coke, and talking about the things they believed in. They seemed to share the same opinions about everything, and it was rare that they disagreed, and it almost frightened Paxton sometimes to realize how much alike they were and how compatible on a broad range of subjects. It was as though they had been destined to meet and become friends. But it worried Paxton at first, because unlike Gabby, the one thing she didn't want was to find a husband. She had come to Berkeley to learn and to make something of herself, and one day she was going to be a great journalist, or at least a hardworking one, and go out and write about the world. She wanted to go to Europe, Africa, the Orient. Sometimes she even thought about spending a year in the Peace Corps. The last thing she wanted was to fall in love, settle down, get married, move to the suburbs and have babies. And she'd told Peter that and he'd laughed. Even his blond good looks were a lot like hers. People told them they looked alike, and he and Paxton looked more like brother and sister, than he and Gabby.

"Are you telling me I look like the type who's going to get married and move to the suburbs? Christ, how insulting." But he was laughing and sitting on her living room floor at two a.m. when he said it. Gabby had just come in from a date, Dawn had been asleep for hours, and most of the time now Yvonne was sleeping at Deke's apartment off campus.

"Did I hear someone say marriage?" Gabby cupped her ears jokingly with one hand, and stopped on her way to the bedroom.

"No, you did *not!*" Paxton was quick to correct her. She was wearing jeans and a T-shirt, and lying on the floor near Peter. She loved being close to him, loved what he thought, and who he was and what he stood for. But she didn't want to love him more than that, didn't want to really let herself fall in love with him, at least not yet. She just couldn't.

"Your friend just insulted me," he informed his younger sister, but as he said it, he stroked Paxxie's golden hair, and smiled down into the green eyes he was falling in love with. "I think she just called me a square, or worse."

"I did *not*!" Paxton sat up, laughing then. "I just said I didn't want to get married, move to the suburbs, and have kids. I want to see the world first."

"And you think I don't?" He still looked mildly insulted.

"He wants to see the world," Gabby assured her, "Monte Carlo, Cap d'Antibes, Paris, London, Acapulco, St. Moritz. You know, the hardship spots." The three of them laughed.

"What do you think I am?" he demanded of them both. "Lazy?"

His sister knew him better than that as she replied, shaking her head, "No, just spoiled. Like me." She smiled benignly and he threw an empty Coke can at her.

"Well, it's true. Can you see either of us wanting to join the Peace Corps, like Pax? Just thinking about it gives me hives, and I can't see you digging trenches or building latrines either, can you?" she asked him honestly, and he shook his head.

"Why do you think I'm in law school?" he teased, but there was truth to it too. He was going to graduate from law school at twenty-five, and with luck he could avoid the draft till he was twenty-six and it was no longer an issue. He liked the deferral status that law school gave him. He had no desire to join the police action in Viet Nam. Only two months before, after the Gulf of Tonkin incident, American aircraft had bombed Viet Nam for the first time, after years of being there as advisers. "To tell you the truth, I can't see myself in Viet Nam, or anyplace else even remotely like it. What makes you want to join the Peace Corps, Pax?"

"I'm not sure I do. I just want to make a difference somewhere," she said seriously, as Gabby left them alone again. "I've spent my whole life watching people indulge themselves and not give a damn about anyone else. I don't want to do that. My father cared about people a whole lot. I think he would have done something like that if he'd had the chance and hadn't gotten married."

"He must have been a nice man," Peter said quietly, as he watched her face grow soft thinking about him.

"He was." There was a lump in her throat as she spoke. "I loved him a lot . . . my life was . . . very different . . . after he died."

"Why?" His voice was gentle in the night, there was so much about her he already loved, but it scared him, too, sometimes, just as it did Paxton.

"My Mom and I are . . . well, pretty different. . . ." She didn't want to say more, not yet, and there was no point. And it sounded too awful to say she had always thought her mother didn't love her.

"Is that what the Peace Corps is all about? To get away from her?"

"No." Paxton smiled. "But Berkeley was." She was very honest with him, they both were. They were just that kind of people.

"I'm glad," he said to her, as his lips brushed hers and they lay close to each other on the floor, propped up on their elbows.

"So am I," she whispered back, and then he took her in his arms and they lay there and kissed for a long time, until suddenly Gabby opened the bedroom door and looked down at them with considerable interest.

"You guys going to bed separately or together tonight, or are you just gonna lie here and neck? It's all the same to me, I just wonder if I should wait up for Pax, or go to sleep now." Peter groaned and Paxton laughed as she rolled away from him, her hair tangled, her cheeks pink from their kissing.

"Has anyone told you lately what a rude pain in the ass you are, Gabrielle?" He knew how desperately she hated the name and he loved to use it to annoy her. "Christ, it's just my luck to fall for my sister's roommate." He stood up then, and held out a hand to Paxton. "I guess you'd better get some sleep, babe. If the mouthpiece here will let you. I don't know how you stand it."

"I just fall asleep when I'm tired."

"And she probably keeps talking." All three of them laughed because it was true and he kissed Paxton goodnight and left. And when he was gone, Gabby pressed her.

"Is it serious, Pax?"

"Don't be silly. We've only known each other for six weeks, and we've got our whole lives ahead of us. He's got three years of law school, I've got four years of undergraduate work to do. What could be serious?" But in her heart, she knew it was, and didn't want to admit it yet to herself or Gabby.

"You don't know my brother. I've never seen him look like this. He really cares about you. I think he's in love with you." And then with an earnest, investigative stare, "Has he told you he loves you?"

"For heaven's sake . . . of course not. . . ." But he didn't have to. Paxton knew it. Gabby was right. And Paxton had never felt like this either. It was just rotten luck that it had happened so fast, and so early. For the moment, finding the man of her dreams was the last thing Paxton wanted.

"Shit. Isn't this just my luck," Gabby complained as they got into bed. "I want to find a husband and you don't, and what happens, you've got Peter drooling over you and looking like he wants to get engaged, and who have I got? No one. Some jerk with frizzy hair to his waist who wants to go to Tibet with me next summer as long as I'll pay for his airfare. Some people have all the luck."

61

"Karma." Paxton grinned as she lay in the dark, listening to Gabby.

"Who's he? Isn't he that guy at the free-speech table on Bancroft?"

"No, it's that thing Dawn is always talking about. Karma. Fate. Kismet."

"They must be sleeping pills. Christ, did you hear her getting sick yesterday? I think she's dying."

"Maybe she's pregnant," Paxton whispered hesitantly.

"When does she have time to get pregnant? She's always sleeping." And with that, they both laughed and turned over and went to sleep. For once, Gabby had nothing left to say and she had to go to her contemporary music class in the morning. And she had a lot to do after that. It was the day before Halloween, and she wanted to work on her costume. She was going to be a gold lamé pumpkin.

It was also the day the Viet Cong attacked the Bien Hoa airbase, fifteen miles north of Saigon, the first major U.S. military installation to be hit.

Five American men were killed, and seventy-six were wounded. And Johnson did not order an attack in retaliation. He was trying to sit tight, especially before the election four days later. Goldwater was promising to bomb the hell out of everyone, and end our involvement in Viet Nam by crippling the north, and Johnson was promising not to get us in any deeper, which was what everyone wanted to hear. And Johnson won by a landslide on November third. The threat of Goldwater involving the country further in Viet Nam had been answered.

And the following week, Peter asked Paxton what she was doing for Thanksgiving.

"Nothing much. It's too far to go home just for a few days." Too far and too expensive, although Thanksgiving without Queenie's turkey wouldn't be Thanksgiving. Paxton was trying not to think of it, and she was planning to spend the day studying for a physics test, and having a turkey sandwich at the cafeteria if she even remembered.

"I was wondering if you'd like to come home with us. I mentioned it to my mother last week, and she'd love it if you used the guest room. It might even give you a rest from listening to Gabby talk to you all night."

"I might miss it," Paxton said shyly. "Are you sure it wouldn't be an imposition?"

"Not at all. That's what Thanksgiving's all about. People overeating together and watching football. In fact, Dad and I are going to the game on Saturday and I'd love it if you came. And I thought maybe we could drive over to Stinson Beach on Friday."

"I'd like that." She smiled. Gabby had said something vague about it a few days before, but then she had forgotten to pursue the subject further. But Paxton couldn't think of anything she'd like better than spending Thanksgiving with them. She hadn't met their parents yet, but suspected from everything she'd heard that she would like them. And going there was a little frightening, too, it would bring her that much closer to Peter. But there seemed to be no way to avoid it. Most of the time they went out with friends, and she had only been out with him alone a few times, but even in a crowd of people, their attraction to each other was so strong that it was impossible to fight it.

He told Gabby that afternoon, and she exploded into their living room while Paxton was studying and surprised her.

"I hear you're coming home with us for Thanksgiving, Pax, that's terrific!" She smiled warmly. She had talked to her mother only that afternoon, and Marjorie Wilson wanted to know more about her roommate and if she was a serious interest with Peter. She had found it strange that he, and not Gabby, had called to ask if Paxton could come home with them. "You're going to love my Mom."

"I'm sure I will." She already did from all of Gabby's stories.

The two were amazingly close, and it was obvious from everything Gabby said that she was crazy about her mother. It sounded as if Marjorie Wilson was involved in causes and auxiliaries and bridge clubs, like her own mother, but unlike Beatrice Andrews, she seemed genuinely to love her children. Paxton wasn't sure what their father did, but she assumed somehow that he was in business.

Peter picked them up late Wednesday afternoon, and as usual Gabby had too many bags, and Paxton only had one small one. She was wearing a serious navy blue dress and her gray winter coat, and the only pair of dressy heels she'd brought, a pair of simple black ones. She looked very pretty and neat, and she had pulled her hair back in a ponytail and tied it with a navy satin ribbon, and she was wearing her grandmother's tiny Victorian pearl earrings.

"You look like Alice in Wonderland," Peter said with a smile as she got into his battered Ford. He had been talking about buying one of the new Mustangs, but said he didn't have enough money saved up from the summer. His father had offered him a trip or a car as a graduation gift, and he had opted for two months in Europe in Scotland, England, and France, and he had no regrets about it as he drove around in the same wreck he'd had all through college.

"Should I have worn something dressier?" Paxton asked Gabby nervously. She had a black velvet dress she could have worn, but she was saving it for Thanksgiving rather than their arrival.

"You're fine. Don't listen to him." Gabby was wearing a red velvet miniskirt and a black sweater, high-heeled red shoes, and her red hair sprang out from her head like Shirley Temple's. "My mother will be wearing a plain black dress and pearls, and my father will be wearing plaid pants and a velvet jacket. Their uniforms." Paxton laughed nervously and hoped she wouldn't embarrass them, especially Peter. Suddenly it all mattered so much to her, and that frightened her too. She had never been "brought home" by anyone, as a potentially serious girlfriend, and she had the sinking feeling that that was what Peter was doing.

They came across the Bay Bridge at full speed, and drove west on Broadway past Carol Doda's place and all the topless bars, and as soon as they went through the Broadway Tunnel and crossed Van Ness, they began to pass the stately homes on Broadway. Paxton was impressed, and suddenly even more nervous. And then they were there. Peter brought the car to a screeching halt, Gabby hopped out, and rang the bell, and a moment later, they were standing in the enormous front hall of a very large brick house with Peter's parents, dressed exactly as Gabby had said, making her feel welcome. Their mother was a small woman with fading red hair, combed into a sleek bun, and bright green eyes not unlike Paxton's, and his father was long and lanky like his son, with once blond hair now turned snow white, and an air of aristocratic good humor. His wife was warm, and when she hugged Paxton, she seemed to mean it.

She had Gabby show her to her room, and a few moments later they were all downstairs, in a handsome wood-paneled library filled with old leather-bound books, overstuffed antique furniture, an Oriental rug, and a fire blazing. It was the kind of room one read about in books, and Paxton had had no idea that they were so wealthy. And suddenly she felt uncomfortable about her dress again, but no one seemed to care what anyone else was wearing. Whereas her own mother would have made comments about Gabby's miniskirt, Marjorie Wilson seemed to find it amusing, and they were talking animatedly about the party she'd gone to the previous weekend, and the boy she'd met whom she considered a "serious hopeful," her favorite term for the kind of boy she'd like to marry. And across the room, Paxton heard Peter ask his father how things were at the paper.

"Interesting, since this recent business in Viet Nam. The attack at Bien Hoa may change things a little bit now, whether Johnson wants it that way or not. We can't sit on our hands over there forever." Peter didn't say much, as he knew his father had been a staunch supporter of Goldwater, although it was a point of view he had chosen not to discuss with Peter.

"I don't think even being there is the answer. We should get the hell out before we get in over our heads, like the French did," Peter said somberly to his father.

"We're smarter than they are, son." His father smiled. "And we can't let the Communists take over the world, can we?" It was an endless conversation they'd had for years, and their views were always different. Peter didn't think the U.S. forces belonged there, but like most people of his generation, his father did, and thought they could kick ass quick, teach them a lesson, maybe even do some good, and get out without getting too badly hurt. But the big question always was, how much was "too badly"?

They wandered over to talk to the women then, and Paxton was amused to see how much Peter looked like his father. He had the same fire, the same zest for life, the same lively blue eyes that she loved in Peter, the same warm manner. They were all warm and lively people, and she found herself totally at ease with them over dinner, more so than she had ever been with her own family in Savannah. She also discovered that they talked about the morning paper constantly, and halfway through dinner, she realized that Peter's father worked there, and then, as they talked about what Peter was going to do the following summer, she found out something more, and for a moment the realization stunned her. Peter was talking about working for corresponding papers somewhere in the country, and as she listened, Paxton understood it all, even why Peter's father had had to keep his support of Goldwater quiet at the office. Because the *Morning Sun* had officially come out in favor of Johnson, and the paper had always been staunchly Democratic. But its owner was not. And its owner was Peter and Gabby's father. In fact, the Wilson family had owned the *Morning Sun* for over one hundred years and as it all came clear to her, Paxton started to laugh, as Peter looked at her in confusion. He had just said that he wasn't sure he wanted to work for a newspaper the following summer at all, but he was thinking of volunteering for a law project in Mississippi or working for Dr. Martin Luther King, especially since he had won the Nobel peace prize in October. And she was laughing.

"What's so funny about that?" He looked surprised, she usually took things like that fairly seriously, and he knew she shared his views about most things, especially that one.

"Nothing, I'm sorry. I just figured something out that neither of you bothered to tell me. I thought you just talked about the *Morning Sun* all the time because your father works there. I never figured out until just now that you . . . that . . ." She looked mildly embarrassed and Peter grinned as his father laughed.

"Don't feel bad, Paxton. When he was a little boy, he used to tell his friends I sold newspapers on Mission Street, at least his humility doesn't go quite that far anymore, or maybe it does. Is that what he told you?"

"No." She shook her head as she laughed, and Gabby grinned. She had never said anything to Paxton either. They had never liked bragging to friends, and Paxton could see why. Although they lived beautifully, they weren't showy people. It was the kind of old money, and discretion, that would have really impressed her mother. "Actually neither of them ever said anything. I never gave it a thought."

"I didn't think it was important," Peter explained quietly, knowing that she liked him for himself and not what his father owned. And Paxton was quick to reassure him.

"It isn't. But it's interesting. At least you can talk about something intelligent at home. All we ever talk about is who's getting married, who bought a new house, and which of my brother's patients is dying."

"Is your father a doctor too?" Marjorie Wilson asked with a warm smile.

"No," Paxton said quietly, feeling sad somewhere deep inside, she wished she still had a father, like Gabby and Peter. "My father was an attorney. He died seven years ago, when his plane crashed."

"I'm sorry," Gabby's mother said softly.

"Me too." It was so different being with them, it was all so normal and so happy. They played dominoes that night, and teased and laughed. Peter talked to his father in front of the fire for a long time, and then he included Paxton. They talked about Viet Nam again, and Diem, and Johnson's position with the Russians since the recent coup d'état had stripped Khrushchev of power in September. And Paxton found herself full of admiration for Edward Wilson. He was intelligent and reasonable and he had great foresight, which she respected, even though their opinions on Viet Nam differed. They talked about the realities of integration in the South, and Martin Luther King, and even the recent developments and student unrest at Berkeley. The Free Speech Movement had gotten out of hand in the past few days, and the Board of Regents were taking a tough position, refusing to negotiate with the students, which Peter's father agreed with, and Paxton said she did too, although it was not a popular view on campus. It turned out that President Kerr was a friend of his, and they had had a long conversation only that morning.

"He's not going to play ball with those kids. There's too much at stake. If he gives in, they'll lose all control at the campus." Peter strongly disagreed with him, and they talked about it for a long time, but Paxton found all of their discussions exhilarating and refreshing. It was exciting being with people who talked about intelligent things, and were aware of what was happening in the world. In Savannah, she felt so cut off from the real world sometimes, so bogged down by the South, and their desperate fight to hang on to the past and a way of life that had to go by the wayside. And Paxton said as much to Ed Wilson.

"You have a wonderful paper down there, though. W. S. Morris and I are old friends."

"I'm hoping to work for him, or for the paper anyway, next summer. I'm a journalism major, or I will be next year." Peter smiled proudly at her, and reached out and took her hand, which did not escape his father. Ed Wilson didn't say anything to him, but he did to Marjorie that night, when they were undressing in their bedroom.

"I think your son is seriously smitten, my love." He looked tenderly at his wife. She loved her children so much, he wondered if it would be hard for her when they finally fell in love and got married and had lives of their own, apart from their parents. "Something tells me he's really in love with that girl."

"I think so too," she said pensively as she sat at her dressing table and brushed the once red hair. "But you know something, I like her. She's quiet at first, but there's a lot to her. She really cares about him, and she's decent and straightforward and very honest."

"And much too young to get married," her husband added. "At eighteen, it would be crazy to even consider marriage."

"I don't think she is considering it. Something tells me that there's a lot she wants to do with her life. I think she's even more levelheaded than Peter."

"I hope so." He sighed. And then as he bent and kissed his wife's neck with a tender smile, "I'm not ready for grandchildren yet."

"Neither am I." She laughed. "But in that case, talk to Gabby."

"Oh, no, don't tell me, not another true love this week. Do I need to worry, or will it be over by next Tuesday?"

"Long before that. Thank God no one's taken that child seriously yet. She's going to kill me."

"Is she?" He returned to Marjorie's side in the pajamas he had made twice a year in London and took the hairbrush from her hand and put it on her dressing table. "I love you, do you know that?" She nodded, and without a word, put her arms around him and kissed him. And then, quietly, she turned off the lights and went to bed, and he lay there with his arms around her. They were happy people with a life that meant a lot to them, and a family they had always cherished.

And it showed the next day, as they sat down together for Thanksgiving. Paxton wore her black velvet dress, and Gabby wore a white Chanel suit her mother had bought her the year before in Paris. It made her look very grown up suddenly and it reminded Paxton of when Jackie Kennedy was setting the fashions. And as Ed Wilson said grace, he looked serious and distinguished. And Paxton caught a glimpse of a private smile that had more than a little spice to it, between him and Gabby's mother.

They had an enormous meal that left them all stupefied with satisfaction, and even Paxton had to admit that it almost rivaled Queenie's. She told them about their Thanksgiving meals, and spoke with obvious love for the woman who had raised her. And in the afternoon, friends came by, and Paxton was impressed to realize that one of them was the governor of California. They were all talking about the demonstration that was taking place at Berkeley that afternoon, led by Mario Savio and the other members of the Free Speech Movement. Apparently Joan Baez was singing there, and a thousand students had staged a sit-in, protesting the university's positions against free speech, no longer wanting them or the other causes to use university property to raise money or pass out leaflets for their causes. The university said that traffic was being blocked and leaflets were littering the campus. Finally the university had compromised, saying they could use the same space they had previously used, but they could not advocate action. To Paxton, it all seemed like a tempest in a teacup, but tempers had flared, liberties had been questioned, and the time was right for a contest of wills and a major explosion. And by that night, almost eight hundred students had been arrested. And Paxton found it fascinating to be in the Wilson home, where everyone was so aware of what was going on in the world, and in close touch with people of action and power.

They all watched the continuing demonstrations on the news the next day, and as a result, she and Peter never went to Stinson. On Saturday, she went to the football game with Peter and his father, while Gabby went shopping with her mother. Paxton had called her own mother on Thanksgiving Day, and spoke to her and George, and Queenie. They seemed to be alright and she had assured them that she was having a good Thanksgiving, although only Queenie seemed worried about it. And she had whispered into the phone that she hadn't made her best mince pie that year, since Paxton wasn't there to enjoy it.

Paxton had a good time at the game, and by the end of the weekend, she felt close to all of them. She felt like a member of the family, as she said good-bye to them, and thanked them for a wonderful Thanksgiving. It had been the best one she'd had in years, the best one since her father died, and her eyes shone happily as she thanked Peter and Gabby on the way back to Berkeley.

There was still evidence of unrest when they got back to school. There were riot police everywhere, in case further demonstrations broke out, and Paxton was shocked to learn that night that Yvonne and Deke had been part of the demonstration and had been arrested. They had already been released by then, but Yvonne had terrible bruises on her arms, inflicted by the riot squad when they dragged her to the paddy wagon.

"It was pretty grim," she admitted with a somber look. "And where were you all weekend?" she asked Paxton and Gabby accusingly as Peter brought their bags up from the car.

"In San Francisco," Gabby answered snappily, not inclined to say more. She had no intention of feeling guilty for not getting arrested. "You don't have to go to jail to prove you give a damn, Yvonne. It's not going to prove shit if I get bruises on my arms, and to tell you the truth, I don't give a damn where they hand out those goddamn leaflets." It was the first time she'd lit into Yvonne, but she was tired of her snide remarks and her veiled accusations.

"What *do* you give a damn about?" Yvonne shot back at her as Peter and Paxton listened.

"Maybe the same things you do. I care about the blacks, I care about Viet Nam, I care about people getting a fair deal, and staying alive to enjoy it, but I'm not going to have my ass dragged down the street and thrown into a paddy wagon to prove it."

"Then nobody's ever going to listen to you. You can't sit around in your living room, filing your nails and thinking someone will hear you, they won't. Nobody heard in the South till people started getting shot and killed and arrested."

"So how come you're here and not there?" Gabby shot back quickly at her.

"Because I'm sick of it. Because I'm sick of the back of the bus, baby. I've had it all my life. And I'm going to stay here until I can go back and kick ass at the front of the bus where someone is going to pay attention."

"Great. But don't pick on me while you're here, because I'm just out here minding my own business."

"I'm moving next month anyway," Yvonne blurted out, annoyed, not quite sure whether or not she had been bested by

Gabby. Maybe she should have been in the South. Maybe she should have been in Birmingham, fighting Wallace's cronies and not sitting in Berkeley. But she had had it with all that, which was why she'd been so glad to get the scholarship to Berkeley.

"You moving in with Deke?" Gabby asked, only mildly curious. She was tired of Yvonne and the enormous chip on her shoulder. It was so large, it obscured her view most of the time, but Paxton, knowing the South as she did, wasn't sure she always blamed her.

But Yvonne was shaking her head in answer to Gabby's question. "No . . . I'm . . ." She looked embarrassed suddenly, as though she realized she'd gone too far, as though she knew she'd taken her anger out on them and they didn't deserve it. "I'm not moving in with Deke. I'm moving off campus with friends." Paxton knew she would live, by choice, with people like herself who were still too angry to enjoy the integration they had finally won and didn't yet know what to do with.

"That's cool," Paxxie said quietly. "I hope you'll be happy there."

"What about your room?" Gabby said matter-of-factly, unmoved by Yvonne's announcement.

"I figure you can find someone to take my place." And then, as she spoke, Dawn wandered into the room in her nightgown.

"I'm moving too," she said hesitantly, ". . . that is . . . I mean . . . I'm leaving." She looked apologetic, but pleased, as she smiled at all of them. "I'm going home."

"You're dropping out?" Gabby looked stunned, she couldn't imagine why anyone would want to leave, she was having so much fun there. But admittedly, Dawn had done nothing but sleep in the three months she'd been there.

"I'm getting married . . . I think . . . at Christmas . . . I'm . . ." She blushed, and looked at them, her only friends in Berkeley. She had hardly been to a single class since she'd been there. "I'm having a baby in April."

The three girls looked at her in amazement, although Paxton realized afterward how stupid they all were. She had every symptom in the books, but they'd only been kidding when they'd said she might be pregnant.

"Dave and I are going to Nepal as soon as the baby's born, to see our guru."

"That's great," Gabby said, still looking amazed, and Peter turned away so the girls wouldn't see him smile. "That's really great, Dawn." And after the other two went back to their rooms, Gabby turned to Paxton with an irritated look. "Shit, now what are we going to do about their room? If the university assigns it, God knows who we'll get, and I don't know anyone who wants to switch midyear, do you?"

"Why don't we trade?" Paxton said pensively. "I know two sets of girls who have doubles and are dying for a quad. We could give this to them, and take one of their deuces."

"Or you could just turn their room into a closet. Or move in with me," Peter said hopefully, looking at Paxton. They had been remarkably good that weekend at his parents. Although he had been tempted to come to her room and try to seduce her, he had forced himself not to. He knew how upset she would have been to do something like that in his parents' home, and he also knew from Gabby that Paxton was still a virgin. He had been thinking about it for a while, and wondering if she would be willing to go away with him somewhere, but so far the right time hadn't come to ask her, and he was willing to bide his time till she was ready. Paxton was someone he wanted with him forever. "Actually, you know, that's not such a bad idea," he said to both of them before he left, "maybe next year we could rent a place together, off campus." The idea appealed to all of them, but next year seemed like a long way off, and Paxton wondered if he would still like her by then. A lot of things could change in a year. It was amazing to think of what already had. In three months, she and Gabby had become good friends, she and Peter had fallen in love, they had lost two roommates, and one of them was having a baby. It was amazing to contemplate when they went to sleep that night. And the next weeks seemed to fly by before they left for Christmas vacation. After Christmas, Peter was going skiing with friends, and Gabby was going to Puerto Vallarta, in Mexico, with her parents. Peter had asked Paxton if she wanted to come skiing with him, but she had told him that it would be awkward leaving her family early to come back to California, and he understood that.

He drove her to the airport on the twenty-first instead and as they stood at the gate, making comfortable chitchat about Christmas, he suddenly looked down at her and her heart stopped when he spoke to her, suddenly looking almost as grown up as his father.

"This isn't going to work, you know." It was almost Christmas, and he was telling her the romance was over.

"What . . . I . . . I . . . I'm sorry . . ." She couldn't look up at him, it hurt too much, and she resisted as she felt his finger under her chin, forcing her to look up at him, her eyes blinded by the tears he had just caused her.

"You don't know what I mean, Pax, do you?" His eyes were damp too, and she shook her head miserably as she watched him. "I can't go on playing like this, pretending we're just good friends and this is just a freshman flirtation. I'm in love with you, Pax. I've never loved anyone like I love you. I want to marry you one day. All you have to do is say when. Tomorrow, next week, ten years. You want to go to the Peace Corps, to Africa, to the moon, that's fine. I'll wait. I love you." His voice trembled, and his lips, too, and he pulled her into his arms so hard, it took her breath away, and this time when she kissed him, he had her whole heart. She couldn't play with him anymore either. She knew just how much she loved him.

"Peter, what are we going to do?" She was smiling through her tears this time, and he was too. Just holding her, feeling her, kissing her, he knew she loved him. "I have three and a half more years of school. I *have* to finish," she added.

"So we'll wait. No big deal. Maybe we'll get engaged sometime. All I want to know is if you love me." His eyes bore into hers and she nodded seriously.

"I love you . . . I love you so much. . . ." she whispered, and this time he took her in his arms and kissed her more gently.

"I hate not to be with you on Christmas," he whispered into her hair, "do you want me to fly down to Savannah after Christmas?" She did, but she didn't dare. If her mother knew that at eighteen she was serious about someone, particularly a boy from California, she'd be frantic.

"No, it's too soon. They won't understand."

"Then come back soon."

They were calling her plane for the last time and everyone had already boarded. "I've got to go. I'll call you from home." . . . home . . . where was home now? "I love you." But what if he forgot her over the holidays? What if he found someone else? If he met someone when he was skiing? All her thoughts were on her face as she pulled away from him and he laughed at her.

"Stop that, you dummy. I love you. And *you'd* better remember that. One day, your name is going to be Paxton Wilson." He gave her a last quick kiss, and she ran to catch her plane, waving to him, and calling over her shoulder that she loved him.

# CHAPTER 5

˅

It was strange arriving in Savannah that night. It was cold and dark, and very late. The plane had been delayed on the way and with the time difference, it was almost midnight when she got home, and everyone was sleeping. Her brother had come to pick her up, but her mother had gone to bed with a bad head cold. Only Queenie was sitting up waiting for her, with hot chocolate and Paxton's favorite oatmeal cookies fresh from the oven. The two embraced without a word, and just holding her old friend, Paxton wanted to share her happiness with her. She had thought of Peter constantly on the plane, and now she could hardly wait to tell her. But George seemed not to want to go. He seemed to feel dutybound to wait until she finished her hot chocolate. He told her the news of people around town, and told her that her mother had been given an award by the Daughters of the Civil War, and Paxton tried to sound excited for her. But all she could do was look at Queenie and smile, telling her with her eyes how much she loved her.

And at last, she went upstairs to bed, and George went home, and she lay in bed thinking of Peter, and trying to feel at home there. But nothing felt the same, nothing felt inviting and warm, and all she could do as she lay there was think of Peter and

California. It took her hours to fall asleep, and when she did at last, she felt lonely without listening to Gabby.

And in the morning, things were worse. She felt like a stranger when she had breakfast with her mother. She congratulated her mother on her award, and after a cool nod of thanks, her mother fell into an awkward silence. They seemed to have nothing to say at all, and Paxton kept struggling to find things to tell her about her classes. She never asked about Paxton's roommates at all, and there was no way in the world she would have mentioned Peter to her. She did mention that George had a "new friend," and told her that she would meet her that night at dinner, although George himself had said absolutely nothing about her when he picked Paxton up at the airport. And Paxton was reminded again how different her own family was from the Wilsons. And she couldn't help wondering how different they might have been if her father were still alive, to warm their hearts and make them all a little more human.

It was late afternoon before she managed to find Queenie alone in the comfortable kitchen, and she told her all about Gabby and Peter and the Wilsons.

"You ain't done nothin' you'll be sorry for, have you, girl?" she asked her sternly, and Paxton shook her head, but the thought had crossed her mind, and now that they had admitted how serious they both were, it was reasonable to believe that, sooner or later, something "serious" could happen. But she answered Queenie truthfully, and knew that there were some thoughts you didn't share, even with Queenie.

"No, Queenie, I haven't. But he's wonderful. You'd love him." She told her all about him again, and the old woman watched her with a tender heart, her eyes alight as she talked about the boy she'd fallen in love with in California.

"You like it there? Are ya happy?"

"I really am. It's wonderful. It's so exciting." She told her about the classes she was taking, the people she had met, the places she had seen, and Queenie could see it all from her descriptions. And then, in a conspiratorial whisper, she asked her about George's new girlfriend.

"You'll see." The old woman laughed. "I think this one may be for real though." But somehow, Paxton sensed that Queenie didn't like her.

"What makes you think so?" Paxton looked intrigued, but Queenie only laughed, and two hours later, Paxton could see for herself why Queenie didn't think much of her. George's new friend, Allison, looked like their mother's double. She wore her hair the same way, had the same cool airs, the same prim, southern-lady manners, only she was much, much more restrained. And everything about her was so taut, she seemed in danger of breaking. But George looked totally at ease with her. He was used to that kind of woman, although in his youth, even George had liked them a little looser. Paxton watched her all that evening, her mouth so prim and tight, she could barely speak, and yet she didn't seem shy about expressing her opinions. And finally after dinner, Paxton exploded into the kitchen, and when they were alone, she let her hair down with Queenie. "My God, she's so rigid and so opinionated, how on earth does he stand her?" But she was exactly what he wanted. In his view, she was the perfect southern woman. He had been well trained by their mother. "What does Mama think of her?" She was curious about that, but Queenie only shrugged.

"I don't know. She don't tell me nothing."

"It must be like looking in the mirror, or maybe she doesn't see it."

The rest of the evening was incredibly boring for her, as was the rest of the trip. They went to church on Christmas Eve and again on Christmas morning. She saw a few of her friends and was shocked to discover that two of her friends who had chosen not to go to college that year were getting married, and another one who'd gotten married after graduation in June was already pregnant. Here she felt years too young even to consider responsibilities like that, and they were already fully embarked on adult lives with husbands and children. It made her think of Peter again, everything did now, and he called her every few days, but most of the time she answered the phone herself so no one was aware of how often he called her. Her mother only mentioned him once, and said she thought it odd that a boy from California would call Paxton all the way to Savannah and she hoped it didn't mean anything unpleasant. "Anything unpleasant" being an involvement with a boy who wasn't from Savannah, Georgia.

Paxton went to the employment office of the newspaper while she was there, and despite Mr. Wilson's offer to smooth the way for her, she didn't take advantage of it, and managed to get hired for a summer job while she was on vacation from Berkeley from June to August. She was looking forward to it, but now anything that would take her away from Peter depressed her. And that bothered her too. She didn't want to be totally dependent on him, and there was still so much she wanted to do with her life, to fulfill the promises she'd made herself. But he had promised he would wait, and she knew he would. He had repeated that promise again and again when he had called her in Savannah over Christmas.

She had agreed to fly home the day before New Year's Eve, and her mother seemed to be so involved with George and Allison and her own friends that Paxton didn't think she'd really mind it. She even admitted to them that she wanted to spend New Year's Eve with her friends at school, and although her mother said she thought that "unkind of her," she actually seemed to accept it. George took her to the airport again, after Paxton spent a quiet morning in the kitchen with Queenie. She had developed her annual chest cold by then, and Paxton had made her promise she would go to the doctor.

Paxton's mother had gone to the hairdresser before she left, and had said good-bye to her earlier that morning. And as Paxton prepared to say good-bye to George, she told him to give her best to Allison, and he almost flinched at the familiarity with which she said it.

"You two are serious, aren't you?" she couldn't resist asking him in the intimacy of the moment. Intimacy was a word which her brother hated.

"I have no idea what that means," he said with a tone of icy annoyance, and she couldn't help laughing softly. He had just turned thirty-three, and if he hadn't figured it out by then, he was in serious trouble. "It's most unladylike, Paxton, for you to ask that." The thought came into her head of how comfortable Peter and Gabby were and it made her sad to realize how different her own life was, and how stiff and stilted her relationship with her only brother.

"I think she really likes you, George. And I think Mother likes her." It was all she could say that was true. She didn't want to lie and say she liked her.

"I'm sure she does," he said miserably, wishing his sister hadn't asked the question.

"Take care of yourself." She leaned forward and kissed him on the cheek, and without another word, took her bag from his hand and walked toward the plane with a last friendly wave in his direction. Peter had done a lot for her. She couldn't bring herself to play their game anymore, the game of frozen feelings, and constant restraint, and endless silent dinners. And as George watched her go, he thought unhappily of what was happening to his sister in California.

When Paxton got off the plane in San Francisco this time, Peter was waiting for her, and her feet barely touched the ground once he saw her. He swept her off her feet and into his arms, pressed his lips onto hers, and held her tight as they laughed and kissed, and passersby smiled as they watched them.

It was nice to see young people in love like that, it warmed the heart, and reminded people of what they had once felt like.

"Oh, God, I missed you," he said fervently as he finally set her down and they walked slowly toward the baggage claim arm in arm. "I didn't think I could stand it another minute."

"Neither could I." She beamed.

"How was Savannah?"

"Awful!" She told him again all about Allison, and George, and her summer job, and everything Queenie had said about them, and with regret, she mentioned how withdrawn and distant her mother had been. "I think she still feels betrayed because I went to Berkeley. That, and I guess she's always been like that but I see it more now, because now I've seen something so different." Like the Wilsons.

"It doesn't matter, babe. You have me now." It was a brave thing to say and it touched her heart. But still, a tiny part of her was still afraid to rely on him completely. What if he changed his mind, or went away, or fell in love with someone else . . . she had learned a long time since that it was very dangerous to love someone completely. She had learned that lesson a long time before with the man she'd loved so deeply, the man who'd been everything to her, and then it was all over in a single moment, when his plane crashed.

"What are we doing tonight?" she asked happily as they walked to the garage for his jalopy. She didn't really care what they did, just so she could be with him. She had never been as happy in her life. Maybe her friends in Savannah were right, the ones who were married and having babies. She had told him about them, too, and about how strange it made her feel, but he understood that she wasn't ready for that yet. He seemed to understand everything, and she had never loved him more as they sat in his old car and kissed until neither of them could think straight.

"What are we doing tonight? . . ." He tried to make himself

think, as she laughed. "I was going to drive you back to Tahoe tonight, so we could spend the weekend there. But there's a storm and they've closed Donner Pass. We're going to have to wait till tomorrow morning and see if they'll open the pass then. Do you want to go to dinner and a movie?"

"Sure." He drove her into town, and she wasn't sure if she was going to spend the night at her dorm at UC, or in the guest room at the Wilsons'. His parents and Gabby were still away, and all the help was off, but he insisted that there was no reason why she couldn't stay there. "Do you think we'll behave?" she asked him honestly while she tried to make up her mind about it.

"Do you want me to behave?" he asked her, holding her gently.

"I'm not sure what I want anymore, Peter . . . I keep thinking we have to wait . . . for that too . . . and then I look at my friends, and think I'm stupid."

"Don't look at them," he said gently. "Look at me, look at you. I'll do whatever you want, Paxxie."

She smiled gratefully at him. "I'll sleep in the guest room." She didn't want to sleep alone in a lonely dorm. In fact she wanted to curl up in bed with him. She wanted much more than that, but she still believed she shouldn't do it. She was almost nineteen, and he was turning twenty-three. They were old enough to get married, to have kids, to do a million things, and yet they weren't supposed to make love yet because they weren't married.

When they got to the Wilsons' house, he carried her suitcase upstairs for her, and then went back downstairs to look for the paper to pick out a movie, and she felt wonderfully at home just being there, in the grandeur of the place that had been built by Ed Wilson's father. And she laughed as she sat down and looked around the pretty guest room. The fabric was a pretty pink flowered chintz, the carpet a pale, sunny yellow, and the bathroom was all pink and white marble. It was every girl's dream, and so was Peter.

"How about *Goldfinger,* the new James Bond movie?" he suggested when he came back upstairs with two beers and a bag of potato chips he held out to her. "Did you eat on the plane?" He suddenly realized she might be really hungry.

"I ate twice." She smiled. "I can't eat a thing." She had kicked off her shoes and changed into her jeans. She felt as though she'd come home again, just being there with him, as he sat down on the bed and curled up close to her.

"You can't begin to imagine how I missed you."

"I missed you too," she said softly as she put her arms around him and they kissed, and slowly they rolled back onto the bed and they lay there for a long time, kissing and holding each other and touching and stroking. They were quiet and at peace in the cozy room, and after a little while, he stopped, and seemed to look around them.

"I never realized how much I love this room. Or maybe it just seems like its yours now." He smiled, kissed her again, and held her closer, drinking in the subtle scent of her perfume. She wore Femme, and he loved it. The word itself made him think of her. Woman. "Maybe we should get up." He looked at her hesitantly, wondering if they should, because he was beginning to feel as if he didn't want to.

"Yeah," she said quietly. "I guess we should."

They got up. She put on a warm sweater and her shoes, and they went out to the movies. They went to the Hippo for a hamburger afterward, and they were home long before midnight. He kissed her goodnight in the hall outside her room, and then went upstairs to his own room. As always, they had talked about a thousand things they cared about that night, their families, their friends, their views, and now their future. And she was already in her nightgown, and still thinking of him, as she heard a soft knock on the door a few minutes after he had left her.

"Yes?" She knew who it had to be, because they were the only ones there.

"It's me," he said with a grin as he poked his head inside the door.

"That's good news." She laughed. "I figured if it wasn't, it had to be a burglar."

"I miss you," he said, looking like a little kid, and as he opened the door, she saw that he was wearing red flannel pajamas, and he laughed as he saw her looking at them. "It took me ten minutes to find these or I'd have been here sooner." They both laughed, and she felt young and happy and in love as she walked slowly toward him.

"I miss you too," she said softly, and without a word, he switched off the light, and they stood in the moonlight streaming in the windows.

"I don't know what to do, Pax . . . I don't want to do anything that'll hurt you . . . now or later . . . I love you so much . . . but it's . . . it's hard to keep my distance."

"I don't think I want you to." They sat down on the bed, just to talk, and then they were kissing again, and lying on the bed, and she was in his arms, and he gently pulled off her nightgown.

"I just want to look at you." He said it so softly, so gently, and his whole body ached as he looked at the sheer beauty of her in the moonlight. She was long and lean and beautiful and perfectly carved, like a beautiful pink marble statue. "Oh, God . . . I love you . . ."

And she loved him, too, and without hesitating, she unbuttoned his pajamas, and they lay there for a long time, holding each other close, and not daring to do more, yet wanting so much more than that, wanting everything they each had to give, forever. He stroked her long silky hair, and ran his hands gently over her breasts and down her thighs, and then back up again, barely daring to come closer to what he wanted. But it was Paxton who decided it for him. She couldn't bear it any longer. She wanted him too much, and she gently peeled away the bottom of his pajamas, revealing his urgency, his fervent desire for her, which he could no longer control as he held her.

"Paxxie . . ." he whispered hoarsely, "are you sure? . . ." But she only nodded with a smile and then kissed him, as he gently rolled her over on her back, and pushed her legs apart with his own and sought what she had saved for him until that moment.

He was infinitely gentle with her and there was almost no pain, there was only passion and desire and youth, and the gifts of love they had to give each other. They lay in each other's arms all that night, making love again and again, and in the morning, when he awoke, she lay there beside him, her hair fanned out across his arm, her face like a child's, sleeping, as with one hand she held his, and he felt a tear sting his eye as he watched her. She was what he had dreamed of all his life, what he had wanted, what he'd hoped to find one day, and only she knew now how much he loved her.

# CHAPTER 6

∨

The rest of the school year seemed to fly by, with only a few very important events to mark it. Over Christmas, Viet Cong terrorists had bombed the Brinks Hotel in Saigon where the American officers were housed. It was Christmas Eve, and officers had come from all over Saigon to share a celebration that ended in shock and grief. Two were killed, and fifty-eight wounded. And once again, Lyndon Johnson refused to retaliate by bombing. Another attack ensued. And finally, on February seventh, the President ordered the first major bombing raids against the North. And two and a half weeks later, "Operation Rolling Thunder" began, the first sustained bombing of Viet Nam. And two weeks after that, the first ground combat troops arrived. On March eighth, the Marines landed in Da Nang, after years of futile "advisers."

Two weeks after that, the American embassy in Saigon was attacked, and the American public began to understand that we had a serious problem in Viet Nam.

At the same time, in the States, the National Guard was obliged to protect the Selma–Montgomery Freedom March, and the University of Michigan staged the first antiwar teach-in.

But the teach-in didn't stop the war, and the bombing didn't stop the Viet Cong. Supplies were still reaching the South by the elusive Ho Chi Minh Trail. And there were more antiwar protests on Armed Forces Day in May. And Peter and Paxton participated in the one at UC Berkeley.

It was almost the end of the school year for them. And Paxton was getting nervous about leaving him to go back to Savannah. The thought of not being with him every day seemed almost frightening to her now. She couldn't imagine a day without him.

He had volunteered for the law project he'd talked about. And he was planning on spending most of the summer in Mississippi. But he had promised to come and see her whenever he could. And she was going to be working in Savannah, on the paper. Gabby was to go to Europe with her parents again, and she had pooh-poohed the idea of getting a job when her father suggested it to her. She had promised to get one the following year but she wanted to play "just this last time," on the Riviera with friends, and in Paris with her mother. Ed Wilson had scolded his wife for indulging her, but like Gabby, she felt that "one more year" wouldn't hurt her.

All three of them left Berkeley on the first of June. Peter and Paxton spent a quiet weekend at a cabin he rented at Lake Tahoe, and they lay in bed together for the last time before they separated for the summer.

"I'm going to go crazy without you," he whispered as he nuzzled the long golden hair. "It's going to be so lonely in Mississippi."

"Savannah's gonna be worse," she said glumly, but they forgot everything as they fell into each other's arms again, and it was a long, happy weekend. His parents suspected that something had happened between them, and so did Gabby, but neither Peter nor Paxton admitted anything. They were together all the time, and their grades were excellent, so no one could complain. And Peter, Paxton, and Gabby had already agreed to look for a house together for the fall so the threesome could live off campus. Paxton knew that the secret of their affair would be obvious to her then, but by then they'd be willing to tell her. It would be worth it, in order to enjoy the luxury of living together off campus.

Gabby left San Francisco first with Marjorie. They were flying to London to visit friends, and stay at Claridge's, before moving on to Paris. And then Paxton left, waving sorrowfully to Peter at the airport. And he left the same afternoon, in time to reach Jackson, Mississippi, for a voting protest that wound almost a thousand people in jail. Peter was among them, and he was quickly bailed out, and felt as though he had been appropriately christened.

Paxton's introduction to her job was a subtler one, and she was bitterly disappointed to discover that she had been assigned to the editor who covered social news, and she was left to coordinate reports of who was entertaining whom, wearing what, and what the Junior League and the Daughters of the Civil War were doing. It was a job her mother finally understood, and actually had a certain respect for, and at the same time it left Paxton feeling utterly useless. She would sit at the newspaper and watch the teletypes in despair, reporting sit-ins in Alabama, and the doubling of our ground troops in Viet Nam, raising the total to a "mere" hundred and eighty-one thousand men, numbers that were staggering. And Johnson doubled the draft that summer. Paxton knew that some of the boys over there were boys she had gone to school with, and in two cases, their younger brothers. One had already been killed, and she couldn't bear to hear it. And suddenly it terrified her. What if, in some insane way, they managed to get Peter?

She called him almost every day and he called her as often, and in late July, he managed to come up from Mississippi for the weekend. He had planned to come up earlier than that, but he had been in jail twice, and the job he had was far more demanding than he had expected. But Paxton had never looked happier than when she took a cab and picked him up at the airport. He swung her into his arms, and he looked handsome and tan, his hair the same golden color as her own as he kissed her.

"Boy, is it good to see you!" He grinned. "I'm so tired of bailing people out of jail, I can hardly see straight."

"Not nearly as tired as I am of garden parties and afternoon concerts! Christ, I thought I was going to be doing something meaningful, and I've done nothing but write about my mother's friends all summer."

He grinned at her and kissed her again, wishing they could go to bed somewhere on the way in from the airport. "How is your mother, by the way?"

"Same as ever. She can hardly wait to meet you."

"Oh-oh. That sounds dangerous." He kissed her again. He couldn't stop kissing her. It had been almost two months since he'd seen her. But she was just as hungry for him. She had rented him a room in a nice quiet hotel just outside town, where she wasn't likely to run into her mother's friends, and she told him that as they drove into Savannah.

"May I make a suggestion?" He grinned and leaned over to kiss her in his rented car.

"Anything you like." She was beaming.

"How about checking out the hotel on the way home?" He grinned mischievously and she laughed.

"That sounds like an excellent idea." She was all his. She had taken two days off from the paper, in spite of a very social wedding they had thought she should cover.

They arrived at the little hotel shortly after that, and Peter looked extremely serious and responsible in his suit and tie as he signed the register Mr. and Mrs. Wilson, and carried the single bag to a clean, simple room that became their honeymoon suite for the next several hours.

It was almost nightfall when he looked at his watch and she gasped. "Good Lord, my mother's expecting you for cocktails."

"I'm not sure I can still stand up, let alone drink," he teased, and pulled her back into bed with him again, but only for a minute. And then they showered together, and dressed. For a brief moment, it was almost like being married. "Does she know we're sharing a house together this year?" He didn't want to put his foot in it and it was a good thing he asked, because Paxton shrieked at the very suggestion.

"Are you crazy? She thinks it's me and Gabby and another girl, and even at that, she's not crazy about the idea." But she had finally relented.

"Great. I gather this means I can never touch the phone." He looked amused, and he didn't mind. All he wanted was to live with Paxton, even if it meant putting up with his sister. His mother had told him on the phone, when she called him in Jackson, that Gabby had chased every man over thirty on the Riviera. "I think she's getting desperate," he said to Paxton on the drive back into town. "She's silly, she's too young to get married." Paxton smiled at the words, and he leaned over and kissed her. "That's different. She's a baby, you're not. But I think you're too young too. For about three more years. And then . . . watch out!" They both laughed. She knew how reasonable he had been, and she never felt pressured by him. He wanted her to do what she needed to, like this summer, working in Savannah, but she had to admit, she had been miserable without him.

George and her mother were waiting for them when they drove in, and her mother looked frankly disapproving at Paxton.

"I thought you'd be home hours ago." Allison was there, and her mother thought Paxton should have changed for their "guest," but Paxxie ignored her.

"I was showing Peter the sights. Peter," she said formally,

"my mother, Beatrice Andrews, my brother, George, and his
. . . 'friend,' Allison Lee." Her mother never failed to tell anyone that Allison was related to the great Confederate general.
And Paxton had waited all summer for George to get engaged
to her, but for some reason he hadn't. At thirty-three, he didn't
want to rush into anything. Anything. Although, at thirty-one,
Allison seemed to be getting decidedly nervous. "This is Peter
Wilson," she explained to all of them as though they'd never
heard of him before. "His sister, Gabby, is my roommate." Everyone murmured polite how-do-you-do's, shook hands, and
George offered Peter a drink, and Peter asked for a gin and
tonic. It was deadly hot and the fan overhead did little to cool
the room, although everyone pretended not to notice. Queenie
had made her best hors d'oeuvres, and Allison passed them
looking demure and as prissy as ever. Paxton had decided long
since that she couldn't stand her.

But Peter was congenial with everyone, and her mother was
painfully polite, while George looked frankly bored, and Allison
appeared not even to know someone was in the room with
them. She almost never spoke to Paxton, and had said to
George several times that she just didn't understand her. And
secretly, she thought Paxton rude and far too headstrong. Allison kept talking to George that night about the new curtains
she had just ordered for her bedroom. Peter tried to explain
what he was doing in Mississippi, but no one seemed to care,
and her mother kept pointedly changing the subject. It took him
a while to realize that it was because she disapproved of what he
was doing there, and she was trying to keep him from embarrassing himself, and when the message finally got across, it
shocked him. They were even worse than Paxton had said. They
were distant and cold, and living in the Dark Ages.

He switched to discussing his parents' trip to Europe then,
which seemed a safer subject. Paxton's mother seemed impressed to hear that they were in the south of France, and she

asked him as genteelly as she could what his father did, and Peter was surprised Paxton hadn't told her.

"He . . . uh . . . works for a newspaper in San Francisco. . . ." It seemed indiscreet somehow to say he owned it.

"How nice," Beatrice Andrews said with a look of obvious disapproval. "And you're going to be a lawyer?" He nodded, speechless at the iciness of her tone. She was everything Paxton had said and more . . . or less, as it were. She was glacial. "Paxton's father was an attorney. Her brother"—her eyes indicated the deadly George—"is a doctor." Now that was obviously a profession that measured up in her eyes.

"That's wonderful," Peter said, feeling wooden and wondering how long he could go on talking to them, and how Paxton could stand them on a daily basis. No wonder she was so unhappy when she came home. She was so unlike them. "And Allison, what do you do?"

"I . . . why . . . uh . . ." She was so startled to be asked, she had no idea what to say. She had been waiting around to find a husband for thirteen years, ever since she got out of high school. "Why . . . I . . . I'm very fond of my garden."

"And she does marvelous work for us at the Junior League, don't you, dear," Mrs. Andrews said encouragingly. And then to Peter, "Her great-great uncle was General Lee. *The* General Lee. I'm sure you know who he is."

"Yes indeed." Peter felt as though he was going to run from the room screaming, and it was the longest dinner of his life, with endless silences, and awkward snatches of conversation, and only an occasional wink or nudge from Queenie, or look from Paxton, to cheer him. It seemed aeons before they went back to his hotel, and he pulled off his tie, and collapsed on the bed with a groan that didn't begin to express what he had felt about the evening, and then he sat up and looked at Paxton. They had pretended they were going out for a little "dancing." "My God, baby, how do you stand them? They are the most difficult, uptight people I've ever met. I know I shouldn't say this about your family, but I thought I'd never get through that dinner."

She grinned from ear to ear. "I know. Aren't they awful? I never know what to say to them. I always feel like a stranger."

"You are. You don't even look related to them. Your brother is the most boring man I've ever met, his girlfriend is the most prissy, uptight, dumb pain in the ass, and your mother . . . my God, she's like an iceberg."

Paxton grinned happily, loving him more than ever. She felt avenged suddenly, and as though she had more in the world than just Queenie. "That's my Mommy."

Peter still couldn't believe there were people like that in the world. They were totally different from his own family, and totally different from Paxxie. "I wish I'd met your father."

"So do I. He would have loved you."

"I'm sure I would have loved him too. But from everything you've said about him, Paxton, I just can't imagine him with your mother."

"I don't think he was very happy with her. I was only eleven when he died, so the subtleties of their relationship kind of escaped me."

"Maybe that's just as well. Thank God you went to Berkeley." He couldn't begin to imagine what would have happened to her if she had stayed in Savannah with them. It would have destroyed her, or her spirit eventually. He had had three gin and tonics just to get through dinner, and they probably thought he was an alcoholic.

Paxton stayed with him as long as she could, and then he drove her home in the rented car, and watched as she went into the house. And much to her surprise, her mother was waiting up for her, which was something she never did, and wasn't necessarily a good omen.

"What exactly does that boy mean to you?" she asked Paxton only seconds after she came through the door.

"He's my friend. I like him."

"You're in love with him." Her mother hurled the words at her like cannonballs, and as though she expected Paxton to fall down and beg for mercy.

"Maybe." She didn't want to lie to her, but she didn't want to stir anything up either. Her mother was sitting on the couch in her dressing gown, and there was a small glass of sherry beside her. "I like his family. His sister is my friend, and his parents have been very nice to me."

"Why?" It was a ridiculous question and Paxton couldn't begin to find an answer.

"What do you mean, 'why'? Because they like me."

"Maybe because they think you're a step up in the world for their son. Have you ever thought of that?" Paxton almost laughed at the suggestion, but she didn't want to be rude to her mother.

"I don't think that's very likely."

"Why not?"

"Mother . . ." Paxton wasn't quite sure what to say to her, but the truth seemed the only solution. "They own the second biggest paper in San Francisco. The *Morning Sun.* They don't need me for anything. They just like me."

"They sound common," her mother said harshly, but in her opinion, all westerners were, including, and perhaps especially, Peter Wilson. Westerners were even worse than Yankees.

"They're not common." Paxton felt suddenly hurt by her mother's lack of warmth for the boy she loved. It was so unlike the warmth she had encountered from the Wilsons. "They're nice people, Mother. Really."

"I don't want you to go back to Berkeley." The words shot from her mouth like flares, and Paxton sat down heavily in a chair, wishing they didn't have to go through this.

"I like it there. It's a wonderful school. I'm doing well. Mother, I'm not going to stay here."

"You will if I tell you to. You're nineteen years old, and don't let that little trust your father left you go to your head. At your age, you are not independent."

"I'm sorry you feel that way." Paxton fought to stay calm, and she was far beyond her years in her wisdom. "But I'm not going to stay in Savannah."

"May I ask why?"

"Because I'm not happy here. I want broader horizons. And when I finish school, I want to go abroad somewhere for a while." Even Peter understood that.

"You're sleeping with him, aren't you?" It was a low blow, and one she hadn't expected.

"Of course not."

"Yes, you are. It's written all over you, like a cheap whore. You went to California and turned into a slut. Even your brother and Allison saw the difference." It was an ugly thing to say and their consensus hurt her.

"I'm sorry to hear that." Paxton stood up, determined not to hear more of the same. "I'm going to bed now, Mother."

"I want you to think about what I said."

"About being a whore?" Paxton said coldly, but her mother seemed unaffected.

"About staying here. I want you to think twice before you go back to California."

"I don't think I'll have to," Paxton said sadly, and walked up the stairs to her bedroom.

She met Peter at the hotel the next day, and she said very little about what had happened. But he knew. He could see it in her face. "She said something, didn't she? Was she upset?"

"Upset?" Paxton laughed, for the first time sounding bitter. "No, my mother never gets 'upset.' Disappointed. She wants me to transfer back to a school here." Peter looked horrified as he listened, but Paxton quickly kissed him to reassure him. "She says I'm turning into a slut out in California, even my brother and Allison can see it. And it's *very* distressing to *them.*"

"The bastards . . . did they . . ." He was spluttering he was so angry, and she silenced him with a kiss again, too wise for her years, too saddened by what had happened.

"It doesn't matter. I'll be back in Berkeley in four weeks. And I don't know if I'll ever come back here. I'm not sure I can. It depresses me too much. They always want to hurt me."

"Can she cut you off?" Peter asked worriedly, although he would have been more than happy to remedy the situation at a moment's notice, but Paxton shook her head. She still looked sad, but she also looked older and more independent.

"No, she can't. My father left me just enough money to go to school and support myself while I do. And after that, I have to work anyway, so it doesn't really make any difference. She'd probably support me if I wanted to come home and spend the rest of my life at the Junior League, but I don't, so it's no loss. It really doesn't make any difference. I just can't come back here. Not to live anyway." She looked certain.

"What about Queenie?" He knew how much she meant to Paxton.

"I'll come back to see her. I'd have to." Paxton smiled, but her life was in California with him now. More important, her life was her own, and she knew it. And so did her mother, which was what scared her. She had very little power now over Paxton.

He left the next day, and Paxton hated to see him go. And he hated to leave her among people who didn't love her. He promised to call her at least every day, more often if he could, and wasn't in jail, he laughed, as he left her at the airport. He kissed her long and hard and reminded her to think about how much he loved her, and not to let her family upset her.

But they did anyway. Her mother was hostile to her after

Peter left, and her brother told her several times, whenever he had the chance, that she owed it to their mother not to go back to California.

"I owe it to myself to make something of myself, George," she told him bluntly, no longer afraid of him, or impressed by him, despite the fact that he was so much older. He seemed pathetic now, a small-town doctor who was still tied to his mother's apron strings and was afraid to have a relationship with anyone of any substance. She was sure that her relationship with Peter was more whole and more mature than his was.

"You can make something of yourself here," George insisted to her one night before she left, when their mother was at her bridge club.

"Bullshit," she exploded. "Look at you. Look at the people we know. Look at Allison . . . look at the girls I went to school with."

"Watch your mouth, Paxton!" He was outraged at the slurs on all of them, but so was she. She had taken too much for too long and she'd had it. "You've filled your head with a lot of wild ideas and ugly words, Paxton, and they don't suit you."

"Neither does this. This isn't me. It never was. And it wasn't Daddy either. He probably just put up with it because he was a nice man and he thought he had to."

"You don't know anything about him. You were a child when he died."

"I know he was a good man with a big heart and I loved him."

"You don't know what he did to Mama." He said it as though he were hiding something terrible from her, and she found that hard to believe about her father.

"What could he possibly have done to her?" She couldn't imagine anything, but George couldn't resist hurting her further. It was his final revenge for her independence, the independence he had never had and never would because he was too much like their mother and not enough like their father, unlike Paxton.

"There was a woman with him when he crashed."

"There was?" Paxton looked startled at first and then, slowly, thoughtful. It explained a lot of things. Her mother's attitude. But it was also easy to understand why he had wanted another woman. She wasn't really surprised. And in a funny way, she was glad. If he had found someone to love and who had loved him, he deserved it. He didn't deserve to die for it. But that wasn't what had killed him. Chance had killed him. Bad luck. His name on a slate, written by a hand in Heaven. "I'm not really surprised," she said quietly, and he looked disappointed. "Mama was always so cold to him. He probably needed more than she had to give him."

"What would you know about that at your age?"

"I know what it's been like being her daughter," she said openly, and he looked shocked. "And your sister. We're very different."

"We certainly are," he said with angry pride. "We certainly are. And you'd better think twice about what you're making of yourself in California. Out there with all those drugs and hippies and demonstrations, all those fools wearing their bedsheets and putting flowers in their hair, and demonstrating for the blacks when they've never even seen one."

"Maybe they know more than you do, George. Maybe they care more. And maybe that's something."

"You're a fool."

"No." She shook her head as she looked at him. "No. But I would have been if I'd stayed here. Good-bye, George." She held out a hand to him, but he didn't take it. He just looked at her and a few minutes later, he left the house, and she didn't see him again before she left Savannah.

Her good-byes with Queenie were more painful this time, because she had already decided she wouldn't be back for

Christmas that year, although she hadn't said it to Queenie. But Queenie sensed that she wouldn't be back for a long time, and she held her close and looked into her eyes sadly. "I love you, girl. Take care of yourself."

"You too. And go to the doctor when you get that cough." But she seemed older and slower now, even without it. "I love you," Paxton whispered, and kissed the warm black cheeks and then she left her.

Her mother didn't take her to the airport this time, nor did George. Her mother said good-bye to her in the front hall, and let her know by her tone that her going back to California was a major disappointment, not because she'd be missed but because she had failed somehow, as a human being, and a Georgian, and as her mother's daughter, and George's sister. It was all more than a little exhausting.

"You're wasting your time out there."

"I'm sorry you feel that way, Mama. I'm trying my best not to."

"They said you did a nice job on the paper." It was the only compliment she could ever remember her mother giving her. "You could have a job working for the society editor one day, if you worked hard." Paxton didn't tell her she'd rather die than spend the rest of her life chronicling her friends' weddings.

"That's nice. Take care," she said softly, sorry to leave them, yet relieved, sorry most of all for what they had never been to each other.

"Watch out for that boy. He's no good."

"Peter?" It was an odd thing to say about him. He was so warm and so good and so decent that her mother's words shocked her. What did her mother know that she didn't?

"It's written all over him. If you let him, he'll use you and throw you away. That's what they all do." It was a statement about herself more than Paxton, and Paxton was sorry for her. It must have been a great blow to her to discover that her husband had been in the plane with another woman. And he had never regained consciousness again to explain it. George hadn't said who she was, or if she had survived the accident, but maybe it didn't matter. And Paxton didn't want to know any more than he had told her.

"I'll call when I know my number." They still had to find a house or an apartment to rent in Berkeley.

Her mother nodded and watched her go. She never reached out to her, or even tried to kiss her. And all the way to the airport in the cab, all Paxton could think about was going back to Berkeley, and Peter. And once she was on the plane on her way back to him, she never had another thought about Savannah.

# CHAPTER 7

⌄

By sheer luck, it only took them two weeks to find a house, on Piedmont, and it was perfect. There were two bedrooms and a huge living room, a big sunny kitchen, and a lovely garden. And it came as no shock to Gabby finally to discover that she was not going to be sharing the bedroom with Paxton, but sleeping alone, while Paxton and Peter shared the larger of the two bedrooms. She herself had lost her virginity to a handsome young Frenchman on the Riviera that year, and she now considered herself a woman of the world, and it excited her no end to discover that her brother and her best friend had been having an affair for months and she didn't know it. But Peter was less amused by her attitude about their affair, and he assured her that if she told anyone, compromised Paxxie in any way, or let their parents know that she wasn't sharing the room with her and he was, she would bitterly regret it.

But the arrangement worked beautifully. The Wilsons came over to visit them, and the girls cooked dinner for them. And the threesome got along to perfection. The two lovebirds got along perfectly, and Paxton and Gabby were as close as ever. The only difficulty was that Gabby seemed to have a new man in her life every week, and it was difficult for Peter to restrain himself and consider himself merely her roommate, and not her older brother. But Paxton reminded him constantly that he couldn't take advantage of the situation. But it was a constant strain on him to keep his mouth shut.

The other strain on him was the amount of work he had to do to keep his grades up during his second year of law school. There was a staggering amount of work, and Paxton had taken on a heavy workload, too, so they seemed to spend most of their time studying or in the library, or in bed, and very little out playing. Paxton was doing a little volunteer work in her spare time, and writing an occasional piece for the university paper as well, and she got a real thrill out of it whenever she saw her byline. It was an idyllic life for them, and they had never been happier.

They were deeply involved with school most of the time. And in mid-October, Peter burned his draft card with Paxton's full approval. At the same time in Viet Nam, B-52 bombers were being called in to support the ground troops, and the air cavalry became a major factor in fighting the Viet Cong, bringing choppers right into the jungle in the heat of the battle. The war had begun to escalate to unknown heights and it frightened Paxton thinking of what was going on there. But when they talked to Peter's father about it, he insisted that what was needed was more bombs, more men, and a tougher stance against the North. And all Paxton and Peter wanted was to see the United States get out completely. But it was impossible to convince his father of the wisdom of their position.

She spent Thanksgiving with his family again that year, and this time she felt like a member of the family, and she was totally at ease with the Wilsons. It was hard to believe that she and Peter had been involved for only a year. It seemed as though they had lived together forever. His parents suspected that was what was happening, too, but they stayed out of it, although more than once Marjorie asked Ed if he didn't think she should say something to them.

"Why? They're responsible kids. Do you think you'll change anything by talking to them?"

"Maybe they should get engaged if that's what they're doing."

"What difference does that make? If they want to get married, they will. And if they don't, they won't. They're too young to get married anyway. Peter will be twenty-four next month. And she isn't even twenty. Just wait. They know what they're doing, believe me."

Paxton spent Christmas with them, too, and by then she was horrified to read in the *Morning Sun* that the number of troops in Viet Nam had escalated to two hundred thousand.

"But that's insane!" she said to Peter, over breakfast.

"I know." He looked unhappily at her, praying he wouldn't flunk out of law school. It was getting so damn tough that sometimes it scared him. And the prospect of getting drafted scared him more. It was terrifying.

"Why don't people see what's happening over there? Boys are dying every day. Not just Vietnamese, our boys too. And they're sending eighteen-year-olds over to fight them."

"I'm too old for this war," he groaned as he poured himself another cup of coffee.

"If they ever call you up, I just want you to know now, I'll either shoot you in the ass myself, or lend you my black lace underwear and buy you a ticket to Toronto."

"I might take you up on that. The underwear anyway. As long as you're still in them."

"That can be arranged." She kissed him over their morning coffee, and Gabby groaned as she wandered into the kitchen in her nightgown.

"Are you two at it again? You make me sick." But in truth, she loved them both. She just wanted to find someone for herself now.

But after Christmas, when they all went skiing together, it

finally happened. Gabby was roaring down the slopes one day and collided with a man who flew into the air, and then came crashing down on her, and they lay in a breathless heap for a moment, untangling their limbs and their skis, trying to make sure that nothing was missing, damaged, or broken.

"That was one hell of a spill, are you alright?" he asked with considerable concern, standing up to his full height and offering a hand to pull her up, and she looked up at him with amazement. His name was Matthew Stanton and he had movie-star good looks and was wearing a one-piece black ski suit. He had dark hair and blue eyes and a well-trimmed beard, and he looked intrigued with her as she dusted herself off and apologized for not looking where she was going. He skied back to the lodge with her, invited her to lunch and dinner every night after that. Peter and Paxton scarcely saw her again except to wave from the lift, or as she ran in to change and go out with Matthew. He was thirty-two years old, in advertising, and seemed thoroughly amused by Gabby's constant antics. So much so that he seemed to appear constantly at the house in Berkeley when they went back, and whenever he did, Gabby seemed not to reappear until the following morning.

"Do you think he's serious?" Paxton asked Peter finally when they were studying for finals a month after Christmas.

"Who knows with those two. I don't see how he can put up with her." But whenever Paxton saw Matt with her, she thought they seemed very happy.

He had admitted to Gabby that he was divorced, but had no kids, and he seemed to be spending a lot of money on Gabby. There were flowers from him constantly, and books of poetry, and bracelets, and things he knew she'd like, trinkets and dolls and silly things that pleased her. He seemed to be imaginative and fun and playful. "And too old to get sent to Viet Nam," Paxton added to her list of virtues. "These days that's a real bonus."

"That's disgusting," Peter said. But it wasn't. Young men were being sent there every day to die for their country. And on January eleventh, student demonstrators had been reclassified 1-A, which had caused a real outrage in California. And three weeks later, Johnson resumed the bombing of North Viet Nam after a Christmas halt. It had lasted exactly thirty-eight days, and now it was all starting again. And all Paxton could think about at times was the war, and the danger of its finally reaching out to Peter.

Paxton had spoken to her family over the Christmas holiday several times, and her mother was hinting broadly that George might have a surprise for her in the spring, which hardly seemed a surprise anymore. If he finally got engaged at thirty-four, it was becoming a lot more surprising than if he wasn't. And Queenie was sick again, and she hadn't sounded well on the phone. Paxton was worried about her, but she didn't get a chance to call again for a long time, and when she did, her old friend insisted that she was much better.

"You're not lying to me, are you?"

"Would I lie to my baby girl?" Yes, she would, they both knew, but Paxton didn't say that.

In March 1966, government troops took Da Nang over from the Communists again, and Peter and Paxton took part in three days of antiwar protest.

Paxton had lined up her summer job by then. Peter's father had offered her a wonderful job as a cub reporter at the paper. She had hesitated at first, not wanting to take advantage of her relationship with Peter. But it was too good to resist, and Peter's father promised that she wouldn't cover a single garden party or fashion show during the entire summer. And all she had to do now was tell her mother she wasn't spending the summer in Savannah.

She went home over the Easter holiday to explain it to them, and George finally got engaged, and they were planning to get married sometime that summer. But Allison didn't ask Paxton to be one of her bridesmaids, which made it easier to explain that she would just be coming for the wedding and then flying back to San Francisco. She told them she had taken a job on a paper there, and her mother, remembering what Paxton had said about his family, immediately blamed Peter for the defection.

"That has nothing to do with it. They offered me a terrific job on an important paper. That's too good an offer to turn down for a job on the paper here."

"Just where are your loyalties?" her mother accused. "Here or there?"

"That's not the point. My real loyalties should be to myself and my future."

"That's all you think of," her mother said through clenched teeth, and Paxton tried to turn the conversation back to George and Allison and their upcoming wedding. The wedding reception was going to be at the Oglethorpe Club, and they said they were only having about a hundred friends. She was so old by then that to Paxton it almost seemed ridiculous to have a thirty-two-year-old bride at the center of an enormous wedding.

Paxton had a chance to visit a few of her old friends, and was amazed to find that even more had gotten married, still more engaged, and some of the early married ones were having second babies. It made her feel ancient, even though she had just turned twenty.

"Do you think he'll marry you?" Queenie asked her about Peter late one night, and Paxton smiled and shrugged. They didn't really talk about marriage anymore. It was not in their immediate plans, but Paxton knew that eventually they probably would, if he didn't mind the wait, while she got all her independent wanderings out of her system. But she was terribly used to him now. She loved living with him, and she could no longer even begin to imagine a life without him.

It was a good visit for her, and the only thing that worried her was how tired Queenie looked when she left, and despite her enormous size, she somehow managed to look frail and Paxton urged her brother to keep an eye on her. No one knew exactly how old she was, but it was clear that she was no longer young, and not as strong as she once had been.

There was still a strain between her mother and herself when Paxton left, but she tried not to think about it, and she promised to come home again that summer, for the wedding. And when she got back to Berkeley, Peter was waiting for her. He had been impatient for her to come home this time. In many ways, their relationship was just like being married.

And when Gabby came home the next day, from a trip to Hawaii with Matt, she had stars in her eyes, and a look that Paxton knew she had seen somewhere before, but she couldn't remember where, and it was late May before she remembered. Suddenly, Gabby was constantly in bed and asleep all the time. She never seemed to go anywhere, except out with Matt at night, but she always had that sleepy look, and a look in her eyes that Paxton recognized almost instantly once it clicked, and she confronted Gabby one day when they were alone in the house, and there was no one else there to hear them. She had just gotten up at two o'clock, and Paxton had just come back from one of her classes. And all she could think of was Dawn. The girl from Des Moines who had slept through the first three months of school. And then gone home at Christmas, to have her baby.

"You're pregnant, aren't you?" She decided not to beat around the bush, and Gabby wheeled where she stood, with a look of amazement.

"That's ridiculous. Why would you say a thing like that?" For a moment, she looked frightened.

"Because you are. Aren't you?"

"I'm . . . no, I'm not . . . that's a stupid thing to say . . .

I'm . . . I . . ." But she couldn't go on with the lie. She sank into a kitchen chair, put her face in her hands, and started to cry as Paxton watched her. And then Paxton sat down next to her and put an arm around her shoulders.

"What are you going to do?" she said gently.

"I don't know . . . I kept thinking I was late, but . . . I just don't know what to do now."

"Have you told Matt?" The redhead shook her head. "How pregnant are you?"

"I don't know. Maybe about six weeks. I started to ask around about abortions last week, but everyone has horror stories about Mexico or East Oakland. I don't want to do something like that. What if I die?"

"You could go to Tokyo, or London."

"Yeah, and say what to my parents? I'm going on a business trip? A research project for my art class? Shit, Paxxie, what am I going to do?"

"What do you want to do? Do you want the baby?"

"I don't know." And she honestly didn't. She had thought about it constantly and she couldn't make her mind up about any of it, she was so confused. It was a relief to be talking about it to Paxton.

"What about Matt? Do you want him?"

"I think so. He's so good to me. And so sweet. I think I love him." It wasn't good enough. At least not to Paxton. But Gabby's standards weren't as high as hers were.

"You have to be sure, especially if you're going to have a baby."

"How can I be? How do you ever know? You've been going out with Peter for almost two years, are you that sure about him?"

"Yes," Paxton said honestly. "I'm not as sure about myself. I'm not quite sure I'm grown up yet. But I do know that I love him."

"Then you're lucky. But you're different than I am."

And she had only been going out with Matthew Stanton since Christmas. And sometimes Paxton thought he was so smooth, and so calculating and so perfectly orchestrated, that it was hard to tell who he really was beneath the veneer. It was easy to see why Gabby wasn't sure. And Paxton also suspected that it meant a lot to him that he was going out with Gabby Wilson. He knew exactly who her father was, and even indirectly, he seemed to enjoy the connection.

"What are you going to do?" Paxton asked her again. "You'd better decide soon, or you won't have a choice." But it was true. After three months, she couldn't even consider an abortion.

"Oh, God, Paxxie, don't say that."

"Why don't you tell him?"

"What if he walks out on me?"

"Then at least you'll know what kind of guy he is, won't you? And maybe you'll have your answer."

"And if he doesn't?"

"Then you have to think about that too. But Gabby, think about what *you* want. A baby is forever." She had too many friends who, at twenty and twenty-one, were regretting the children they had and the marriages they had either rushed or been forced into.

They were still talking about it that afternoon when Peter walked in and both of them fell suddenly silent. "Christ, what's with you two? Did I say something I shouldn't have?"

"No. Don't be so paranoid." Paxton kissed him hungrily. "How did your exams go?" He had almost finished his second year, and they both knew that this one was the hardest.

"I think I flunked everything. I should be on a plane to Viet Nam by tomorrow morning."

"Don't joke about stuff like that." Paxton looked upset as she poured him a cup of coffee.

"Don't be so sensitive," he said as he put the cup down and

kissed her again, and then watched his sister leave the kitchen. She looked as though she had been crying. "What's with her?" he asked in a whisper. "She break up with that guy?" Peter never seemed to remember his name, which wasn't a good sign. "He's too old for her anyway. And he's too interested in my father." Paxton thought so, too, but under the circumstances, she had no intention of admitting it to Peter.

"I think it's just a little spat. I'm sure it's nothing," she said noncommittally, and Peter knew instantly that she was lying, but he didn't press her. She obviously knew more than that, but she wasn't telling. When Matthew showed up that evening to pick Gabby up, she was wearing a bright orange minidress, and huge cube-shaped plastic earrings. But she looked surprisingly somber, considering the outfit. And she looked closer to hysterical when she came back less than an hour later. And this time, she looked straight at Paxxie, as though her brother didn't even exist.

"He says he has to think about it. How do you like that?" She burst into tears and then ran into her room and slammed the door as Peter stared at her in confusion. And then suddenly it clicked, and he looked at Paxton.

"Shit. She's not, is she? Tell me she's not . . . please . . . or I'm going to kill her. And then I'm going to kill him." His whole jaw was taut, but Paxton quickly grabbed his arm and almost shook him.

"You're not going to do anything. You're going to let them work it out."

"Oh, Paxxie . . ." There were tears in his eyes as he sat staring at her in disbelief. "How could she? The guy is a jerk, can't she see that?"

"Maybe he isn't. Maybe he's okay. Maybe he'll come through for her." She certainly hoped so. If not, Gabby was in big trouble.

"I think she should get an abortion. She is pregnant, isn't

she?" He was right, of course, and she nodded. "How could she let that happen?"

"It was an accident."

"Those kind of accidents don't happen. They don't happen to you. Doesn't she take the pill?" Paxton shook her head sadly.

"Christ. What are my parents going to say?"

"Nobody's going to say anything. Let her work it out first. She doesn't even know what she wants yet."

"She was so fucking desperate to get married, and now look at her, she gets knocked up by a ski bum."

Paxton laughed at him. "Stop it. He is not a ski bum. She met him on a ski slope, and for all we know he's the perfect husband for her." And just as she said it, the doorbell rang, and it was Matthew, looking somber and drawn, and asking if he could see Gabby.

"She's in her room," Paxxie said quietly, and then glanced at Peter, praying he wouldn't strangle the baby's father. "Why don't we go out for a pizza or something."

"Because I'm not hungry," Peter snarled, glaring at him, and then let Paxton force him out of the house, as he argued with her once they were outside. "Why can't I talk to him?"

"Because he doesn't want to talk to you. He wants to talk to Gabby. Leave them alone, for heaven's sake."

"Why? Look what happened when they were alone before."

"Well, it can't happen again. So mind your own business."

"She's my sister."

"I think he has priority now. Besides, I'm hungry."

"Don't tell me you're pregnant, too, or I'll throw up."

"Is that what you'd do?" She looked at him with interest as they stopped at his car, and he looked suddenly serious as he watched her.

"No, that isn't what I'd do, just for the record. If that ever happens to us, Pax, I don't want you to do anything stupid.

Hell, we're practically married now. We'd just make it legal, and I'd keep the baby for you while you go to the Peace Corps."

"You almost make it sound tempting." He was teasing her a little, but he wanted her to know that he'd marry her in a minute.

He walked around the car to her, and put his arms around her. "I love you, babe . . . a lot. One day I'd love you to have my baby."

"So would I," she whispered into his neck, but she couldn't imagine it yet. And she couldn't imagine Gabby with a baby either.

Gabby and Matt were sitting on the front steps when they got back, and she wasn't crying, which Paxton thought was a good sign. And he stood up nervously and looked at Peter.

"I'd like to talk to you," he said, looking him straight in the eye.

"What about?" Peter had no intention of making it easy for him, but Gabby was too nervous to listen. She jumped up and looked at her older brother.

"We're getting married." She glanced at him and then at Paxton, and then she started to cry, as Paxton put her arms around her, and gave her a hug and told her she was happy for her.

"Have you spoken to Mom and Dad yet?" Peter asked cautiously, knowing full well that they hadn't.

"Matt is going to have lunch with Dad tomorrow."

Peter looked at both of them, and it was obvious that he was still upset. "Is he going to tell him you're knocked up?"

"No," Gabby said, with a trembling lip, "are you?"

"I don't know yet," Peter answered, but suddenly Matthew stepped in, and put an arm around Gabby's shoulders.

"That's enough. There's no reason to tell anyone." He looked at his future brother-in-law. "That's between the four of us. There's no reason to upset your parents, or Gabby. This has been traumatic for everyone. It kind of knocked me off my feet, too, when Gabby told me. But we might as well make the best of it. I love her, she loves me, and we're going to have a wonderful baby." He pulled her close to him again, and kissed the top of her head as she fought back tears and looked up at him with gratitude. He could have told her to go to hell but he hadn't. But Peter also knew that there were a lot of benefits to being married to Gabby Wilson. He had a lot less to lose than she did.

Peter looked hard at his sister then. "Are you sure that's what *you* want to do?"

She nodded, looking at him. "Yes, it is. I just didn't know what to do at first." She glanced nervously at Paxton. It was a big step to take. From college co-ed, she was suddenly leaping into being wife and mother.

"What are you going to tell Mom and Dad?"

"That we want to get married . . . soon . . . like in a few weeks, or a month maybe."

"You don't think they'll know? Mom will be real disappointed if you don't want a big wedding."

"I'll just tell her Matthew feels strongly about it because he's divorced." She shrugged. "And then the baby will be two months premature. Lots of babies are." She smiled happily up at Matt, as Paxton watched them. It was amazing, in the space of a few hours, her friend's whole life had changed and suddenly she seemed to belong not to them, but to Matthew. She went home with him that night and when Paxton saw her again a few days later, she seemed to have changed completely. He had bought her a ring, and all she could talk about was getting married. She had finally gotten what she wanted out of school. A husband. But Paxton still wasn't sure that Matt Stanton was the perfect answer.

Ed Wilson felt the same way, too, but all his entreaties to them to wait held absolutely no sway, and finally he gave up. She was so headstrong, he knew she'd run off to Mexico and marry him if she had to.

Their wedding day was set for June, and they had insisted they wanted only a few friends, and a luncheon at the house. And just as Peter had predicted, Marjorie Wilson was bitterly disappointed.

And on their wedding day, on the fourth of June, Paxton stood beside her and cried, because she knew Gabby was doing something that she really wasn't sure of. And in January, they were going to have a baby. Ed Wilson suspected it, too, and even Marjorie wasn't fooled. But they all went along with it for Gabby's sake, and prayed that Matt would turn out to be a decent husband.

Peter and Paxton drove back to the house in Berkeley afterward. They had to move out in another week, and they still had some packing to do. They were giving the house up and moving to a smaller place, and there was no longer any pretense about being roommates. Only Paxton's mother didn't know for sure, and there was no reason to tell her. She was far enough away to believe the charade they had lived for the past year. But with Gabby gone, things were going to be a little different.

"Well," Paxton said seriously, as she took off her hat when they got to the house and looked at the sea of boxes all around them. Gabby and Matt were already on their honeymoon. They had flown to New York that afternoon, and after two days there, at the Pierre, they were flying on to Europe. "What do you think? Do you think he'll do?"

"I don't know, Pax." No one knew. They could only pray, for her sake.

"He's nice to her at least."

"He'd better be," Peter growled, and she leaned over and kissed him.

"What are we going to do with all this stuff?"

"I don't know. Give it away?" Most of it was books, and a lot of it was Paxton's.

"I'm never going to have time to pack all of this before I go to Savannah."

"Don't worry about it. I'll do it for you."

"You're a saint." She smiled. She was leaving the following week for her brother's wedding in Savannah. They had decided to get married in June too. And she felt as though she was on a merry-go-round, packing, moving, unpacking, and flying to Savannah for the wedding.

And when Paxton arrived, Queenie didn't look well to her again this time, but her mother seemed a little more relaxed than usual. She seemed to get along very well with Allison, which took some of the heat off Paxton.

Two days later, after the wedding, Paxton came back to San Francisco to start her job on the paper. Peter had taken a job for the summer in a law firm in Berkeley. It was almost like being married now that they'd moved. They had their own place, a cute little house with a big living room, a kitchen, a dining room, a garden, and a big bedroom upstairs, with a little den where Peter kept all his lawbooks. She cooked for him at night when she got home from work, or sometimes he met her in the city and they went out for dinner. And she was crazy about her job at the paper. They gave her interesting stories to do, and sometimes she just stood there and read the Teletypes, feeling as though she had a finger on the pulse of the world. And she'd never been happier. And neither had Gabby.

She showed by September when Peter and Paxton went back to school, and she was thrilled about taking the year off. And Paxton suspected she'd never go back. Her parents knew about the baby now, and Matt was being good to her, so everyone was very happy.

It was hard to imagine where the time went that year. It was her third year at Berkeley. Paxton went home to Savannah for Christmas this time, and Queenie was clearly ill. She looked pale, if that was possible, and she coughed all the time, but even though her daughters thought she should retire now, she still insisted on working, especially while Paxxie was home, which really scared Paxton. But George insisted there was nothing he could do for her, when Paxton pressed him. He wasn't terribly interested anyway. All he could think of was Allison. She was expecting their first baby the following summer, in August.

And Gabby's baby came three weeks after Paxton got home at Christmastime, a little girl with bright red hair like her mother's. And as Paxton stood in the hospital, looking at her, it was hard to believe that Gabby was a mother. But Matt was thrilled, and the Wilsons were too. And Paxxie felt an odd empty space in her heart as she drove home to Berkeley with Peter.

"You okay?" He had noticed it, and she hadn't said much on the ride home, but she looked at him when he asked, and smiled strangely.

"Yeah. It's funny to see her with a baby, isn't it? We've been together for such a long time, more than two years, and we know each other so well. And they've only known each other for a year, and there they are, happily married, with a baby. It seems kind of weird, doesn't it?"

"Yeah, I guess it does." And then he grinned. "But it could be arranged, if that's what you want."

"It isn't. Not now anyway." She smiled almost sadly, because in some ways she did. She wanted everything, and she was tired of school. She missed the job that she'd had at the paper that summer. And now it was back to exams, and papers, and quizzes, and blue books.

There were four hundred thousand American boys in Viet Nam by then and nothing made sense anymore. It was easier if you didn't care. But she did. She cared too much, and in five more months, Peter would be out of law school.

She was still sad when she went to bed that night, and realized when Peter held her that she was jealous of Gabby's baby.

"What are you thinking about?" Peter asked her in the dark, with his arms around her.

"How dumb I am." She grinned and he laughed.

"There's a cheerful thought."

"I get ahead of myself sometimes."

"Are you thinking about the baby again?" The baby was cute, but what had struck her was how happy they were, and how complete, and yet she couldn't see herself having babies for years, but a part of her knew she would love that.

"Look, if you want to, we can get married when I graduate in June. I'll have a job by then . . . baby, I'd love it." He was beaming in the dark, and from a draft standpoint too, it would be safer.

"I just don't think we should. Look at Gabby, she'll never go back to school. I want to finish what I started."

"What about the Peace Corps?"

She grinned. "I think maybe I could sacrifice that. I'm not so sure I'd be so great with all those cockroaches and leeches."

"Is it a date then?" He was smiling too. "June sixty-eight, when you graduate?" It was only seventeen months away, and it actually sounded pretty good to Paxton. "What do you say, babe?"

"I say yes . . . and I love you. . . ."

"I love you too." He beamed. "Does this mean we're engaged?"

"It sounds like it, doesn't it?" She almost giggled.

"Can I buy you a ring?"

"Maybe we should wait." That seemed like such a big step, and it meant she had to tell her mother and listen to her rant and rave that she wasn't marrying someone from Savannah. "Why don't we wait till Christmas? Then it won't be such a long time till the wedding."

"I'll start saving," he said, and snuggled close to her, as they fell asleep in the cozy little house in Berkeley.

# Chapter 8

$\vee$

Peter graduated from law school in June 1967, and his parents gave an enormous lunch for him, at the Bohemian Club in San Francisco. It was a serious affair attended by every important person in town, including Peter's new boss at a very impressive law firm. The Wilsons introduced Paxton to everyone as their future daughter-in-law, and she didn't seem to mind it. And Matt and Gabby were there. She looked beautiful and slim, and she talked constantly about the baby.

"I'm ready for another one," she confided to Paxton when they went to the ladies' room. And Paxton noticed that she had never looked prettier or better.

"What about school?"

"I don't want to go back anyway. I'm not like you. You want to be a journalist, you want a career, you want to prove something. Hell, Pax, I just want to be married and have babies."

Paxton smiled ruefully at her. "You sound like my mother's dream. At least Allison will keep the heat off me. She's having her baby in August. I guess I'll have to fly back there then to see it." Although she was planning to work for the *Morning Sun* again over the summer. And she only had one more year of school, and then they were going to give her a permanent job as a reporter. "So when's the next one due?" Paxton teased. They

119

had named the baby Marjorie Gabrielle, and called her Marjie. "A boy this time, I assume."

"That's what Matt wants." Gabby beamed. She was twenty-one years old, married, and a mother. And Paxton had lived with Peter for three years, and he was an attorney, and all she was was a student. She wanted to get on with it now. To finish school, get a real job, and get married. In that order.

"Is he good to you?" Paxton asked, but she knew she didn't have to.

"Yes, he is," Gabby said quietly, with a serious look at her old friend and roommate and future sister. "I was lucky. He could have turned out to be a real shit, but he didn't. And he's terrific with the baby."

"I'm glad," Paxton said honestly as they left the ladies' room finally and wandered back to their table.

"What were you two doing in there? I was looking every-where for you," Peter complained when he finally found her. "I wanted to introduce you to my boss's wife. She's English and I think you'd like her." But they couldn't find her again, and it was a long, happy day and they were both exhausted when they finally went home to the little house in Berkeley. They had decided to continue to rent it for another year, so it would be easier for Paxton during her last year at UC Berkeley. And when she graduated, and she went to work for the paper, and they were married . . . then they would move into the city.

"It was a wonderful day." She smiled at him. "I'm so proud of you . . . you did it!" He looked pleased, too, and his parents had been so proud. They were happy with both their children, and they loved Paxton, too, and she really loved them. They chatted about his graduation day all that evening.

The rest of the summer sped past them. He was busy at his job, and Paxton was busy night and day at the paper. And then she flew home just before she went back to school, to see her mother and George's new baby. He had had a little boy, and he was so pleased with himself he could hardly stand it. They had called the baby James Carlton Andrews, and he was cute and Allison was fine. And even her mother had unbent a little.

Only Queenie seemed to have aged a dozen years, and suddenly seemed barely able to move with crippling arthritis. "Why don't you do something for her?" Paxton accused, and George brushed her off. He had other things to do than worry about his mother's ancient servant. "She won't go to anyone else, George. She trusts you."

"There's nothing I can do. She's old, Pax. Hell, she must be close to eighty."

"So what? She could live to be a hundred if someone took care of her properly." But although he didn't say it, he didn't think so. She had been failing for the past couple of years, and whether or not Paxton wanted to admit it, she wasn't going to live forever.

But Paxton reminded him again before she left, and she spent most of her last afternoon with Queenie.

"You finally gonna marry him?" she asked grumpily when Paxton mentioned Peter.

"We've been talking about next June, when I graduate, or maybe sometime next summer." She really wanted to start working first. She still had strong feelings about remaining independent.

"What you waitin' for, girl? Gray hair or a full moon? You been lovin' him for three years now."

"I know. But I want to finish what I'm doing."

"You can be married and go to school too. You smart enough to do both. So what's the problem?"

"I'm silly, I guess. I keep thinking I have to do one thing and then the other."

"Don't wait too long." She looked pointedly at the girl she'd raised, and thought to herself that Paxton was prettier than ever. She looked older and more mature, and her features seemed more sharply etched, her body slightly fuller in the right places.

"What do you mean?" Paxton looked suddenly worried.

"Maybe he'll find someone else who don't wanna wait, or maybe some girl chase him and catch him . . . or I dunno . . . life is funny sometimes, sometimes it makes you sorry when you wait for somethin' too long, like you shouldda done it while you could, but you cain't no more . . . baby, I think you should get married." But Paxton thought maybe the old woman just wanted to see her married while she was still well enough to enjoy it. And she knew Peter would wait. He wasn't the type to go running off with someone else. She was sure of that. And they had waited this long. They could wait one more year until next summer.

And on the day Paxton flew home to him, President Thieu was elected in South Viet Nam. And by a month later, thirteen thousand Americans had died in Viet Nam and seven hundred and fifty-six were missing.

And Gabby told her she was pregnant again then. The baby was due the following June. It seemed a long time away to Paxton, almost as long as their wedding.

Her fourth year at UC seemed almost anticlimactic to her. Paxton felt as though the days were flying by, and she and Peter kept talking about their plans after graduation.

They all spent Christmas together at the Wilsons that year, and after Christmas, as they had before, Peter and Paxton went up to Squaw Valley to go skiing. They had a terrific time, and laughed about how Gabby had met Matthew there two years before and how so much had happened to them in the three and a half years they'd been together. It didn't seem long to wait anymore. June and Paxton's graduation seemed just around the corner. And then she was going to decide about a serious job, and get married by the end of the summer. It was less than a year now.

But when they came home, there was a letter waiting for him in the mailbox from his draft board. They had called him. Paxton could almost feel her heart stop as she read the letter.

"Christ, what'll we do?" Paxton asked with a look of terror.

"We pray," he said, and later that evening he called his father. His father admitted that he had no pull as far as the draft board was concerned, but he asked him point-blank if Paxton was willing to get married. "I'm sure she would," he said quietly, and she guessed instantly what his father had asked him, "but we really want to wait till next summer." He knew how important it was to Paxton to wait and do things in the proper order.

"I don't think you should wait. If that'll get you out of this, do it." And they all knew it might, but nothing was certain anymore. It was up to the individual draft board whether or not they'd accept marriage as a deferral. And lately, eleventh-hour marriages weren't being respected for deferrals. It was probably too late. And Peter really didn't want to push Paxton to get married before graduation.

"We'll see, Dad. Maybe they'll change their minds when I go to the physical. I'll be twenty-six in six weeks. It's hardly worth it. They want the young ones." But when he hung up, there were tears in Paxton's eyes. She was terrified that they'd take him.

"Don't be silly, babe." He pulled her close to him. "I'm too old. They're not going to take me."

"And if they do?"

"They won't."

"Let's get married." It was what she wanted now, but he really didn't think it would help now.

"That's not the way to do it. We haven't waited three and a half years in order to rush out in a panic and have a shotgun wedding."

"Why not? Peter, I don't want to wait." She suddenly remembered Queenie's words . . . sometimes life makes you sorry when you wait too long. . . . "I want to get married."

"Stop panicking." He tried to sound calm. It was the first time he had ever seen her so frightened. "I'll talk to my boss tomorrow." But he shared Peter's view. They weren't going to draft someone a month from the cut-off age, it just didn't make sense. And if they wanted to, he could probably stall them. It was only six weeks, after all.

But when he went to the Oakland Induction Center for the physical, they took him. It was done. He was in. And neither of them could believe it. Paxton felt like the world had come to an end. She wanted to hide him but he wouldn't hide. He didn't believe in the war. He had even burned his draft card, she reminded him. But he was a responsible adult now, he said, the son of the publisher of the *Morning Sun.* And he had to go now, or at least that was how he saw it, even if he didn't like it.

And if he got married now, it was too late. He was in, and there was no discussion.

It was like a bad dream. And in Viet Nam, two words that gave Paxton nightmares now, twenty thousand Communist troops moved south for surprise attacks during the Tet, Chinese New Year celebrations. And on January twenty-third, the North Koreans had seized the USS *Pueblo.* It was the same day Peter had to report to Fort Ord for basic training. Paxton wasn't going to see him again for six weeks, and after that, God only knew where they would ship him. The only thing that encouraged him was that as an attorney, they would probably give him a desk job somewhere, and at least he would never see combat. But even though he reassured Paxton and his parents, he was still scared. This wasn't what he had planned to do with his life seven months after he finished law school.

"Peter, please . . . let's go to Canada . . . I'll do anything," she begged him before he left, but he didn't want to hear it.

"Don't be ridiculous. I want you to finish school." He knew how much it meant to her, and how well she was doing there, and he didn't want to run away now. He might as well face it and make the best of it. It would certainly put a crimp in his career plans but two years wasn't the end of the world, he told himself. He could have trained as an officer but that would have extended his time. He preferred to do two years as a "grunt" and come home quicker.

There was nothing he could do to stop it now. But Paxton begged him not to go right up until he left. She even drove him to Fort Ord and cried copiously when she left him. "I'll see you in a few weeks, sweetheart. Now stop it." And he had insisted that she go back to San Francisco and stay with his parents. But after a few days she went back to the house in Berkeley. She had been so happy with him there that she wanted to be in the house they'd shared. And she waited every night for him to call her. When he finally could, she felt as though she had died, waiting to hear from him. It had been six weeks since she heard his voice, and she hadn't studied anything. She couldn't think of anything but Peter. But as soon as he called, he told her he was coming home that weekend. He was, but not with great news. He was coming home to tell them that he was leaving for Saigon five days later.

# CHAPTER 9

Peter's last days in town were an agony for everyone, and most especially Paxton. They all wanted to be with him, to talk to him, to let him know how much they loved him. His father even tried to pull some strings, to no avail. His only friend on the local draft board said he couldn't help him. Everyone was in the same situation these days, there were too many families desperate to save their sons, but there was nothing anyone could do. He had to go if he'd been called, and all he had to do after that was stay alive once he got there. He had been assigned to Viet Nam for a standard tour of thirteen months. Three hundred and ninety-five days, he had told Paxxie. And after that he'd be assigned somewhere in the States and it would be all over. It meant a slight delay in their plans, but nothing more than that, he claimed. Although they both knew different. It meant that for the next thirteen months they would both be holding their breath and praying, that nothing would happen to him, that he would stay alive, that he would make it home again. And more than anything Paxton felt guilty now for not having married Peter sooner.

"Let's go to Canada," she whispered to him late one night, as they lay in the guest bed at his parents'. The Wilsons wanted him to stay at home for his last few days, and they had invited

Paxton to join them. They still expected them to sleep separately, but Peter crept silently into her room at night, and back to his own in the early hours of the morning. They couldn't sleep anyway. Paxton was too upset, and he was tense. He was so busy reassuring everyone, and at night he had his own fears to contend with.

He had lost weight at Fort Ord in the past two months, and "muscled up," but now his eyes had a look of pain that tore at Paxton's heart. His were eyes that said, "I don't want to do this," but he felt he had to.

"We can't go to Canada, Pax," he said calmly, and lit one cigarette from another. He had hardly ever smoked before, but in boot camp, it had become a constant habit. "What the hell would I do there?"

"You're a lawyer now. You could take their bar, and start there instead of here."

"And break my father's heart. Pax, I'd never be able to come back here."

"Bullshit. One day they're going to let everyone come home again. There are too many of them there, they're going to have to."

"And if they don't? Then I can't come home again. Baby, it just isn't worth it." And if he didn't come home at all? Was that worth it? Disbelief struck her again. This couldn't be happening to them. He was twenty-six now, an attorney, engaged, and they were sending him to Viet Nam. It was a nightmare.

"Peter, please . . ." In the dark she reached out to him. And he held her as she cried, and he cried too, but he wouldn't agree to what she wanted. He wouldn't run away. He had never wanted to go, didn't believe in the war. It had been years since he'd burned his draft card. But still, he knew he had to go, and when it came right down to it, he was willing to serve his country. In boot camp, they had gotten them all fired up about "Nam," and how much he was going to hate "Charlie." They

127

told them horror stories of children carrying machine guns there, and VC hiding in the brush, and booby traps, and tunnels filled with Viet Cong waiting to kill him. But there were other things they didn't say, the heartbreak, the agony, the grief of losing a friend, the horror of stepping on a mine, or killing a woman with a baby because you were so scared you couldn't think straight.

Still, he felt he was prepared, and over and over again he reassured Paxton in his last few days that he was going to be careful and not do anything crazy.

"You swear?" She extracted another promise from him before he went back to his room, and he kissed her.

"I swear," and then with a slow smile, "I swear I'll come back to you . . . in one piece . . . and ready to get married and have fourteen babies. You'd better be ready for that, Pax. I'll be an old man by then." But then she'd be more than ready and she'd have gotten all her independence out of her system.

"We could get married before that, you know." She was willing to marry him right then, and he knew that. But he didn't want to get married this way, in a frantic rush, hysterical, afraid. And he didn't want to take the risk of making her a widow. He was willing to wait, and he knew she'd wait for him. He wasn't afraid of that, and after all their years together they both felt married. "I love you . . ." she whispered again, and he kissed her and went back to his own room as the sun came up. It was the last of March 1968, and he was leaving for Viet Nam the next day. And he had a lot to do today. It was Sunday.

Gabby and Matt and the baby came for lunch that day. Marjie was fifteen months old and she had just learned to walk and she was into everything. And Gabby was seven months pregnant. Peter spent a long time talking to her, and after lunch they went for a walk in the garden. They both looked as though they had been crying when they came back. But everyone cried that day. Even Peter's father.

And that night after Gabby and Matt went home, they all sat and listened to Lyndon Johnson. He promised to reduce the bombing again, and promised peace. And then he stunned everyone by announcing that he wouldn't run for reelection. At least it was something to talk about. Something other than the fact that Peter was leaving in the morning.

That night he came to Paxton's room before his parents even went to bed. He didn't want to wait a moment longer, and he lay all night and held her in his arms as they both cried. He didn't want to die, didn't want to kill anyone, and didn't want to leave the girl he loved, and yet there was no question in his mind that he had to.

Paxton still blamed herself for not marrying him long before and yet it had seemed so sensible to wait until she finished college. But what was sensible now? What made sense? A war half a world away, in a place that no one really cared if we won or lost, a war we couldn't win and never would, in a country where we couldn't defend ourselves because we were too afraid of retaliation? Nothing made sense to them, or anyone. And none of it made sense to Paxton.

They stood at the window and watched the sun come up, and then went back to bed and made love for the last time, and when Peter finally left her room, as he walked back to his own, he ran into his father.

"Morning, Dad." He smiled sadly at him, and tears filled Ed Wilson's eyes as he nodded. He had held him when he was a baby and now he was a man, and he was desperately afraid he might lose him.

They all had breakfast together that day. They were all perfectly dressed, wide-awake, their faces looked alert and serious, and they ate in total silence. It was Peter who finally spoke first, as he slowly pushed his chair back from the table.

"Well, you guys, I probably won't have a breakfast like that for a long time." Certainly not served by a maid in uniform, in a formal dining room, on Limoges, with silver service, and Porthault napkins. Nor with people he loved and who loved him, in clean clothes, and in a room where no one could hurt him. "I'm going to miss you." The honesty of his words broke the dam, and they all began to cry, Peter, his parents, and Paxton, each promising the other to be brave, that he'd be home soon, and telling him how much they were going to miss him. And Paxton realized more than anyone how lucky they were that they were able to say what they felt to him. Had her brother gone, no one would have been able to say anything about how afraid they were, how sad, or how much they loved him.

And half an hour later, the foursome set out for Travis Air Force Base in Fairfield, with Peter in a brand-new uniform and carrying an enormous duffel. He had been told to report there by noon, and he didn't know exactly what time he'd board the plane, but once he left them, it didn't really matter.

It was a warm sunny day, and Mr. Wilson's driver said not a word as he drove them there, but when they arrived, he got out and shook Peter's hand with admiration.

"Good luck, son. Give 'em hell." He had fought in World War II and to him the idea of war still had some meaning. When he had gone, he had known who the enemy was, who the good guys were, and why he was fighting. Peter was less sure of it as he nodded.

"Thanks, Tom. Take care." He repeated the same words to everyone, and for a long moment he held his mother. "Take care, Mom . . . I love you. . . ." She wanted to sink to her knees and wail at the thought of seeing her son sent off to war, but she bravely nodded, kissed him again through her tears, and squeezed Ed's hand until he thought his fingers would break, while Peter said good-bye to Paxton. "I love you too . . ." he whispered, unable to speak by then. "Take care. . . ." And then, he turned away from them, and disappeared into the cavernous building. They could go no farther with him, and Ed Wilson thought it was just as well. It was already painful enough saying good-bye to him here, and he thought it might be too much for Marjorie to watch the plane take off, carrying her baby into danger.

He helped them all back into the limousine, the two women crying with their arms around each other.

"I should have married him. . . ." Paxton sobbed openly, and Marjorie only shook her head in fear and grief.

"You couldn't know what would happen." No one could. No one knew anything about the war he was going to, and the price he might pay to be there. "My God, I hope he's careful," his mother said softly as they crossed the Bay Bridge back to San Francisco.

Paxton had lunch with them, but they were all too spent to say very much, and that afternoon, she packed her things and went back to the house in Berkeley. She had an exam that afternoon, in her last eco course, but she had already decided not to take it. She couldn't remember anything anyway, except where Peter was and where he was going. All they knew was that he was flying to Hawaii, and then Guam, and then on to Saigon, and if he could he'd call her. But where he was going after Saigon wasn't clear yet. And Paxton hoped nowhere. With any luck at all, they'd put him at a desk and leave him there, she had urged him again and again to trade on the fact that he was a lawyer. But he hadn't been assigned to the legal corps. If he had been, he would have been kept stateside. They didn't need lawyers in Viet Nam. They needed grunts to fight their war and look for mines, and hunt Charlie down in his caves and tunnels.

Peter's parents had urged her to call, and to come to dinner, or stay with them, anytime she wanted. But all she did that first day was lie on the bed they had shared and smell his after-shave on the clothes he had left in their closet. He hadn't had time to pack up anything, even though they were giving up the house in July, and Paxton hadn't wanted him to. She wanted to be there with his things, and with him. This way she didn't feel as though she'd lost him.

Gabby called her that afternoon. And they both cried. She said it even made her depressed about the baby.

"I just want him to come home," she wailed. They had always been so close, especially in the last few years during the time he'd spent with Paxton.

"So do I," Paxton said mournfully, looking around the silent kitchen.

"Do you know what day this is?" Gabby asked typically, but Paxton didn't know or care, although she knew she'd never forget it. "It's April Fools'."

Paxton almost smiled. "Does this mean they send him back tonight and say they're sorry?"

"They should . . . the assholes . . ." But then Paxton could hear Marjie crying in the background and Gabby had to go, after promising to call her later.

Instead, Peter called when he stopped in Guam. It was midnight, but Paxton wasn't sleeping. She was lying in bed, thinking of him, and it was like a gift hearing his voice over the crackling line. He only had a few minutes between flights, but he just wanted to tell her he loved her.

"I love you too . . . take care . . ."

"I love you!" And then he was gone, and she lay in bed again, awake until the morning.

That day, she skipped classes again. She just needed time, and she had two papers to turn in, but lately, ever since he'd been at Fort Ord, she couldn't face it. The strain was too much for her, and her midterm grades had shown it. From an A she had slipped to an Incomplete in almost every subject. But later she went to the library to pick up some books they had been holding for her since early March. She figured she had nothing else to do now, and she was beginning to feel vaguely panicked about her papers.

The next morning, Peter's mother called. She knew Paxton wouldn't have heard anything from him yet. She already knew about the call from Guam, from Gabby. But she just wanted to see if Paxton was alright. And she was, except that she had that odd feeling again, the same feeling she'd had when her father died, and John Kennedy was shot, the sensation that she was moving underwater. Everything seemed to be in slow motion, and the voices she heard seemed to come from a great distance. It was almost as though she didn't care, as though nothing that happened mattered anymore. She just wanted to hibernate somewhere until Peter came back, whenever that was. Although he had promised to meet her in Hawaii for R and R, or wherever they'd let him go, he actually wasn't sure how far he could go, or when he could leave, but one thing was sure, as soon as he could go anywhere, he was going to meet Paxton.

"Take care of yourself," his mother said, and Paxton promised her, just as Peter had. And after she hung up, for a moment, Paxton thought about calling Queenie in Savannah. But she didn't want to upset her.

Paxton turned on the news the next night, knowing that by now, Peter was in Saigon. And suddenly it all mattered to her, every report, every word, every image sharply etched, fearing that any one of those soldiers could be Peter. But it wasn't the news from Viet Nam that jolted her that night, it was what came after that. It was a re-hash of a story that had run for most of the day, but having stayed home all day again, Paxton hadn't heard it. They were talking about Dr. King, and then showing confused images on a screen of people running . . . a hotel . . . someone shouting . . . and then the words registered. Martin Luther King, Jr. had been killed in Memphis. Killed. Dead. Shot. She stared at the television, unable to believe it. The world had gone mad. Peter was in Viet Nam, and

Martin Luther King had been killed . . . shot . . . someone had wanted him dead, and everything he stood for. And in the house in Berkeley, she sank slowly into a chair, and stared at the TV, listening to what they said. But nothing made any sense anymore. And that night, when the riots began, she heard them. They started in cities everywhere, they were an anguished cry of a generation that had tried to live on past the murder of Kennedy five years before. They had passed the torch from hand to hand, and now their hearts and hands were too tired to carry it any further.

Paxton sat in the darkened living room, crying for him, and this time when the telephone rang, she didn't answer it. Because she knew it couldn't be Peter. It would only be friends, wanting to grieve with her, to ask her if she knew, to share their disbelief with her, and she didn't want to hear it. She didn't want to talk to anyone. She didn't want to be part of a world that killed people like him. It made her sick to think of it, and as she watched the news again that night, she found herself crying for his children.

"Why?" She asked the silence in the house. "Why? . . ." She shook her head again, and dried her tears, unable to understand it. And on Friday morning, the next day, she awoke feeling the terrible weight of depression. Everything seemed to be going wrong, starting with Peter leaving for Saigon on Monday.

It was a depressing weekend, and although she sat in the house day after day, she couldn't seem to study. She had a terrible nightmare on Sunday night, about birds swooping down on her and trying to attack her face, and she awoke with relief to the sound of the telephone on Monday morning. It was a sound she didn't recognize at first, as she held the phone to her ear, and then she realized that no one was there, and it was not the telephone, but the doorbell. She couldn't imagine who it would be, and she quickly put Peter's robe over her nightgown, and went to peek out one of the kitchen windows. But she couldn't quite see who was there, and finally she went to the front door, barefoot and still looking sleepy, and her eyes opened wide when she saw that it was Peter's father.

"Hi . . . I . . . this is a surprise . . . how are you?" She kissed his cheek and as she did, she saw the dampness in his eyes, and took a quick step back with a look of terror, as though if she didn't stand too close to him, whatever had brought him here wouldn't touch her. "Is something wrong?" She stood there, looking young and beautiful, and very, very frightened, and he could only look at her and shake his head as he fought back tears. But he had wanted to come here to tell her himself. He knew that that was what Peter would have wanted.

"They called us last night. . . ." Marjorie was still in bed, sedated by their doctor, when he left the house to see Paxton. "Paxxie . . . there's no easy way to say this." He took a long stride closer to her, to where she had fled, and pulled her close to him, and held her, and for the briefest instant, she wanted to pretend to herself that it was not him, but Peter. "He died in Da Nang." He said the words so softly, she almost didn't hear them. "They sent him up north as soon as he arrived, and he was out on a patrol at night. As green as he was, they made him a point man." She didn't know what that was and she didn't care. She wanted to put her hands over her ears so she didn't have to hear it. "He was the one out ahead . . ." Ed Wilson began to cry. ". . . He didn't take a hill . . . or get shot . . . or level a village . . . he didn't even step on a mine . . . he was killed by what they call 'friendly fire,' one of our own boys panicked and thought they heard a VC in the brush, and they shot Peter instead. . . . It was a mistake, they explained . . . a mistake, Pax . . ." He couldn't stop crying, even though he had come here to help her. ". . . But he's dead . . . our little boy is dead . . . his body will be home on Friday." As he said the words he felt a great rock pull through his chest, and she felt as though she were going to die in his arms. But she wanted

135

to hit him first. She wanted to force him to un-say it. She began to flail at his chest, her hands and hair flying wildly around her.

"No! . . . no! It didn't happen like that! . . . It didn't! It's not! . . . I don't want to hear it!"

"Neither did I . . . but you have a right to know. . . ." He looked at her miserably, the man who had believed in bombing the hell out of Viet Nam, had lost his son to it. "He died for nothing." And all he could remember now was how he had looked as a little boy, not how he had looked as a man when he left only a week before, on April Fools' Day. He had lived one week in Viet Nam, less than that, because he had only gotten there on Wednesday their time, and he had died on Sunday. Five days. Five days it had taken for him to be killed. For nothing. Killed by "friendly fire." How friendly was that if it had killed the man she loved, the man who'd been his baby?

"The service will be a week from today . . . but Marjorie thought you might like to come home with me . . . I . . . I think it might be good for her. . . ." Without saying a word, Paxton nodded. She wanted to be with them, too, they were the only family she had right now, and she wanted to be close to them. Maybe if she stayed with them, he'd come back and tell them the call from Nam had been a joke, the guy had only been shooting blanks, and he was fine, and still planning to meet her in Hawaii.

Paxton walked into the bedroom they'd shared, feeling numb and strange, and she put her jeans on and slipped her feet into loafers. She put one of Peter's sweaters on, and it still smelled like him, and she threw everything she could think of into a bag, and walked out to the car with Mr. Wilson. He reminded her to lock the house, and carried the bag for her, and she sat in the car, alone with him, feeling wooden.

"It's my fault, isn't it?" she asked as they drove across the bridge, staring straight ahead, at the city still shrouded in fog. The city looked sad today and she was glad. Too many people had died recently. Dr. King, Peter . . . it seemed as though everyone was dying.

"Don't say a thing like that, Paxton. It's no one's fault, except the boy who pulled the trigger. It was an accident. The hand of fate. You have to know that."

"If I'd married him, he'd have had his deferment."

"Maybe not. Maybe something else would have come up. He could have gone to Canada, run away, done a lot of things. I think basically he felt he had to go because they called him. I could have forced him to go to Toronto, too, but I didn't. I could blame myself too. We can't . . . if we do that, it'll drive us crazy."

She looked straight at him as he drove, wanting to know the truth from him. "Do you hate me because I didn't marry him?"

"I don't hate anyone." His eyes filled with tears again, and he patted her hand and looked away. "I just wish he were still with us."

She nodded, unable to say more, and grateful for the absolution. And she sat very still and straight, wishing the tears would come to wash away her pain, but after the initial anger, all she felt now were hatred and resentment.

When they arrived at the house on Broadway, Gabby was there, and Marjorie had just gotten up, still looking very groggy. But they were both crying, and little Marjie was staggering around aimlessly, eating cookies. Mr. Wilson said he had some things to arrange, and he went into the library, and he left Paxton with the other women. And it was here that she was able to vent her grief, with them, the other women who had loved him. They cried for what he had been to them, what he had said and meant and done, and they seemed to spend the whole day telling stories about Peter, as a child, as a man, as a son, as a brother, as a lover. Sometimes they laughed, sometimes they cried, and sometimes they just sat in silence, thinking. It was hard to believe he was no longer alive somewhere, that he wasn't going to call and tell them he was fine, and he was really sorry for the scare, but when the official telegram came twelve hours after the call, it only reconfirmed it. And they all started to cry again. And that night when Gabby and the baby went home with Matt, Paxton went to the guest room feeling absolutely exhausted.

She spent the rest of the week with them, helping Mrs. Wilson to sort through some things, and letting her talk when she needed to, and it gave her someone to talk to too. She thought of calling home more than once, but the truth was, she didn't want to. She didn't even want to tell Queenie. Telling them would make it real, and she didn't want it to be real yet, or ever. But it was much too much so, when the Presidio called them on Saturday morning, and informed them that they could pick up his "remains." Mr. Wilson came into the library with a somber look, and an hour later, Paxton and the Wilsons went to the Survivors' Assistance Office, and stood there with two other sets of parents. The two other families were black, and their sons had both been eighteen years old and cousins. Their grief was just as strong, their hearts ached just as much, and the boys they had loved were gone forever.

Peter was in a simple pine coffin draped with the flag, and Mr. Wilson had arranged for a hearse from Halsted's to join them. It was already waiting there when they arrived, and the Wilsons were ushered into a small room alone with Paxton. And there it was . . . the proof . . . the boy he had been and no longer was . . . in the coffin. In spite of herself, Paxton began to sob, and Mrs. Wilson sank quietly to her knees beside it, as her husband stood beside her, trying to support her.

"Take it easy, babe . . ." Paxxie could hear Peter say to her. "It's okay . . . baby, I love you. . . ." The memories were so clear, the voice still so strong, it was impossible that he was gone. Impossible, and unbearable. But he was gone. Forever.

They stayed that way for a long time, and finally Peter's

father helped his wife to her feet, and taking Paxton's arm, they walked slowly back into the April sunshine. Life seemed to have less meaning now. It seemed to matter less what one did, where one went, what one wore, who one saw, what one said. Without him, nothing mattered.

They drove slowly back to the house, and the hearse took Peter to Halsted's, and that night when his body had been moved to another coffin, in a quiet room, Paxton went to see him. She couldn't believe it was really him in the mahogany box, but she didn't want to look to see, just to prove it. Instead, she knelt there beside it, and touched the wood, and the brass handles, with the tips of her fingers.

"Hi . . ." she whispered alone in the room, ". . . it's me . . ."

"I know . . ." she could almost hear him say, the voice so familiar, the eyes so blue, the hair so like her own . . . the lips the same ones that had kissed her only a week before. That same face was in the box, that boy was the one she loved, and always would, and yet now they wanted her to believe that he had left her. "You okay?" her heart told her he was asking, and she could only shake her head as her eyes filled with tears again. She wasn't okay, and she never would be. Just as she hadn't been when her father died. How could you be okay again when you lost someone you loved that much? What did you believe in after that, except loss and pain and sorrow. A part of you felt vulnerable for the rest of your life, and in a secret part of you, you always knew that at every moment.

She knelt there for a long time, feeling him close to her, and wanting to feel at peace, but she couldn't. All she felt was pain and loss, and anger at the boy who had accidentally pulled the trigger. Even the terminology was wrong. "Friendly fire," as though that made it all right, because he had been killed by an American and not the North Vietnamese Army. What difference did it make, if he was dead now?

The service on Monday was heart-wrenching and brief. The news of Peter's death had appeared on the front page of the *Sun,* and several other papers. And everyone he had ever gone to school with came, along with teachers and friends and relatives and colleagues. And the Wilsons introduced Paxton to everyone. In the end, it was almost as if she and Peter had been married. And she envied Gabby now. If she had had Peter's baby, she would always have had a part of him with her. She was twenty-two by then . . . twenty-two, having loved Peter since she was eighteen, and lived with him for three years. And she knew that who and what he was, was lodged in her heart forever.

She stayed with the Wilsons for another day, and then, feeling strange, she went back to Berkeley. She had fallen so far behind that it seemed almost pointless to go back there, but she knew she had to. It no longer seemed possible that she would graduate in June, but she didn't really care.

And in May, she had just gotten an extension to complete all her classes over the summer, when her brother called her. She hadn't heard his voice in so long that at first she didn't realize who he was, but the accent gave him away quickly.

"Hi," and then sudden realization. "Is something wrong?" It was the only thing she could think of now. Ever since Peter had died the month before, she seemed to expect nothing but bad news, and it was almost a relief when no one called her.

"No . . . I . . ." He didn't want to lie to her, but he didn't know what to say either. They had never been close and he knew this wasn't going to be easy for her. "Mama thought I should call."

"Is she sick?" Or was it Allison, or the baby? Paxton couldn't figure it out as she waited.

"No, she's fine," he drawled on, and then, there was no way out. He had to say it. "Paxton . . . it's Queenie." Her heart stopped at the words, and she wanted, ever so gently, to set the phone down before he could tell her. Instead, she said not a word, and clutched the phone as she waited. "She died in her sleep last night, Pax. She had no pain. Her heart just gave out . . . that's all . . . Mother just thought you should know and she asked me to call you." She could have called and extended her condolences herself, but she didn't.

"I . . . yes . . . I . . ." She couldn't form the words. She felt as though the last person who had loved her had disappeared, and there was no one left now. "Thank you, George." Her voice was an anguished croak, and he felt sorry for her. "Do you know when the service is?"

"One of her daughters picked her up today, and I think she said the service is tomorrow. Mother said she'd send flowers from all of us, but I don't think you should go, if that's what you're thinking." The funeral would be in the black district, and most people wouldn't have understood the love the two had shared. And there was no doubt that she would have been the only white person at the service.

"Yeah, I guess so." She sounded vague. "Thanks for calling." Paxton hung up then, and wandered around the house, and that afternoon she drove into the city. She went out to the beach, and walked along the waves, and she thought of them, the people she had loved so much and who were gone . . . Queenie . . . and Peter . . . and eleven years ago now, her father. It was as though she had friends waiting "out there" for her somewhere, people she loved and whom she knew really loved her. But it seemed cruel to her that she had to live alone now. She had to go on, with no one there, no one she cared about, and she couldn't imagine caring about anyone again. A few boys had asked her out since Peter's death, but she was horrified. She couldn't imagine going out with anyone. Even Gabby had tried to fix her up with a friend of Matt's, but Paxton told her bluntly that she had no interest.

She stopped at the Wilsons that afternoon on the way home,

but they were out, and she found herself wondering how they could go on living without him, knowing that he was dead and gone, that he had died for nothing, and in a sense had been murdered. It was a tough one to swallow, and there were times when Paxton wanted to die too, she just wanted to go to sleep and never wake up, so she wouldn't have to be without him.

They called her the next day, when they heard she'd come by, and she noticed that his mother sounded a lot better. She was excited about the baby now. And she talked about Peter, but she didn't sound as unable to control her emotions.

Paxton's own mother also called her that afternoon, to say she was sorry about Queenie and wanting to know the details about graduation. It was only a month away, and she and Allison and George were planning to come to San Francisco. Paxton had been meaning to call them for weeks, but she hadn't.

"There's been a change in plans," she announced, and her mother sounded startled.

"What's that?"

"I won't be graduating until September. I won't be graduating with my class. I'm just going to finish my work, and they're going to mail me the diploma." And then I'm just going to spend the rest of my life trying to figure out why Peter and I didn't get married. "It's no big deal, Mom. I'm sorry you're going to miss the graduation." But she didn't really care. She didn't care about anything anymore. Absolutely nothing mattered.

"Is that how they do it out there? They just *mail* you the diploma? How disappointing."

"Not really. It's all right." Paxton's voice was almost completely toneless.

"Why aren't you graduating in June?" There was a tone of faint accusation.

"Oh . . . I've had a lot on my mind this spring. And I've been pretty busy."

"Doing what?" She knew better than to continue to ask if she was still going out with Peter. It just set them at each other's throats. And she had even suspected for the past year that they might even be living together. As long as she didn't try nonsense like that in Savannah. What she did in California was up to her. She was over twenty-one, and Beatrice Andrews was smart enough to know she couldn't stop her. "Going to too many parties?" She was just making idle chitchat.

"Not really."

"Well, if you're not graduating in June, when are you coming back to Savannah?"

She sighed. "I don't know . . . I don't know anything." And she had to fight back tears as she said it, but Beatrice Andrews didn't hear it. "If I have to go to school, I can't start work until September." She had been planning to work for the *Morning Sun.* But she had also been planning to get married sometime that year and now that wasn't going to happen either. Nothing was. Nothing was ever going to happen to her again. And in the midst of it all, Savannah seemed totally unimportant. "I don't know when I'll come home, Mama."

"Well, try and come home for a few days this summer. Little James Carl is so cute you won't believe it." It seemed odd to hear her getting excited about her grandson, but Paxton was pleased for her. Even that didn't matter to her anymore. The hope of any semblance of a relationship between them was long since over.

"I'll see how school goes." But she was only pacifying her. She had no real desire to go there. She was just planning to finish school, go to work, and maybe, if she had no choice, she would go to Savannah for Christmas.

But most of the time, she didn't think of them. All she thought of was Peter, as she tried to finish her courses. There were dozens of papers she had left undone, tests she had to retake. As she looked back over her work for the past four or five months, it was miraculous that they were willing to let her graduate at all, but when the dean had called her in and wanted to know why her grades had slipped, she had told him about Peter dying in Da Nang, and as far as they were concerned that explained it.

She was almost beginning to get a grip on it in June, when she was coming home from the library late one night, and heard a piercing scream. She looked around her, and a few people nearby were running. She couldn't begin to imagine what had happened. An accident? A demonstration? Other people had heard it too, and people began asking each other what had happened. And it was like 1963 again, people were crying and running, clutching radios and hurrying inside to watch television, and Paxton could feel a chill run down her spine as she watched them. She didn't know what or who, but it was obvious that something terrible had happened.

"What is it?" she asked someone standing next to her as they crowded around a girl with a radio, sitting on the steps and crying.

"RFK . . . he's been shot . . . in L.A. . . . ."

"Kennedy?" Someone nodded. Another Kennedy. Another death. His brother and then Martin Luther King and Viet Nam . . . and Queenie . . . and Peter . . . and now this . . . it was too much, too often, too long . . . and too much to hurt for. They had all cared so much, about so many things, and now all the people they had cared about were dying. It was a hard way to grow up, to grow old, to give up hope, to become a "grown-up." And who cared anyway? Who wanted what they had to give? What was it that was so sacred that it killed everyone who cared. The torch had finally come to burn everyone's fingers.

"Is he? . . . Shhh!" The radio was turned up louder and the announcer's voice cracked as he said, "Robert Kennedy is dead." He had been shot as he gave his victory speech after the primary in California. He had won, and lost, and died, all in one moment. And so had his children and his wife, and the people who loved him.

Paxton listened and turned away, and she walked home, leaving her books on the steps of the library. It didn't matter. She didn't want them.

She sat in her kitchen that night, alone, thinking, looking out the window, and knowing there was nothing left for her here, nothing she wanted to do or learn, or take with her. She had learned all she wanted to, and the lessons had come dear. And all she felt now was sadness. Not grief, not pain, not despair, just sadness. Robert Kennedy was gone, and too many others had gone with him. At that precise moment twenty-two thousand nine hundred and fifty-one men had died in Viet Nam.

That night Paxton packed a few of her things, and she arranged the rest of her and Peter's things, neatly in the closet. In the morning, she drove into town and went to see Ed Wilson at the paper. He looked at her as she came in, and saw the toll it had all taken on her. Everyone at the paper was going crazy over Kennedy's assassination. Another Kennedy. Another brother. Another victim. But Paxton seemed oddly aloof from it, strangely cool, and sadly older. She was a beautiful girl, but she had aged. The years were in her eyes, in the way she moved, in the things she didn't say but felt. She had lost too much, and believed too strongly. She had believed in good, and happiness, and trust. And they had all been lies. The happy ending doesn't always come. And Camelot does not go on forever. For anyone. You grow old, you die, or sometimes you die young. Too many had in her short lifetime, and Ed Wilson, with his wealth of years, and his own sorrow over his son, felt sorry for her.

"What can I do for you, Paxton?" He looked serious, but he smiled at her as he leaned over and kissed her. "You're getting too thin. You need to come in and have dinner with us more often."

"I left Peter's things at the house just now, in Berkeley." The way she said it seemed strange to him, and he looked at her oddly.

"Are you going somewhere?" He frowned as he watched, there was something so sad in her eyes, he wondered if anyone would ever touch it.

"That depends on you," she said calmly. "I've decided to leave school."

"I thought you got an extension to graduate in September." She had told him that when she'd gotten it and he was relieved for her. He knew how important finishing school was to her, so her announcement that morning surprised him. "What's this all about, Paxton?" He almost sounded like a father, and she smiled. In the past four years, he had been more than a father to her, and she wondered if he would give her what she wanted now. But if he didn't, she knew someone else would.

"I want a job."

"You have a job here anytime. You know that. But doesn't it make more sense to stay at Berkeley this summer and get your degree? What's the hurry?"

"I'm not going to finish school." She knew that morning when she left, she would never go back there. She had taken the only things of Peter's that she wanted. Three poetry books he had given her, the watch he had worn since he was a boy that the Wilsons had given her and she wore now, and his dog tags. "I want to work for you, Mr. Wilson."

"Here?" Something in her eyes told him that there was more to it than she was saying. And he was right. She shook her head quietly when he asked her.

"No, not here. Not yet anyway. I want to go to Saigon." She said it quietly and calmly, but his eyes widened as he watched her. She wanted to go for all the wrong reasons. To find Peter. To die. To avenge him perhaps. Or maybe just because she had lost faith in her own country. He knew only too well that this second Kennedy's death, so soon after Martin Luther King's, was going to shake the nation's youth to their core, and it was obvious that it had already shaken Paxton. She had a broken look in her eyes, and she was sitting ramrod straight in his office, a girl who had given everything up, or lost it all, or maybe both. But whatever she wanted to do in Saigon, for whatever reason, he was not going to help her.

"That's out of the question."

"Why?" Her eyes shot bullets into his, and he could see that however wrong she may have been, she meant it.

"Because that's a place for seasoned correspondents. For God's sake, Paxton, that's a war zone. You know better than anyone what can happen there. And even if we never send you to the hot spots, you can get blown up sitting in a bar, or from 'friendly fire,' just like Peter." The mere mention of him hurt them both, but he knew he had to say it, for her own sake. And nothing she could say to him would change his mind, or so he thought, but she was bitterly persistent.

"There are people going there to fight and be killed who are four years younger than I am."

"Is that what you want?" Tears filled his eyes as he asked her. "To die in the same place he did? Is that your gift to him? Is that all you can do with your life, Paxton? I know how you feel, you and your whole generation think this country is going to hell in a handbasket and right now I'm not sure I disagree with you. But going to Saigon on a suicide mission is *not* the answer."

"I want to tell people here the truth, whatever that truth is. I want to see it for myself. I want to know what's going on, without having it fed to me on the evening news. I'm sick and tired of sitting in a library for the rest of my life, nice and safe, reading about other people dying."

"So you *want* to die, is that it?" He was trying to force it out of her, but if that was the truth, she wouldn't admit it.

147

"No, I want the truth. Don't you? Don't you want to know why he really died? What's *really* going on over there? I want to see us get the hell out of Viet Nam, and I want to know why we haven't gotten out yet. And if I go down there, I'm not a tired old correspondent with jaded political views and an ax to grind and an ass to protect, and no, I don't want to die, but if I do, so what, maybe if I die, it'll be for a good cause, the cause of truth, maybe then it might even be worth it."

"Paxton . . ." He shook his head from behind his desk. "It'll never be worth it. Nothing was worth Peter dying for. And it won't be worth your dying for that misery over there either. I was wrong. You are right. And so was Peter. We don't belong there. I don't think we can win. I'd like to see us get out too. And I never thought I'd hear myself say that. I met with the new Secretary of Defense in Washington last week, Clark Clifford, and he's convinced me. If you want a story, go talk to him. Sure, I'll give you a job. Go anywhere you want in this country and get a story. Be a roving reporter, a troubleshooter, be anything you want, but I'm not sending you to Viet Nam. If anything happened to you there, I couldn't live with myself. We owe it to Peter's memory to take good care of you, and you owe him that too." He looked sternly at Paxton, but it didn't convince her.

"I owe him more than that." Her eyes narrowed as she looked at the man who had almost been her father-in-law but now never would be. "And so do you." She stood up with a determined look. "Mr. Wilson, I'm not going to sit here like a coward, waiting for other people to find the answers. I'm going, whether you send me or not. If I have to, I'll go on my own, and sell my stories from there. Maybe someone will want them." He stood up and faced her across his desk, as he reached out and touched her arm.

"Paxton, don't . . ."

"I have to." He stood there for a long time, looking at her, knowing she had changed since just being the girl who was going to marry his son. She had grown up, the hard way, with heartbreak and grief and bitter disappointment.

"Can't I reason with you? Can't you wait? Think about it for six months. Maybe we'll even be out of there by then." He sounded hopeful.

"We won't be. They're lying to us. That's what I want to see for myself now."

"Paxton, all you've done is work for the paper here in the summer, you have no idea what it's like being a correspondent in a place like that. It takes years to prepare for an assignment of that kind."

She smiled sadly as she listened. "Funny, they don't take years to prepare the grunts, do they. They just ship them over to die, ready or not. I'm ready, Mr. Wilson, I know I am." And a part of him knew that she had the right attitude. She was sad, she was tough, she was smart, and she cared . . . because of Peter. The old newspaperman in him was convinced, but the father of his son felt he had to do everything to stop her. "Will you send me?" She looked him straight in the eye, and he felt like crying again. He wanted to do anything but send her, but he knew that she meant business. And if he didn't send her, someone else would, someone who would send her right into the combat zones and maybe get her killed. Maybe if he hired her, he could protect her.

"I'll agree if you swear to me you'll do just what we ask for, and follow orders to the letter." Her eyes lit up like the Fourth of July, and for the first time in months she looked happy. "Did you hear me?" He spoke to her like a wayward child who was being allowed to go to the county fair, but only under certain conditions.

"No garden parties and no fashion shows, right?" They both laughed. They were not likely to be the daily fare in Saigon.

"You're really serious about this, Pax? You're sure I can't

dissuade you?" He sat down heavily in his desk chair again, with a defeated look as she shook her head. And she beamed. She had won. All the night before she had known what she had to do, and for the first time in a long time, if she wasn't happy, at least she felt peaceful.

"I know I'll do a good job for you. I swear." She sounded enthusiastic and excited and alive again. In a way he was relieved for her, but he was also frightened. He would have preferred it if she had looked like that because of a boy she had met at the library. Even at Berkeley, that would have been safer.

"I'm not worried about your doing a good job. I'm worried about your ass," he confessed bluntly. "You'd better take care of it, or I'll come over and kick it myself, and I mean it." And then he groaned and ran a hand through his white hair that was so much like Peter's. They had the same hairline, the same look, the same eyes, but Paxton tried not to see it. "Marjorie is going to kill me for this. And Gabby . . . oh, my God . . . I almost forgot." He looked horrified as he looked at Paxton. "She had the baby last night . . . a little boy. They're calling him Peter." It wasn't surprising. Nothing was anymore, and Paxxie was happy for her. A life for a life. As Robert Kennedy left the world, at the hands of a madman, Gabby's little boy entered it, with a life full of hope before him, and Peter looked on, wishing them well, and lending him his name, because it was no longer needed. The spirits came and went, changing places, changing hands, some dreams ending as others began. It was strange to think of.

"I'm happy for them. Is she okay?"

"She's fine. She called us right after he was born, naturally, and according to Matt, it was very easy. I'm sure they'd love to see you." Paxton nodded, but it would be odd seeing the little boy who bore Peter's name. Paxton knew there would be no babies for her now, and no man. She wanted nothing except to go to Viet Nam and find the truth about the war. It was odd how her life had changed. All the dreams she had once had were gone. Harvard, and then Berkeley, and Peter . . . now all she wanted was to see what was really happening and tell people in the States, so they would know why their husbands and sons were dying in Viet Nam.

"How soon do I go?" Paxton wanted to pin him down and he knew it. He glanced at his calendar, made some notes, and then he looked up at her.

"These things take a little time. I have to talk to our bureau chief there, and see what we need . . ."

"I'm not going to wait six months."

"I know you're not," he said quietly. "I was thinking about a week, maybe two, three at most. You'll need that long to get organized, be briefed, have the shots you'll need. Let's say two weeks. Does that sound reasonable to you?" She nodded, amazed she had won. She smiled slowly at him. She'd done it.

"Very reasonable. I thought I'd go home for a few days, to say good-bye to my mother."

"Do that. I'll call you there and tell you when we need you back here. You can start the shots there. I know you'll need quite a few. Your brother can take care of it for you, if he's willing." He wondered if her family would try and stop her too, but he knew her well enough to know that now that she'd decided, nothing would stop her. She was a strong girl with a good heart, and he knew better than anyone that part of it was broken. He stood up again then and walked around the desk to her. "It's been a hard year for all of us, Pax. I just hope you're not making a terrible mistake." He held her close to him and kissed the top of her head. "We don't want to lose you too."

"You won't," she whispered as she clung to him. And oddly, she felt, as she stood there, that she'd be alright, because she had Peter's blessing.

# Chapter 10

Paxton arrived in Savannah on a Friday afternoon, two days after Robert Kennedy had been shot, in time to watch the train cross the country on TV on Saturday, bringing his body home, as people waved from every town, crying for another hope lost, another heartbreak. And this time, no one met Paxton at the airport.

She had called her mother to say she was flying in, but her mother had to go to a tea being given by her bridge club. And Paxton didn't mind, it gave her a chance to go home alone, and sit in the kitchen and think of Queenie.

Her mother had hired a new girl after she died, and she was black, too, but she was younger and she only worked days, and she was out buying groceries when Paxton arrived, which was a relief in a way. It gave her a chance to be alone in Queenie's kitchen. It was odd being there without her, and Paxton felt a terrible ache, remembering her last words the last time she'd been home . . . sometimes if you wait, life don't give you a chance to do what you want. She'd been right. But Queenie knew that by now. Because if there was a Heaven, surely she was with Peter.

The slam of a door broke into Paxton's thoughts and she

heard rapid footsteps in the front hall. It was the new girl, and she almost screamed when she saw Paxxie.

"I'm sorry. I'm Paxton Andrews. I just got home from California. I didn't mean to scare you." The girl looked wild-eyed for a moment and then relaxed. She was about Paxton's own age, and she had a sweet face, but she was short and heavyset and not very pretty.

"You go to school in California?"

"That's right."

"You jus' graduate?" She said it carefully, like it was something very important.

But Paxton shook her head in answer. "No, I didn't." She didn't tell her that she'd come home to say good-bye to her family before she went to Viet Nam. She had to tell her mother first. She just chatted amiably, and helped the girl carry the groceries into the kitchen. And her mother came home half an hour later.

She looked older to Paxton somehow, and she wasn't sure why. She looked well, and her hair was freshly done, but her face looked tired and a little more lined than it had the last time Paxton saw her. But she said she was feeling well, and told Paxton she looked thin, and then asked Emmalee to bring them tea and cinnamon toast in the front parlor.

And after the first sip, Beatrice Andrews looked at her pointedly and asked her why she'd come home. She was no fool, and she had sensed that there was a reason for the trip, other than just a friendly visit. She knew that Paxton didn't like to come home, and if she didn't have to, she wouldn't.

"Are you getting married?" she asked, with an odd look. It was a look of disappointment because she knew who the boy would have to be and he wasn't from the South, and there was also some excitement because her only daughter was about to be a bride, but Paxton only shook her head, sorry to disappoint her.

153

"No, I'm not. I'm afraid that's not in the picture." She sounded calm as she said it, and her mother looked at her strangely, sensing more, but Paxton didn't want to say it.

"Have you stopped seeing that boy?" Peter had always been "that boy" to her, and the words made Paxton smile now. He had been gone for two months, and the first shock of grief was slowly fading. All that was left was the dull ache of disbelief and the quiet sorrow that she felt as though it would go on forever. But she could function with it, and no one knew how much it hurt, except maybe the Wilsons, and the others who had suffered losses like it. But now that she was going to Viet Nam, for some odd reason, even though the pain was still there, she felt better.

"I . . . uh . . ." She groped for the words. "It's a little hard to explain. It's not important." It's not important, Mom, he's just dead, that's all. But she couldn't imagine her mother sharing her pain, which was why she had never told her. Telling her would just have been too painful.

"Is something wrong?" Beatrice Andrews would not let it lie, and her searching glance was making Paxton squirm, much to her own chagrin. There was no way to avoid her. "What happened?"

"He . . . uh . . ." She could hear the ticking of the grandfather clock in the corner of the room, and she concentrated her gaze on the curtains so she didn't have to see her mother's face when she told her. "He . . . went to Viet Nam . . . and he was killed in Da Nang in April." There was an endless silence, and Paxton cursed herself as her eyes filled with tears, and then suddenly, next to her, she felt her mother move. She turned in surprise, and she saw the woman who had been a stranger to her all her life, sitting next to her and crying.

"I'm so sorry . . . I know how you must feel . . . how terrible . . ." She put her arms around Paxton, and all of a sudden, Paxton found herself sobbing, with her arms around her mother, she was crying for Peter again, and for the Kennedys and Queenie and Martin Luther King . . . and even her Daddy . . . why had they all died? Why were they gone? Why had he flown his plane into the storm? And why hadn't she married Peter when she could have? She tried to tell her mother what she felt, but all the words came out in a jumble, and her mother rocked her gently back and forth, as she never had before, and Paxton was oddly reminded of Queenie. "Why didn't you tell me?" They were words of gentle reproach, but the look in her eyes told Paxton that she cared more than she had ever suspected.

"I don't know. Maybe telling you would have made it more real. I guess I just couldn't."

"How terrible for his family."

"His sister Gabby just had a baby two days ago, and she named him Peter." But that made Paxton cry all over again, because now she would never have his babies. They sat like that for hours, crying and drinking tea, and crying all over again. She seemed to be crying for everyone and for everything, and making up for a lifetime. And finally, she put her arms around her mother and thanked her. It was the first time they had ever really made contact.

"I know how you feel," her mother said, much to Paxton's amazement. "I remember how I felt when your father died . . . I was confused for a long time . . . and angry and sad. It'll take you a long time, Paxton. It may even hurt forever. Not every day, every minute, but when you think of him, there will always be a sad place in your heart for what happened." She patted her daughter's hand then. "One day there will be someone else, you'll have a husband and children, but you'll still remember him, and you'll always love him." Paxton didn't tell her that she couldn't imagine another man in her life, or children who were not his, but she knew that her mother was right that she would always love him. And then her mother asked her

155

the question Paxton wished could have come later. "Will you be coming home now in September, dear? There's not much point now to your staying in California." They had won after all. She was coming home. Her love affair with "that boy" was over. But Paxton slowly shook her head, and waited, searching for the right words to tell her. Suddenly, she didn't want to hurt her. Her mother had finally given her something she'd needed for a long time, and she wanted to thank her, not give her grief. But there was no choice now.

"I left school yesterday." . . . and the house where I was so happy with Peter. . . . I left everything . . . because Robert Kennedy was killed and I can't stand the insanity of this country a moment longer. So she was going to a place that was even more insane, but at least there, the insanity was out in the open.

"You left school for good?" Her mother looked shocked, because she knew that giving up was so much unlike Paxton.

"I just couldn't do it anymore. I could stay for the next ten years and I can't write another paper, take another test. It doesn't make sense to me anymore. I can't even remember why I wanted to do it in the first place."

"But this is your last term." She looked confused, and she suddenly wondered if Paxton had gone a little crazy. "You could graduate in the fall if you finish now. Paxton, you don't want to waste everything you've done. You're only inches from the finish."

Paxton nodded miserably. It was true. Her mother was right. But she just couldn't do it. "I know. But ever since Peter went away, I haven't been able to think straight. Ever since he left for basic training in January, I haven't been able to do a single paper."

"That's understandable, of course. Maybe you could finish here. And get a job on the paper. You know how badly they want you." She was trying to offer encouragement, and Paxton felt sorry for her. She had no idea what was coming.

"Mama . . ." She reached out and touched her hand, still grateful for her solace over Peter. "I took a job yesterday." Paxton spoke very softly.

Beatrice Andrews's face fell. "In San Francisco?"

There was a long pause, as Paxton thought about how to phrase it. "With the *Morning Sun*. But not in San Francisco."

"Where then?" She couldn't begin to imagine.

"I'm going to be a correspondent in Saigon." There was an endless silence in the room, and then suddenly her mother dropped her face into her hands and began to sob, and this time it was Paxton who held her. And then she turned to look at the child she barely knew, as though she were the total stranger she always had been.

"How can you do such a thing? Are you trying to get killed? To commit suicide? I felt that way after your father died too," she said, blowing her nose daintily in a lace hankie, "but I had you and George to think about. And your future. I know things look bleak to you now, but they won't in a while, Paxton, you have to be patient."

"I know, Mama . . . I know how it looks. But it's something I have to do now. I can't just sit here, or there, and wait for life to take its course. I want to be in Viet Nam. I want to understand what happened. I want to stop it from happening. I want to help stop it sooner. I want to make people care. Every night, we sit around watching people get killed while we eat our dinner, and no one cares, no one even flinches. Even if what I do takes ten minutes off the war, then maybe that's enough. Maybe in those ten minutes five people would have been killed . . . maybe something I can do will save them."

"And if you're killed, Paxton, instead? What if it's you and not someone else? Have you thought of that? . . . and what it will do to me? You're a woman. Good God, you don't have to go to war. You're still crazy after that boy died. You have to stay home and heal your wounds. Stay here, don't go back."

She was begging her, and it was breaking Paxton's heart, but she knew she had to go. It was her fate now.

"I have to go, Mama. But I promise you, I'll be careful. I'm not looking to get killed." She knew that Ed Wilson had thought the same thing, which made her wonder. And there were times when she was tempted to join Peter, times when she drove across the bridge, and thought of stopping the car and jumping. But she hadn't. And now she knew that there was something she had to do that was a lot more important than escaping.

"Please don't go . . . Paxton, I beg you . . ."

"Mama, don't." And for the second time in what seemed like a lifetime, the two women embraced. The ice had been broken, the bond had been formed, but it was too late for Paxton to turn back. She had come home to say good-bye, and by the next day, her mother knew it.

They spent the next two weeks talking quietly, about her father, and how her mother felt when he died, and finally she even talked about the other woman. She had been a woman he worked with, and Beatrice had known about the affair. She had known how lonely he was, but she just couldn't give him what he wanted. And she even admitted she'd been relieved when someone else could. It only hurt when he died, and everyone found out that there had been another woman in his life. It seemed an odd way to think of things to Paxton, but even now, with their newfound exchange, she recognized that she and her mother were very different. The one so cool, so distant, so aloof, so afraid of letting go, of being out of control, of too much feeling, the other so warm, so open, so passionate, so deeply involved and committed, even in her grief after Peter's death. And in so many ways, Paxton was so much like her father.

Her brother George tried to talk her out of going to Viet Nam, too, but like his mother, within days he realized that there was no point, Paxton was determined. He administered her shots, and in the end, when Ed Wilson called and told her to come back to be briefed, George and Allison and her mother took her to the airport, and this time even Paxton cried when she left them. She felt as though she were leaving home for good. Even if she came back, it would never be the same, and she knew it. She had left as a child, and she would return different, battle-scarred, wiser, or perhaps more bitter. But she would never be a child again. The child that been Paxton Andrews was gone, with the others.

# CHAPTER 11

⌄

The good-byes in San Francisco were no easier than the ones in Savannah. In fact, despite her mother's reaching out to her over Peter's death, the good-byes said in San Francisco were much harder. Gabby cried nonstop, and Peter's mother was still heartbroken that her husband had agreed to the job in Saigon. And she told him point-blank that he was as crazy as Paxxie.

And the night she left, they all took her to the airport. She had been given a seat on a military transport out of Travis Air Force Base, and she had her vaccination certificates, and her passport, and her visas, and her papers from the *Morning Sun,* and all her instructions about who she was to report to and where, and where she was to stay. They had booked her into the Hotel Caravelle on the Tu Do, and the *Sun* had even given her a Vietnamese phrase book. But this was still the hard part. Saying good-bye to them was awful. Being at Travis reminded them all of when they had said good-bye to Peter. And even Peter's father cried when he held Paxton in his arms, and kissed her firmly on the cheek and reminded her for the ten thousandth time to be careful.

"And for God's sake, if you get there and change your mind, don't be a fool, you turn right around and come home. I think you're making one hell of a mistake going over there, don't be too proud to admit it and come back quickly."

"I won't," she promised him with tears in her own eyes, "I love you." She had learned to say it all while she could. You never knew what was going to happen. "You all take care." She kissed them all again, as her flight was being called. "I've got to go. Promise you'll write."

"Take care of yourself," Marjorie exhorted her, trying not to think of her son. "Be careful what you eat!" They all laughed, and Gabby and Paxton embraced. It had all started with them. The two girls who loved each other like sisters, and had for four years now.

"I love you, you crazy girl. Be careful, Paxxie, please . . . if anything happens to you, I'll die. . . ." Paxton only shook her head, and ruffled the bright red curly hair.

"Just don't get knocked up again before I come home." The baby was only three weeks old and Gabby laughed through her tears.

"Take care of yourself, Pax. We're going to miss you." Matthew hugged her gently, and then she stood back and looked at all of them.

"I'll be home in time to trim the tree." That was the deal she had made with Ed Wilson. Six months in Saigon. And home by Christmas.

They all waved as she slung a large tote bag over her shoulder and picked up her one small suitcase. She was wearing stout boots that looked like combat boots, and jeans and a T-shirt, and she had a new Nikon slung over her shoulder. She turned at the gate and gave a last wave, trying hard to fight back tears as she thought of Peter, and then she turned and ran toward the plane, and as she ran up the steps to the C-141, she collided with what looked like someone's kid brother. He had wheat-colored hair like her own, and a round baby face and he looked about fifteen as he ran up the steps behind her, carrying his

161

duffel. And then she knew what he was. Just another green kid, going to fight the war in Viet Nam, and as she took her seat on the plane, he hurried to the back to join a hundred others like him . . . eighteen . . . nineteen . . . twenty . . . she felt like an old lady next to them . . . and as they took off, and headed across the Pacific, she looked down and prayed that the boys flying to Saigon with her would still be alive by Christmas.

They had given her six months. Six months to find herself, to see the war, to come to terms with what had happened in Da Nang, and to see it all for herself . . . six months to tear her heart out and give it to them, to atone for her sins, and tell the world what was really happening over there. Six months in Nam. Maybe she was crazy, she knew, but she felt she owed it to Peter. And as she closed her eyes, and laid her head back against the seat, the lights of California dwindled swiftly behind them.

# PART II

$\vee$

# Viet Nam:

*June 1968–April 1975*

# CHAPTER 12

$\vee$

Paxton was wide-awake from Travis Air Force Base to Hawaii, even though when they arrived it was almost midnight for her, and she was still awake most of the way to Guam, and found herself talking to some of the men, as they all took turns waiting for the bathrooms. Most of the boys looked like the one she'd collided with boarding the plane. They looked barely eighteen years old, and they were young and scared, and when they relaxed a little, they were full of mischief. Several of them asked her for dates, some showed her photographs of girlfriends and mothers and wives, and for the most part they were the rawest of new recruits. The epitome of the word they were about to hear thrown at them night and day once they arrived: *Green-seeds.*

A few of the older ones traveling with them had been to Nam before, and through their own choice, they were returning for another tour of duty. These were the ones Paxton was interested in, and two of them shared the whiskey in their flasks with her as they passed the night on their way to Guam, roughly halfway by then between San Francisco and Saigon.

She wanted to know what it was like over there, why they wanted to go back, why they hated it or loved it, the essence of it and what it meant to them, but as she listened to them, she

165

wasn't sure she understood them. They talked about what a bitch of a place it was, about what bastards the VC were, about how Charlie had killed their friends, and in the same breath they spoke of the country's beauty, the mountains, the streams, the green of the hills, the stink, the smells, the perfume, the women, the whores, the friends they loved, the buddies they'd lost, the danger. It was hard to make head or tail of it unless you'd been there. And they seemed to have an odd respect for the enemy and their fierce loyalty to their cause, how hard they fought, how tireless they were, how they never gave up until they died. It was an odd kind of respect for their opponents. They talked about Charlie a lot, and about what jerks their COs were, how they never knew what in hell was going on. And more importantly, how there was no way America could win the war in Viet Nam.

"Then why are you going back?" she asked quietly, and both men looked at each other and then away. And she waited for what seemed like a long, long time. And when they answered her, she almost understood it.

"It doesn't feel right being stateside anymore," one explained. "No one gives a damn. All the kids hate you for being there, and you feel like a traitor when you come home. But back in Nam, your buddies are dying in the dirt, stepping on mines . . ." The man talking to her gritted his teeth as he spoke and was totally unaware of it. "I watched my best friend's face get blown away . . . my other two best friends are MIA . . . I can't . . . I can't go home and sit on my ass over there . . . I gotta be back here helping them, at least till someone gets smart and gets us the hell out of here."

"Yeah." The other man nodded, knowing full well what he meant. "There's no room for us back there. We're the shitheads now. Not Charlie. Not the President. Us, we're the bad guys . . . us, the guys who're getting killed for them. The truth is, lady, no one gives a damn. We got our asses stuck over there, and the guys in charge won't let us really do some real damage to them, because they're afraid the Russkies or the Chinks'll get pissed off. So they let us get our balls shot off in Viet Nam. You wanna know why I came back? I came back to help my buddies out, until we can all go home together."

He had no wife, no kids, and all he cared about were his friends in the army.

But they were intrigued by her too. And eventually, they turned the questions on her. "What about you? What are you doing over here?"

"I came to see what was really going on."

"Why? What difference does it make to you?" She thought about it for a long time, and she wasn't planning to tell everyone, but it was late, and she knew she'd never see these boys again. She reached into her shirt, much to their surprise, and pulled out Peter's dog tags, which she brought with her. She pulled them out and extended them toward them, and both men nodded, they knew what it meant. "He died in Da Nang. I just want to see what's going on."

They nodded again. "It's a crazy place." And then the older of the two men smiled. "How old are you?"

She hesitated and then smiled at him. "Twenty-two. Why?"

"I'm two years older than you, and this is my third tour, and lady, I seen stuff over there that I wouldn't want no little sister of mine looking at. You sure you know what you're doing going to Saigon? It's a bokoo long way from home."

"I figured that." In fact, she was counting on it, but she still couldn't imagine it. And eventually, she said good night to them, went back to her seat, and fell asleep the rest of the way to Guam.

They landed in Guam at what was nine a.m. for them, two a.m. local time, of the next day. They stayed for an hour, to refuel and then flew on to Saigon. They were scheduled to arrive at five a.m. local time. And it was odd, as they flew on, she kept thinking that Peter had come this way only a little more than two months before.

They flew into Tan Son Nhut Airport on the main military base, on schedule, shortly after five a.m., and Paxton was disappointed she couldn't see the countryside. Everyone talked about Viet Nam being so green. Instead all she could see were fireworks as she came down, and wondered what they meant. But the soldier sitting next to her laughed at her when she asked if it was a national holiday.

"Yeah, you could call it that, I guess. They call this a war. That's artillery . . . those are tracer bullets going off . . . oh . . . I'd say somewhere in the vicinity of Bien Hoa. . . . Lady, you're gonna love it here. We got fireworks anytime when our birds drop their eggs on Victor Charlie." His attitude annoyed her, he was faintly condescending and somewhat amused by her. And it was embarrassing to realize that she had made a blunder.

She carried her own bags when she got off, and the boys who had talked to her seemed to have forgotten her by then. They had their own troubles now. And they were all loaded into trucks almost as soon as they arrived at the airport.

There was no one at the airport for her, and as she picked up her bags and went to look for a cab, she felt very brave. She spoke not a word of Vietnamese, and suddenly she felt as though she didn't have a friend in the world.

A string of battered cars were outside the terminal, and there were U.S. soldiers everywhere. This was the main military base for Saigon, and for a last few moments, she felt safe there.

"Hey, Doughnut Dollie, welcome to Saigon!" a voice called out to her, and she turned to see who they meant, and was annoyed to discover that the black man with the accent from the Deep South meant her.

"Thanks a lot!" she called back, letting him hear her Savannah drawl.

"Louisiana?" he called back, and this time she laughed.

"Georgia!"

"Shee-it!" He smiled, and hurried on. It was still before dawn, but there seemed to be plenty of people awake and busy. And she signaled to one of the drivers of a waiting cab. It was a blue-and-yellow Renault, and the driver wore sandals and shorts, and he had a flat narrow face and shaggy black hair.

"You Wac?" he asked, speaking too loud. The noises seemed remarkable here. Even at this time of the morning, in the distance she could hear loud voices and horns. And there was a pungent smell in the air, a kind of perfume made of flowers, spices, and oil. She could smell the jet fuel everywhere, and as she looked around her, there seemed to be a haze of smoke just above them.

"No, not Wac," she explained, wondering why he cared.

"Wave?"

"No." She wanted to put her bags in the car. She had been traveling for more than twenty hours. "You take me to Caravelle Hotel, please."

"You prostitute?" he asked, finally impressed, and she didn't know whether to laugh or cry or just admit it to him.

"No," she said firmly, as she put her bags in his car. "Journalist." She already knew from a phrase book she'd brought that she was a *bao chi*—in Vietnamese, a correspondent. But she didn't yet dare to try the unfamiliar language. He shook his head. He refused to understand, as he slipped behind the wheel and turned to look at her, wondering what she was *really*.

"You military?" Shit. It was obvious she was never going to get to Saigon.

"Newspaper," she tried again. And this time the light dawned.

"Oh. Very good!" He was almost shouting at her, and as they left the base, he kept his hand continually on the horn. The noise was almost deafening, but all around them, despite the hour, there seemed to be a cacophony of horns. "You buy drugs from me?" he asked chattily as they headed toward Saigon. It was all so simple here. You prostitute? You buy drugs from me? It must have been overwhelming for the young boys she'd seen who'd never left home before.

"No drugs. Hotel Caravelle." She repeated again just to be sure he understood. "On Tu Do." It was supposedly the main drag, or so the man in charge of foreign correspondents at the *Sun* had said. And Ed Wilson had insisted that they book her there because it was one of the best in town, and the cleanest. The CBS office was there, and he thought she might be safer there than at some of the other hotels in Saigon.

"Cigarette?" he offered as she prayed he wouldn't offer her anything else on the four-mile ride to town. "Ruby Queen," he identified Viet Nam's favorite smoke.

"No, thank you, I don't smoke," she explained as several motor scooters and an ancient Citroën seemed to sideswipe them all at once. He responded by putting both hands on the horn, as did everyone else. And as she sat back against the seat she tried to take a deep breath again, but the continuing smell of fumes almost choked her.

But as she watched their route into Saigon, she saw the buildings around them become more beautiful, and there was a look of Paris as they came closer to the center of Saigon. There seemed to be foot traffic everywhere despite the early hour, and the curfew, but people were scurrying along. There were some on bicycles, people in pedicabs, and everywhere the sounds of voices and horns all around her.

Some of the buildings were colored in washed pastels, others were in solemn stone. And as they reached Saigon, he drove her past the Presidential Palace and the Basilica of Our Lady of Peace, and then onto Nguyen Hue Boulevard, bordered by lovely trees, until they passed City Hall. And then they went past the Salem Building on the square, and she suddenly recognized the famous Marines Statue. And as soon as she saw it, Paxton had a better idea of where she was. She knew that there on the square, in the Eden Building, she would find the Associated Press and the NBC offices. And a few minutes later, she identified the Continental Palace, as they turned onto the Tu Do and she knew from the man at the *Sun* that there was an interesting bar there called the Terrasse, and the *Time* magazine office. And as they drove past the National Assembly building, the driver slowed and turned to her with a half-toothless smile. It was impossible to determine how old he was. He could have been anywhere between twenty-five and sixty.

"You wanna see Pink Nightclub in Hotel Catinat tonight? I pick you up for dinner."

"No, thank you." She tried to take a firm tone with him. "Caravelle Hotel. Now, please. Tonight I must work for my newspaper." She tried to sound firm and uninviting.

"Not prostitute?" he continued to ask hopefully, as she prayed he would take her to her hotel and never come back to find her.

And then suddenly, they were there, at the Caravelle, and all she wanted was to get out and run away from him, check in, and go to bed. She was exhausted but exhilarated just being there. He told her how much she owed and she knew that he was cheating her, but this time she was too tired to care. She walked into the lobby of the Caravelle, carrying her own bags, and it was slowly coming to life as a few young Vietnamese girls began to clean the lobby. It was still early morning, but soon the sun would be up and the hotel would be busy. The lobby would be full of high-ranking uniforms, visitors from abroad, mostly from Europe, and the pretty Vietnamese girls who came to meet them.

"Andrews," she gave her name to the pretty female desk clerk in a white *ao dai,* the traditional Vietnamese costume of

171

trousers and a slim-fitting long tunic. Most were white, but some were prints or brightly colored.

"Andrew?" She looked blankly at Paxton for a moment.

"Paxton Andrews. From the *Morning Sun* in San Francisco." Paxton was too tired to be either patient or charming. All she wanted was a shower and her bed. Even at that hour of the morning, the air was stifling. She hadn't been prepared for the suffocating heat, and the ceiling fans seemed to do nothing, as the girl checked the register and shook her head at Paxton.

"Mr. Andrews not here yet. You his wife? His lady?"

Shit, she muttered to herself. "No," she explained. "I *am* Paxton Andrews." She noticed two young Vietnamese boys listening to her, smiling, as two men met in the lobby. One had come from the plane. The other from the street outside. They were off to an early start and both men gave Paxton a careful look of intense appraisal. One was rugged and dark-haired and somewhere in his middle thirties, the other one was considerably older with a lined face that looked worried. She noticed them but she wasn't interested in talking to them or knowing who they were. All she wanted was her room, and shower, and her bed, for the moment. And meanwhile, the girl at the desk still appeared not to understand her. "I *am* Paxton Andrews."

"You Mr. Andrews?" The girl giggled, and even Paxton had to laugh. In the two hours she'd been in Viet Nam, she'd been called a man, a Doughnut Dollie, and a prostitute. It was certainly an interesting beginning.

"Yes," she explained again. "I am Paxton Andrews. Do you have my room?" The girl finally nodded agreement, and as the two men watched, while trying to appear not to, the girl at the desk signaled for a boy who couldn't have been more than eight years old, and handed him a key to a room on the third floor, well below the well-known bar in the penthouse.

Paxton followed him up the stairs, and he struggled with her single bag while she managed her tote bag, and when they reached her room, she gave him twenty-five piasters, and he grinned and bowed and ran away downstairs. He was a cute child, and it was hard to believe these were the children she'd been warned against. She'd been told that the children in Viet Nam were either thieves or beggars or VC, or all three. But this one looked innocent as he ran back to the lobby. And she walked into her room in time to see a horde of cockroaches dash across the carpet. She let out a small scream, and then forced herself to walk into the room, kill those she could, and look into the bathroom. It was clean, and done in old white tile, and still seemed reminiscent of the French influence in the city. Nothing had changed much since they'd left it. Certainly not the heat, the war, or the roaches. The only things that had changed were the battered, trembling air conditioners in constant use in all the rooms now. It was a touch of home she was grateful for. Her clothes stuck to her skin from her journey from the airport to the hotel in the torrid, humid heat that had left her looking and feeling like a dishrag.

She washed her face, and ran the tub, and it was eight in the morning local time when she got to bed, and when she opened the windows she could still smell the gas fumes below them and hear the noises as Saigon sprang to life below her. The smell of fuel seemed to be pervasive everywhere in the city. And as she lay there, she wondered what it had been like for Peter when he'd arrived, but he probably hadn't seen much. He had been one of the boys loaded on trucks and whisked off into the night to places like Long Binh, or Nha Trang, Pleiku, Da Nang, Vinh Long, Chu Lai, the places she had come to see, and now could only dream of.

She closed her eyes but slept fitfully, there was too much on her mind, too much to think about, and see, and discover. And as the sun settled high in the sky over Saigon, she stirred and opened her eyes and stretched. And she smiled as she looked up, there was a bird sitting on her windowsill, chirping loudly.

"Welcome to Viet Nam." She rolled over slowly and as she said the words, she heard a sound, and sensed a presence in the room, and sat bolt upright, covering herself with the sheet as a tall, good-looking blond man walked into her bedroom. He was wearing fatigues, but he wore no name, and his fatigues did not say "U.S. Army." "What are you doing here?" She wanted to scream, but she wasn't sure if she should or not, as she backed out of the bed, still carrying the sheet around her.

"You left your key in the door last night. I wouldn't do that here if I were you." He was looking at how beautiful she was, but nothing on his face showed that he had noticed. He had been told by one of the bellboys that there was a new arrival in that room, a very pretty girl, the boy had said. And Nigel had tipped him twenty piasters. He had also heard about her from his two colleagues who had seen her early that morning in the lobby. And now he reached across the bed and handed her the key with a solemn expression. "I was just going to leave it on the nightstand beside you." She noticed that he had an accent, and for a moment she wasn't sure if he was British or Australian.

"I . . . uh. . . ." She was blushing furiously, wondering if he could see through the sheet as she stood there. "I . . . thank you . . ."

He smiled, mildly amused at her distress. "No problem. I'm Nigel Aucliffe, by the way. United Press. From Australia." A twinkle in his eye told her that he was something less than innocent or wholesome.

"Paxton Andrews, from the *Morning Sun,* in San Francisco." But she didn't attempt to shake his hand, for fear of losing the sheet she was holding.

"I'm sure I'll be seeing more of you." His double entendre made her even more uncomfortable and with a brief bow, he left the room as swiftly as he had entered it, and she sat down on the bed, still wrapped in the sheet, with her heart pounding after the encounter. This was definitely not going to be an ordinary experience. And how could she be so stupid as to leave her key in the door in a war zone?

"Christ," she muttered to herself, "talk about stupid." She locked the door from the inside this time, and looked out the window, down the Tu Do, and if you squinted, you could almost tell yourself you were in Paris.

She had to report to the AP office that afternoon at two o'clock in the Eden Building in the square, and she bathed and dressed in a light cotton pale blue dress that seemed more appropriate than blue jeans in the weather. And she hurried downstairs to the main restaurant for lunch. There were quite a few people dining there when she arrived, most of them men, several in fatigues or comparable outfits, others in lightweight shirts, and two Vietnamese women in lovely white *ao dais*, the traditional white dresses worn over balloon trousers that seemed so airy and yet molded their figures so gracefully. For the moment, Paxton seemed to be the only Western woman in the room, and in the far corner she saw Nigel Aucliffe laughing about something with a stranger and the two men she'd seen early that morning, and she wondered if they weren't laughing about her. She felt extremely green and new to it all, as she ordered consommé and an omelet. The touch of France was still visible here in the decor, the food, and the menu.

And as she finished her omelet and sipped a cup of coffee, while making a few notes to herself, Nigel Aucliffe and his group stopped at her table.

"Good morning, again." His eyes teased openly now and seemed to evaluate her all over again and the other men watched her, intrigued by the suggestive greeting. He had already told them about her, and had told them she was so green she looked like leaves in spring, and was obviously somebody's very headstrong daughter. He figured it wouldn't take long for Viet Nam to teach her some lessons, and the thought of it defi-

175

nitely amused him. "Having brunch, I see." His eyes seemed to caress her, and his attitude annoyed her.

"Good morning," she said coolly. He had somehow managed to make it sound like he'd spent the night with her, and the chill in her tone suggested that he was quite mistaken. Her eyes took in the other three, and as he didn't introduce them, she held out a hand and introduced herself. The younger dark-haired man she'd seen when she arrived was Ralph Johnson from New York, AP; the older man was Tom Hardgood from *The Washington Post;* and the third man was Jean-Pierre Biarnet from *Le Figaro,* in Paris. They had been out covering an important press meeting since seven a.m., and had treated themselves to a long, lazy lunch. And Nigel and Jean-Pierre had been talking about knocking off for the rest of the day, when Nigel saw her, and told them what a pleasing sight she had been, wrapped in her bedsheet when he woke her. All three men looked intrigued by her, and most of them were almost old enough to be her father, a thought they would have denied had someone said it. She stood up, ready to leave, and she looked young and lovely and statuesque beside them, and for a moment all four men could barely resist hungry longings. There was an odd silence as she looked at them, well aware of their observation of her novice status.

"What are you doing over here?" Johnson asked her bluntly. He was curious about her and what she was doing in Saigon, as were the others, but they were too proud and supercilious to ask her.

"Same as anyone else, I guess. Looking for a story. Covering the war. I'm here for six months to write for the *Morning Sun,* in San Francisco."

Johnson looked stunned. It was a good paper. And he'd known another correspondent they'd sent for a while the year before. It surprised him that they'd send this green girl, but maybe there was another reason.

"Have you ever done anything like this before?" She shook her head honestly, and for an instant, beneath the bravado, she looked scared, and she was. She had absolutely no idea what she was doing. She had been told to report to the AP office for now, and do whatever assignments they gave her. And Ed Wilson had specifically and personally instructed them not to let her go anywhere alone, and to keep her well out of combat. "How old are you?" Johnson asked bluntly again, and for a moment she considered lying, but then decided not to.

"Twenty-two. I just finished Berkeley." She didn't tell him she'd dropped out, as she signed the check and they all walked slowly into the lobby together. And then he smiled at her.

"I graduated from there sixteen years ago." Johnson looked at her with amusement. "And I was about as green as you are when I started. I almost shit. I was 4-F, and *The New York Times* sent me to Korea. But I learned some stuff I would never have learned sitting on my ass in New York, I can tell you that." And he surprised everyone by holding a hand out and shaking hers. "Good luck, kid. What did you say your name was?"

"Paxton Andrews." They shook hands with her all around then, and the group broke up. Nigel and Jean-Pierre had decided not to quit for the afternoon after all, and instead were going to Xuan Loc to cover some maneuvers. And Ed Hardgood was going to MacVee headquarters at Tan Son Nhut, where Paxton had arrived the night before, for a private interview with General Abrams.

"Are you going to the AP office?" Johnson asked Paxton almost as an afterthought, as she walked out to the street and nodded. "I'll show you where it is," he said, smiling at her again, and the others left, promising to see him that night, as Paxton strode along beside him.

The AP office was in the building she'd seen on the way in the night before, the Eden Building on the square across from the statue of the marine that seemed to be a reference point to everyone in Saigon. And the AP office was in the corner of the building. She had her orders waiting there. She was to "orient herself to Saigon" and be at the U.S. Information Service auditorium at five o'clock, for what Ralph Johnson informed her were called the Five O'Clock Follies.

"I see they're either giving you a slow start, or putting you on Pablum. My first day in Seoul, they booted me right out to the front lines and I almost got shot. It was one way to be introduced to the war. This ought to be a little nicer." But she felt somehow put down, and she wondered what he meant by "putting her on Pablum."

"What are the Five O'Clock Follies?"

"A lot of propaganda. They tell us everything they want us to hear, to tell us how great the war is going. We lose a hill, we really didn't. A bunch of guys got killed, the enemy lost more; Charlie captured some of our equipment, all of it was obsolete anyway so who cares. Body counts that make things sound a little better than they are, the usual shit they want you to feed the folks back home to convince them we're winning."

"And are we?" she asked bluntly.

"What do you think?" he asked coldly. His eyes told their own tale.

"That's why I'm here. I want to know the truth."

"The truth?" He looked at her cynically. "The truth is, it's hopeless." It was what she'd suspected all along, what Peter had thought all along. Before the place had killed him.

"When do you think they're going to admit that and get our boys home?" she asked with innocent fervor in her eyes, and he shook his head with a look of exasperation.

"That, my friend, is the million-dollar question. We have half a million guys here now, a thing called a DMZ, which means don't step on Uncle Ho's toes, and a bunch of kids getting shipped out of here in body bags by the thousand." As he said the words, he saw her flinch and it annoyed him. "If you're shy about that, you'd better get over it quick, or go home. This isn't a place for the fainthearted." He wondered if they knew what they were doing telling her to orient herself to Saigon. Maybe she was just someone's kid playing tourist. But something about her told him that there might be more to her than that. He wasn't sure yet. "I've got a meeting with some guys." He looked at her then, a question in his eyes. "You interested in seeing some of the real Nam, or are you just here to play for a while and tell the folks back home you saw it?" The question was an honest one and she appreciated at least the chance to prove herself as she looked him in the eye and let him know she meant business.

"I want to see the real thing."

He nodded. He had somehow suspected that, despite the good looks and blond hair, she didn't look like a Doughnut Dollie. "I'm taking a crew up to a firebase near Nha Trang tomorrow. You want to come?" His eyes were hard, but he was giving her a chance. He'd been young once, too, and they'd gone to the same school, and for some unknown reason, he thought she deserved it.

"I'd love it." And then, meaning it, "Thank you."

"You got boots?"

"More or less." She'd bought the toughest ones she could find from Eddie Bauer's.

"I mean real ones. You gotta have steel shafts in the soles in case you step on a bamboo spike." She looked blank, but he knew his stuff. He'd been in Saigon since '65. "What size shoe do you wear?"

"Seven." She was in awe of him. If she made anything of herself at all here, she thought it might be thanks to him, and she was truly grateful.

"I'll get you a pair."

"Thank you." And as soon as she said the words, he'd vanished. He had an appointment with the assistant chief of the bureau, who was frowning as Ralph walked in.

"What happened to you? You look happy this afternoon," Ralph teased him.

"You would too. I've had ten Telexes from San Francisco this week about some Greenseed who must be someone's nephew. They don't want him up north. They don't want him out of Saigon. They don't want him to get hurt. They don't want him anywhere, except high tea at the fucking palace. I've got enough headaches in my life without visiting firemen, bored movie stars, and other people's fucking nephews."

"Relax. Maybe he won't even show up. Half these kids talk their socks off about coming here, but they never have the balls to get here. We have a new Doughnut Dollie in our midst, by the way."

"Great. Just what we need. Try and keep your pants on, Ralph. I need you alive for another month, if you can swing it." The two men exchanged a smile. They had been friends for years, and had a strong respect for each other. "Who's the girl?"

"I forget. West Coast. She went to my alma mater. She looks smart, but scared, and green. I offered to take her to Nha Trang tomorrow."

"Who does she work for?"

"I forget that too. She's okay. And if she isn't, she'll be scared shitless and on the next flight home by tomorrow."

"Just watch your ass. It's hot up there right now. But I want you to take a look at this for me." It was a "borrowed" document someone had given him, indicating enormous troop requests for fresh battalions.

"Christ, aren't they ever going to get smart and start sending the boys home?" Ralph Johnson looked dismayed when he read it.

"It makes you wonder, doesn't it?"

"It makes me weep." They went over some other things. A report of increased action in the A Shau Valley, and some crazy reports about Agent Orange. They talked about the trip to Nha Trang the next day, and by then the new girl was all but forgotten.

Ralph Johnson stopped for tea in the suburb of Gia Dinh that day, on some personal business. And by five o'clock he was back in town, picked up his messages at the office, and was only ten minutes late at the Information Service to hear the news delivered at the Five O'Clock Follies. It was the usual reports that day. Who had been killed where, fantastic body counts from the Viet Cong, statistics no one believed and hadn't for a long time, and an enemy document everyone had a chance to examine. Tom Hardgood was also there, and Jean-Pierre, but Nigel wasn't. And Jean-Pierre waved when he saw Paxton. After it was all over, he went over to her, and thought she looked hot and tired and still a little stunned by her arrival. He explained that Nigel had gone on to Xuan Loc, but he had decided to stay in Saigon.

"Well, mademoiselle." He smiled. "How do you like it?"

She smiled tiredly at him. She had spent the last two hours exploring the city. It had been excruciatingly hot all afternoon, and she was overwhelmed by the sights and smells, the endless noises, the sound of planes, the smell of fuel, and the smoke that burned her eyes in the Chinese quarter. She had gotten lost several times, had rented two pedicabs, been picked up by at least a dozen GIs, and she couldn't make head or tail of her Vietnamese phrase book. "I'm not sure," she said honestly, with a tired smile, wondering what purpose these five o'clock briefing sessions served. They seemed so perfectly orchestrated and so artificial. But if you wanted to, you could sit here and report on the war based on what they told you. But she knew that was not what she had come for.

"These things are ridiculous, I can assure you." He was still wearing his fatigues and he looked hot and sweaty. He was a photographer, and he'd been out since four o'clock that morning, and after his lunch with the others, he'd covered a tremendous story.

A group of children had been killed by a terrorist bomb, and the photographs he had taken had been awful. He tried to explain it to her, and his voice was almost a monotone as he told her. He couldn't allow himself to feel anything anymore. It was all too painful.

"I got a perfect shot. Of two dead little girls holding hands," he said in a perfectly even tone. "My paper will be very happy." There was something ghastly about being here, and they all knew it. It ate at you, and destroyed something within. And yet, they also knew they had to be there, for whatever reasons.

"Why did you come here?" she asked quietly, sobered by what he'd said, yet intrigued by all of them, as the others started to drift away from them.

"Because I wanted to know what had changed. I wanted to know why the Americans thought they could win, and *if* they could, after we didn't."

"And can they?" She seemed to be asking everyone, but she wanted to know what people thought, people who knew, the people who'd really seen it.

"No. It's impossible," he said, looking very French, "and I think they know it now, but they don't know what to tell your people. They're afraid to admit disgrace, to say they can't win, and must come home now. It's not American . . . it's not proud . . . or brave . . . it took us a long time too," he said by way of explanation. And she agreed with him. The Americans were staying in Viet Nam in order not to lose face, but they already had. And they were losing boys daily, in the meantime. To the Viet Cong, to booby traps, to mines, to snipers, to "friendly fire," like Peter. And it was odd, now that she was here, she had been less obsessed with him. She had hardly thought of him all day, she was so busy trying to figure it all out, see everything, and discover Saigon. It was a relief in a way. Maybe now that she was here, the pain would dim. Maybe she could put him to rest one day. Maybe she had been right to come here.

And as she thought of it, she saw Jean-Pierre watching her, and he smiled, not understanding what she was thinking. "This is a serious place. You were very brave to come here. Why did you do it?"

"It's a long story," she explained vaguely, looking around. By then, Ralph had left, and Tom Hardgood, and Jean-Pierre asked if she'd like to have a drink at the Terrasse of the Continental Palace Hotel.

"It's an amazing place. True Saigon. You really have to see it."

"Thank you," she said shyly, touched by all of them. Although she knew Nigel regarded her with a certain condescension, at least Ralph seemed willing to give her both a chance and a helping hand, and Jean-Pierre seemed pretty friendly. She noticed that he wore a wedding band, but his invitation seemed more platonic than sexual, and she was right. When they got to the Terrasse, he told her all about his wife, a successful model in Paris.

"I met her when I was doing fashion photography ten years ago, then I got fascinated by this, photojournalism. She thinks I'm crazy. She meets me in Hong Kong once a month, and it keeps me sane. I don't think I could stay here without that. How long are you planning to stay here for?" he asked, with casual interest.

"Six months," she said bravely, sounding very young, and he smiled.

"You have a boyfriend here? In the army?" She shook her head, but some women did. He knew a lot of civilian nurses who had come over because their boyfriends had been sent to

Saigon. But sooner or later they all regretted it. The place broke your heart, the boyfriends were wounded or killed, or shipped back to the States and the girls stayed and tore their hearts out caring for maimed children. Some felt they couldn't leave, some did, but no one was ever the same. "Once you've been here," he said knowingly, "you won't forget it." She nodded, willing to take the chance, as she looked around her in amazement. They had sat down at a table on the terrace of the Continental Palace Hotel, and there were limbless beggars everywhere, crawling like insects between the tables. At first she didn't understand what was happening, she thought they were looking for something, and then suddenly one of them was looking up at her, half his face blown away, one eye gone, and both arms, and he looked up at her and moaned as she almost fainted. Jean-Pierre brushed him away and Paxton looked mortified, as shoeshine boys, and prostitutes and vendors of drugs and assorted wares accosted them, and everywhere the smell of flowers and fuel, the voices, the horns, the shouts, the cars, the bicycles, the people. It was like a circus.

"I'm sorry," she apologized for her weakness when confronted by the faceless beggar.

"You're going to have to get used to that. There's a lot of it here. In Saigon, some of the time you can pretend nothing is happening, and then one day a bomb goes off, a bar blows up, one of your friends is hurt, or you see children bleeding in the street, crying for their mother, lying in front of you, dead from a VC bomb. You can't always hide from it. And in the North, it's worse. Much worse. There you really see the war." He looked at her carefully over their drinks, curious about her, she was just young enough to be his daughter. "Are you sure you want to be here?"

"Yes," she said quietly, sure of herself now that she was here, even if she still wanted to cry when she saw the beggars and the limbless children. But she had only been there for a few hours. Fourteen exactly.

"Why?" he asked pointedly.

She decided to be honest with him, as she had been with the boy on the plane. "Someone I loved died here. I wanted to see it. I wanted to understand why he died. To come here and speak the truth about the war through my paper."

He smiled sadly at her. "You are very young and idealistic. No one will care, and when you cry in the darkness, no one will hear you. You want to send a message from here . . . but to whom? For your friend it is too late. And for the others? Some will come here, if they have to, some will live, some will die. Nothing you can do will change that." He made it all sound so hopeless, but Paxton didn't believe him.

"Then why are you here, Jean-Pierre?" She looked directly into his eyes and he wondered if she would sleep with him. He knew Nigel wanted her. Ralph had France and her boy . . . and of course he had his wife in Paris. But she was a long way from there, and this girl was so fresh, so pure, so full of her ideals, so clean and yet at the same time so strong, so sure. He smiled to himself then and Paxton asked why and he laughed as he answered.

"I think you remind me of . . . Joan of Arc, I think you call her. We call her Jeanne d'Arc, she believed in all the same things you do. The truth, the power of the sword in the name of God, and freedom."

"That sounds pretty reasonable." Paxton smiled. "But you didn't answer my question." She was a journalist, after all, and she was smelling the place out, and the people in it.

"About why I am here? I don't know." He shrugged his shoulders, looking, and sounding, very Gallic. "I wanted to see it, so I came for *Le Figaro*. And then I stayed, because it intrigues me. I wanted to 'see it through' . . . and I like it here. It is a sinful place," he said, smiling at her, "if you want it to be.

I like my friends. And perhaps . . ." He shrugged. "Perhaps like all men, I like the danger. Paxton, don't let men lie to you. We all love to play with guns, to pretend we have an enemy, to take a hill away from a friend, or a house, or a mountain . . . or a country. We love it . . . it makes sense to us . . . until it kills us." There was truth to what he said, and instinctively she knew it.

"Is it worth dying for?"

"I don't know." He shrugged, smiling sadly at her. "Ask the men who died . . . what will they tell you?"

"I think they'd say it wasn't worth it," she said philosophically, but he disagreed.

"That's because you are a woman. Maybe it was worth it to them." He loved the argument, the exchange, the philosophy, and she liked him. "But to a woman it is never worth it. The men who die are their sons, their lovers, their husbands. A woman can only lose in war, never gain, and for her it holds no excitement. The faces of the women I photograph are all filled with pain, as they hold their dead babies, dead men, dead children. They do not care if they die themselves. I think they are much braver than men. But they cannot bear losing their loved ones." His voice grew gentle then. "And you? The man you lost? Was he a lover or a friend?" He was curious about her.

"Both," she said, feeling calmer than she had in a long time. "We were going to be married. We had been together for . . . for four years . . . and I should have married him." She looked away, still guilty over it. "I should have . . . but I didn't." Her voice was very soft at the end and he touched her hand.

"If you didn't, it is because you were not meant to. My first wife died in an accident. In a plane I was supposed to be on with her. I missed the plane. She went anyway. She was killed in Spain. And I felt guilty forever. She wanted children, I never did, and afterwards I thought if I'd let her have a baby, then I'd still have a part of her. But you know," he shrugged, "it just wasn't meant to be that way."

"Do you have children now?" Paxton asked softly.

He shook his head with a smile. "We've only been married for two years, and my wife is twenty-eight. She wants to finish her career as a model before we have any babies." And if something happened, Paxton asked herself, would they regret it? Was Gabby right with her simple, married life, and her pretty babies? Was she crazy to be here? Was Jean-Pierre right, that her marriage to Peter just wasn't meant to be, or would she feel guilty forever?

"How old are you, Paxton?" he asked, increasingly attracted to her with each sip of Pernod. Eventually he switched to Scotch, and eventually Paxton switched to water.

"Twenty-two," she answered him, and he smiled.

"I am exactly twice your age." But he didn't seem to mind it. "I think I can say with absolute certainty that you are the youngest journalist here, in Saigon. And surely," he toasted her, "the most beautiful."

"You haven't seen me in the morning," she said by way of conversation, and a voice behind her took her by surprise.

"No, but I have." She wheeled around in her chair, and it was Nigel. "I'd say you look very nice in the morning. Why, is this a serious question?"

"Not exactly." Paxton smiled, relieved that he had joined them. Jean-Pierre had had a little too much to drink by then, and she had a feeling he was going to start getting amorous with the next Scotch. Nigel's arrival made it all a great deal simpler. "I thought you went to Xuan Loc." She smiled at him.

"I decided to go tomorrow." In truth, he had come across an appealing whore, and delayed the trip till the morning. "Have you two eaten yet? I hope not, I'm starved, and I don't want to eat alone."

"No, we haven't eaten," Jean-Pierre volunteered, but it was

nine o'clock, and Paxton was still feeling jet-lagged. "Where do you want to eat?"

"I don't know. What about something quick somewhere, and then going to the Pink Nightclub to go dancing?" Nigel had his eye on Paxton, too, and the whore had only offered him temporary comfort. But Paxton was looking at her watch. She had to get up at four o'clock the next morning.

"I don't think I should. I'm going to have to take a raincheck. Ralph Johnson is picking me up at five tomorrow morning."

"What's he up to?" Nigel looked annoyed, and Jean-Pierre was rapidly getting too drunk to really care. And he only had another week before he met his wife in Hong Kong. And there was still lots of time to seduce Paxton.

"We're going to Nha Trang with a film crew," Paxton explained.

"It's hot up there," Nigel said with a frown, and then remembered how green she was, "and I don't just mean the weather. Lots of Victor Charlie around. Watch your pretty little ass. Because if I know Johnson, he won't watch it for you. He gets the story if it kills him. He's been wounded twice, and I think he's out here for a Pulitzer, although he won't admit it." Paxton smiled at the obvious rivalry between them.

"I'll be careful."

"Coming back tomorrow night?" Nigel looked intrigued by her, and she was a damn pretty girl. But she had no interest in him, or any of them. That wasn't why she'd come to Saigon. She had come to learn what she could and write good stories for her paper. But there were plenty of men here if that was what she wanted.

"I don't know when we're coming back," she answered Nigel's question. "Ralph didn't say. Wouldn't he have said something if we weren't coming back?"

Nigel laughed. "Not necessarily." They all stood up, and the flurry of movement drew the beggars toward them. Nigel and Jean-Pierre waved them all away, and one child really tore at Paxton's heart, a little girl with no legs being pulled along on a cart by her slightly older brother. Paxton looked away, unable to stand it any longer. You couldn't change things for them, couldn't make the war go away, couldn't bring their limbs back.

"You should do a story on the Quakers," Jean-Pierre suggested when they left. "The American Friends Service Committee has a fabulous center. They fit all these kids with prosthetics. I got some fantastic photographs there. It's really incredible what they've been doing."

"I'll check it out. Thanks." She smiled at them both, thanked him for the drink, and they dropped her off at the hotel before going on to another bar to drink longer and harder. They had decided to skip dinner for a while and go on drinking, since she wouldn't join them. And when she got back to the hotel, she saw several nicely dressed couples going upstairs to the penthouse restaurant for dinner. But she was too tired to even think of food. She walked into her room, lay on the bed, and fell asleep as soon as she set the alarm, and before she even took her clothes off.

And it seemed only moments later when she heard the alarm go off. It was a strange buzzing sound, and she was dreaming that there were insects coming after her, and then bees, and she was trying to escape by pedicab and the driver didn't understand where she was going. And the droning noise went on, and then finally she opened an eye and looked around the hotel room. It was still dark, and she took a shower and washed her hair and climbed into the jumpsuit she had brought for occasions like this one. It was a dark khaki green, and she put on the boots she had, in case Ralph hadn't had the time to get her the ones he had promised.

She was downstairs at exactly five a.m. and the lobby was deserted, but the streets were already coming to life, with vendors and bicycles and cars, and people hurrying home or to work or to somewhere, and she could see the women in their pointed *non la* hats and graceful *ao dai*s. She walked outside and smelled the air, and you could still smell the pungent aroma of fruit and flowers, and still the smell of fuel and the cloud of smoke that always seemed to hang over the city, and then just behind her she heard steps, and turned and saw Ralph coming up the steps of the hotel in fatigues and a bush hat and combat boots exactly like the ones he carried, and he had a heavy vest on, and he was carrying another one, and when she joined him, he handed it and the promised boots to her.

"You got the boots! Thank you." She was amazed.

"No problem." And they weren't. He had bought them on the black market where you could buy absolutely anything stolen from the PX, from tampons to nylons to army issue. "I brought you the flak jacket too. It's not a bad idea, if you can stand to wear it." And he had a spare helmet he gave her, too, and with that, he lifted her into the truck they were taking all the way up Highway One to where they were going. They had an army driver with them, and Ralph had a crew of four, two cameramen, a sound man, and an assistant. He introduced her to everyone, and they all looked like GIs. Everyone had on fatigues and camouflage and boots and helmets, and the sound man laughed nervously as he looked around, and the assistant unscrewed a huge thermos of steaming coffee.

"Shit, if the VC grab us on the way, they're going to think they caught themselves a truck full of regular army." He looked at Paxton, who was similarly outfitted too. "Got any high heels in your purse?"

"I'm too tall. I never wear them."

"I meant for me." Everyone laughed, and they watched the sun come up as they headed out of Saigon. It was a beautiful summer morning. It was late June, and suddenly Paxton realized why people talked about the beauty of the country. As they left the city, everything was lush and green, and there was a delicacy and simplicity to everything that reminded her of antique silkscreens. And then here and there, you'd see craters, from bombs, or children standing by the roadside on crutches.

The group fell silent as they drove, and Paxton was awestruck by the beauty of it, the red earth and the rich green. She just kept watching as they drove north, and finally Ralph Johnson leaned back over his seat to offer her some doughnuts.

"Pretty, isn't it?"

"I'm finally beginning to understand what I've heard. Saigon is very different." It had been pretty once, when the French were there, but it was dirty and loud and corrupt, and full of prostitutes and urchins. This had a natural beauty which Paxton had never seen before and touched her deeply. And yet even here, the country was battle-scarred, even far, far out in the country.

"I was over here when they burned Ben Suc a year and a half ago . . . that was a beautiful place. It was a crime to burn it down."

"Why did they do it?"

"To flush out the Viet Cong, cut off their food supply, their hiding places. Most of the time, they can't tell the good guys from the bad guys. So they burned it all down, and turned the whole thing into a parking lot. They claim they relocated everyone, but you can't replace something like that. It was lovely and old, and they moved everyone into Quonset huts." It was how he had met France, but he didn't say anything about that. He didn't know Paxton that well yet. "How'd it go yesterday?" he asked.

"Okay. I kind of poked around Saigon, and kept getting lost." She smiled. And then she decided to let her hair down. "The Five O'Clock Follies sure are bullshit, aren't they? What's that all about?"

191

"I think they call it PR. Another word for it is propaganda, for our side."

"What's the point?" She looked annoyed. She had come here for the truth, not to be lied to. As they talked, she took her helmet off and tied her ponytail in a bun. It was just too hot even to have hair, let alone have it hang down her back from under her helmet.

But Ralph only laughed. "It gives us something to write about when we run dry, which doesn't happen too often." And then he smiled. "My buddies at the AP office were going crazy yesterday, apparently some guy's nephew was due here and everyone has been instructed to keep him out of trouble."

"What's he doing here?" Paxton looked amused too.

"I don't know. Visiting, I guess. Mustn't be too smart. Viet Nam is a good place to stay out of."

She looked him in the eye with a steady glance as the others chatted over their doughnuts. "Does that mean you think I'm dumb too?"

"Maybe." He was honest with her. He always would be. "But I think maybe you're different. I'll tell you what I think when we're through today, but I think you're one of those crazy people who have to be journalists no matter what, who have to have the truth if it kills them."

"Thank you" was all she said, and she put her helmet back on her head and finished her coffee.

They stopped briefly in Ham Tan, and then they pressed on to Phan Rang and Cam Ranh, and then they could hear gunfire in the distance. It was like the roll of thunder coming down from the mountains. The driver of the truck was in constant contact by radio with his base at Nha Trang, and he warned them before they got there, that they would be moving inland. They were going to a firebase that was under heavy attack, and they would be coming in from the rear. They thought they'd be pretty safe because the fire base was well protected and well armed, but they'd been under heavy fire all week, and this was exactly the story that Ralph wanted. It had taken him all week to get permission to be there.

"Their RTO's been telling me things are pretty hot there," the driver explained, and by now Paxton knew that "hot" always meant VC and never weather. The weather itself was unspeakable, and she wondered at times how she would breathe when they got there. As they approached the base, they were told to get down low in their seats, keep their flak jackets on, and wear their helmets. It was seven a.m., and they were stopped two miles before they got to the remote artillery base where they were going.

"I've got journalists here," the driver explained when he was stopped by heavily armed rear sentries. They were carrying standard M-16's, which Paxton already knew from Ralph were inferior to the Soviet AK-47's carried by the Viet Cong, because our weapons jammed and theirs didn't.

The sentries looked inside, and Paxton recognized an M-60 machine gun and the sound of a 150mm howitzer in the distance. She had tried to read up on everything, but it was different seeing it all now in action, and it was more than a little scary. She could feel her heart beating, especially when they looked at her, and continued to question the driver.

"What about the Delta Delta?"

The driver smiled. "Same thing. She's a journalist too. Right?" He turned and smiled openly at Paxton.

"Yes, sir. I'm with the *Morning Sun* in San Francisco." She fumbled for her papers, and they waved them on without any further questions while the driver and Ralph exchanged a smile, and she wondered what had just passed between them. "What was that all about? The Delta Delta stuff I mean."

"You're going to hear a lot of it while you're here." Ralph grinned.

193

"They call you that at first too?" she asked innocently, and he laughed out loud at that one.

"Not likely, sweetheart. I'd better tell you what it means. Delta Delta are the radio call signs for D-D. Doughnut Dollie." Everyone in the truck laughed and Paxton wanted to stamp her boots.

"Shit! I came all the way out here, and I didn't do it to pass out goddamn doughnuts!"

"You tell 'em, lady!" The driver cheered and even Paxton laughed. It was infuriating to be treated like some beauty queen who had come over to see if anyone would whistle.

"Delta Delta, my ass!" Everyone knew "Doughnut Dollies" were nice women who did a lot for morale, but it was still no compliment to Paxton.

"You'll get used to it," Ralph laughed, and she threatened to hit him. But a few minutes later they were told to get down as artillery fire began to whiz over their heads. They all climbed gingerly out of the truck when told, and the cameramen and the sound man began assembling their equipment. Ralph was telling them what he wanted from them, and after conferring with some of the troops, the driver was explaining to Ralph which entries into the camp were safest. But from the sound of it, none of it was perfectly clear, and a young black private who came running down to them told them what they already knew, that "they were hot hot hot," and as he said it, he stared longingly at Paxton.

"Hey, there, where you come from?" he whispered as they got down low near the truck, and Ralph confirmed to her that what she heard were howitzers in the distance. The South Vietnamese Army, the ARVN, were supporting the American troop movements. But the Americans liked to rely on their own.

In their opinion, their own guys were always better, and they were fighting the NVA, the regular North Vietnamese Army, unlike the Viet Cong, who were really just farmers although braves ones.

"I'm from Savannah," she said, trying to appear calm as she talked to the young black guy.

"Yeah? Me too." He gave her an address that didn't mean much, and she smiled, suddenly thinking of Queenie.

"How long have you been here?" she asked with interest.

"In Nam?" He grinned. "Hell, baby, I'm two weeks short. I'm starin' my DEROS right in the eye. If I can just keep my ass out of trouble for the next two weeks, I'm takin' that freedom bird home to Georgia." His DEROS was his date eligible for return from overseas. And two weeks short meant that he had been there for 380 days, 375 days longer than Peter had lived when he got there. "What's yo' name?" She was beautiful, and all he wanted to do was talk to her and touch her. He had a girlfriend at home, but that didn't stop him from wanting to talk to Paxton.

"Paxton."

"Yeah?" He looked amused, and Ralph glanced at them over his shoulder.

"Keep down," he told her firmly.

They were all taken into the firebase after that, and it was an incredible view into a picturesque-looking little valley, all green and very beautiful and smoking with the constant exchange of fire. There were planes flying low overhead, and other planes were dropping bombs in the distance. The men called them "birds dropping eggs." The commander of the firebase came to meet Ralph and his crew, and Ralph was careful to introduce him to Paxton.

"San Francisco, eh?" he asked, chewing on a cigar. "Great town. My wife and I love it." Everyone loved someplace. San Francisco, Savannah, North, South, New Jersey, it didn't matter where you were from. You were alive and you were new, and they were so desperate to go home and just stay alive, just touching someone from anywhere meant everything to them. "We've had a lot of heat around here," he explained. "The NVA are determined to get through, and we're just not going to let them. We held this area pretty solidly last year, and then we lost it. And now that we have it back, we're not letting it go again." But Paxton couldn't help wondering how many men it had cost them. Taking a hill, a valley, a village, it all meant such loss of life. So many boys dead, and so many wounded. He explained again that they were doing pretty well. They had lost only five boys so far, and had a few dozen wounded. Was that okay, then, she asked herself, *"only* five boys" was fine . . . but which five? How did one choose? How did God? And why had he chosen Peter? "Would you like to come up a little closer? We're taking a lot of shells, just stay in the areas my boys tell you."

Ralph was pleased. He wanted a better view for the camera of the forward movements. And they stayed there all afternoon only falling back finally at three in order to eat some C rations before they went back to the heat of the action. And so far, no one had been hurt. It had been a pretty tame day all in all. They were just holding their position relentlessly, and now and then they claimed that they could see Charlie. But the truth was, you couldn't. You couldn't see anything, except smoke and gunfire, and the bushes.

"Well, kid, how's it feel? You're in it now." Ralph sat next to her for a few minutes to smoke a cigarette and finish a cup of coffee.

"How did it feel when the *Times* sent you to Korea?"

"It scared the shit out of me," he said with a grin.

"That's about right." She smiled nervously at him. Her stomach had been in a knot since early that morning.

"Did you eat?" She shook her head. "You should. It'll help. You've gotta keep eating and sleeping no matter what they're doing out there, or you may get careless and do something stupid. Keep your judgment sharp. That's the best piece of combat advice I can give you."

She was grateful for him. He was a nice guy, and a terrific reporter. She could see why the others were jealous of him. He was good, very good, and constantly on the alert for anything that might happen. "Thanks for the boots," she said to him, and he patted her on the shoulder.

"Keep your helmet on and your head down, and you'll be fine." And with that he was off again, climbing rapidly through some trees behind some soldiers, while she wondered if she admired him or thought he was crazy. And just as she thought that, there was a huge explosion. The cameramen ran down to where he'd been, and the sound man right behind them, and without thinking of anything but him, she found herself running too, and when she got there, there were men lying all over the place and he was holding one of them, with the boy's chest hanging wide open.

"We need medics here," he said calmly but firmly, and someone ran to get one, and suddenly there was a radio operator in their midst calling for a "Dustoff." "I've got six men down," he said into the phone, and as he said it Paxton felt one of them touch her. His arm was blown off, and there was blood everywhere, and he had the face of a child as he looked up at her, and all he said was "I'm thirsty."

She had a canteen at her side, but she wasn't sure if she should give him anything. What if he wasn't supposed to drink? If giving him something would kill him . . . Two medics arrived and a priest in a helmet who was attached to the unit and they started going around to the boys who'd been wounded. But the boy in Ralph's arms had already died, and he was helping them with another.

"I'm thirsty." No one had come to her boy yet, and he looked at her with anguish. "What's your name?"

"Paxxie." She stroked his face and laid his head down gently in her lap as blood poured all over her legs and she tried to pretend she didn't feel it. "My name's Paxxie," she said softly, stroking his hair back gently from his face, and fighting back an urge to bend down and kiss his cheeks like a baby, as she cried for him. She tried to smile through her tears but he didn't see it. "What's your name?" she asked, to keep him talking.

"Joe." He was sounding vague from the loss of blood and shock, and he started to close his eyes as she held him.

"Come on, Joe, wake up . . . you can't go to sleep now . . . that's right . . . open your eyes." She smiled at him, and all around them everything was frantic. They were trying to carry the wounded boys into a clearing. The priest was helping them, and Ralph and the cameraman, too, and one of the medics was pounding on someone's chest, and in a minute she could hear the helicopter whirring overhead but they were shooting at it from the brush and it had to move away again as the medic who'd been pounding the boy's chest shouted, "Shit!" He had lost him.

"Where are you from, Joe?"

"Miami." It was only a whisper.

"Miami. That's great." There were tears in her eyes and a lump in her throat and she felt sick and her legs were soaked with his blood as she held him, and the radio operator sitting right next to her in the grass was telling the helicopter to take off again. It was just too hot there.

"The hell I will . . ." the voice came back to them. "How many you got down there?" The voice was steady and strong and he wasn't going anywhere without their wounded.

"I've still got four who need you pretty bad." And just as he said it, there was another huge explosion.

"Shit!" someone said, and the medics were off again, and someone came back to talk to the radio operator and give him a report on the wounded.

"Make that nine. I've got five more for you, Niner Zulu. Can you get me another bird down here quick? We've got some guys who aren't gonna wait too long." And as she listened, Paxton closed her eyes, and knew that the boy on her lap was one of them. She tried to catch the operator's eye, but he was too involved on the phone, and Ralph was long gone with his cameramen somewhere else.

"You okay?" a passing voice asked, and she heard herself respond, much to her amazement.

"We're fine. Right, Joe? Right . . ." He was drifting off to sleep, and she touched his cheek to wake him, trying not to look at the arm that wasn't there and the bloody stump that was bleeding onto the ground beside her. She thought of trying to fashion a tourniquet, but she was afraid of making things worse, and a moment later a medic was with him.

"You're doing fine, son, just fine." And then he smiled up at Paxton. "You're doing okay too." And then she realized, the man reassuring her was the boy from Savannah, and she felt as though they were old friends now.

"This is Joe." She kept her voice light but glanced worriedly at the arm as the helicopter hovered, and she could still hear the pilot's voice on the radio near her.

"This is Niner Zulu. We're going in. But we're coming in quick. We're not coming down. Just toss 'em in as fast as you can and we'll make a quick exit."

"Shit," she heard someone say. It was the word of the afternoon, but it seemed appropriate so far, from what she'd seen around her. "How the fuck does he think we're going to 'toss 'em in'?" the RTO asked anyone who would listen.

"Don't worry about it," one of the men said unhappily. "If he waits much longer, we won't have to." Of the second five, two had already died. They only had seven wounded left to transport, and four had died in all. It had been a stinking day, after a good beginning.

But the chopper came down and hovered long enough for the

medics and the troops to put four men on board, and then a second helicopter came for the others. They were Huey medevacs and they looked beautiful to Paxton as they came in. She watched as two of the men loaded Joe, and she found herself praying out loud that he would make it. And as she turned around, she suddenly saw two of the others on the ground, their eyes open and unseeing, and the ARVN boys beside them. And she stumbled away, and was sick in the bushes: Ralph found her there a little while later, looking ravaged and pale, with her fatigues covered with blood, and even her hair smeared with blood where she had touched it.

"Don't feel bad, kid. I got sick every day for six months when I was in Korea." He sighed and sat down for a minute beside her. Things had calmed down a little bit, but the touch of death was everywhere, but at least the shelling didn't seem as intense now. He was thinking of going back to Saigon that night, instead of staying. "We got a lot of good stuff today," he said, and Paxton looked at him with horror.

"Is that what you call this, 'good stuff'?" She was suddenly reminded of Jean-Pierre, and his perfect shot of the "dead little girls holding hands." It broke your heart to see it.

Ralph said with open irritation, "I didn't start this war. I came to cover it. And maybe if I make people sick enough, they'll make it stop. But if you came to cover cocktail parties at the officers' club, you're in the wrong pew, because this war isn't pretty. And if what you want is laughs, maybe you should wait till Bob Hope turns up for Christmas."

"Oh, go fuck yourself." She was angry and tired and depressed and sick from what she had seen. "I'm here for the same reason you are."

"Are you? Good. Because this war needs more people like you and me. People who are willing to tell the truth about what they see, and maybe even die for it. People who aren't afraid of the truth. Is that why you're here?" She glared at him. He was pressing her, but he liked the way she responded. She was tough and strong and she cared, and had guts. There were a lot of things he liked about her. She was "number one," as the men called the things they approved of.

"Yeah. That's why I'm here." She glared at him. "I'm here to tell the truth about this fucking ugly war. Just like you, mister."

"Is that the only reason?" he asked pointedly, as they both calmed down a little bit, and she decided to tell him what she'd told Jean-Pierre about Peter.

"My fiancé died here almost two months ago."

He thought about it for a long time and then he looked at her and said something that shocked her. "Forget him."

"How can you say a thing like that?" She was horrified, and hurt on behalf of Peter.

"Because whatever the reason is that brought you here, you have to forget it now, if you're going to do a decent job here. He's gone. You can't help him. But you can help other people like him, you can help a whole country by reporting honestly and objectively. If all you want to do is avenge him, or chase after his memory, you won't do anyone any good, not him, not yourself, not the people you've come to write for." He was right, and she knew it, but it still hurt to hear it. In one day, he expected her to grow up and give up the memory of the boy she'd loved all through college. But he was right. As a writer, she had to tell the world what she saw, not tell them the story of Peter. It was a terrible thing he'd said to her, but they both knew there was a lot of truth to it.

They moved on to Hai Ninh that afternoon, halfway back to Saigon, and they came across some fighting there, and some developments that interested Ralph. And by the time they were ready to go, the commanding officer there told them it was too dangerous to go back that night. They would have to wait until morning. They slept in trenches with the men, and Paxton lay there, looking up at the stars and thinking of Peter. Had it been like this here for him? Had he been scared? Did he think it was beautiful? Had he thought of her? And in the end, did it even matter? Maybe Ralph was right. Maybe none of it mattered, except the truth, and the people who knew it.

"You okay?" He moved closer to her and offered her a cigarette, but she declined. She was so tired, and sick from what they'd seen, that she hadn't even eaten dinner. And the C rations they'd been given weren't too tempting. The rice and *pho,* a white noodle soup, the ARVN ate looked a lot better.

"I'm fine."

"You don't look it."

She smiled. "You don't look so great either." But she had to admit he looked better than she did.

"I'm sorry if I was hard on you today. But this is a tough place. And you can't compromise your ideals, or ever forget why you came here. Once it gets personal, it's all over. And even if your trip started out that way, it's not too late to change your sights and keep a nice clean, objective goal in mind. Just remember who you're writing for, and what you want to say to them. It'll keep you human. But you can't make this a personal vendetta. Some of the grunts do that, their buddies die, and they go half crazy, they run out into the bushes to go after Victor Charlie, and they live about fourteen seconds until they step on a mine and it blows their heads off, and they go to the big PX in the sky, as they put it. Whatever you do here, you can't ever stop thinking. The guys who survive here don't forget that for a minute." It was good advice, and she knew it.

"I keep thinking about that boy today . . . Joe . . . from Miami . . . I don't even know his last name . . . I keep wondering if he's still alive."

"He probably is," Ralph reassured her. "He was lucky. In Nha Trang, we were right near the 254th MDHA unit. They probably had him on an operating table in fifteen minutes after he got picked up. You probably made all the difference." He patted her arm, and tried to reassure her even if it wasn't true. It didn't matter. She had done her best, and maybe the kid had lived because of her. There were so many of them, and he had seen so many die and get wounded. You got jaded after a while, and tired and bitter. All those kids being turned into raw beef. It made you sick. It made you wonder why a girl like her wanted to be there. They all had to be a little crazy. And if they weren't when they started, they were when they left. He smiled at her then. "You know, I can never get your name straight. I know the last name is Andrews. But the first name is something like Pattie, or Patton, isn't it?"

"Paxton." She grinned. "Just make sure you don't call me Delta Delta."

"I might have to if I can't remember Paxton." And then he thought about it for a while, and suddenly he started to laugh as they lay there in the trench side by side and she found herself staring at him in irritation.

"What *is* it? My name?"

"No, I like your name . . . but I just had the funniest goddamn thought. You're from the *Morning Sun* in San Francisco, right?" She nodded. "Do you have an uncle there?"

"Not really." She blushed, but he couldn't see it. "A mentor, I guess you'd call it. My almost father-in-law is . . . pretty high up on the paper." She didn't want to tell him he owned it.

"And the bureau chief here said he was getting frantic telexes from all the powers that be at the *Sun* that someone's nephew was coming over here for them, and whatever the hell he did, he was to keep him out of trouble, and away from combat." He looked her in the eye with a grin. "Miss Paxton, I think that means you, and no one figured out you were a girl. Shit . . . and what do I do? I take you to the two hottest spots we've got in one day." He started to laugh and so did Paxxie.

"I'm glad no one figured out who I was."

"So am I." He smiled at her as they lay there, listening to the sound of an occasional sniper. "I don't know how you write. But you're a good sport, and you've got guts. The rest ought to come pretty easy."

"Thank you." She smiled at him.

"Anytime. You can come out on missions with me anytime you want. Providing you don't tell your uncle."

She smiled again, and as she lay there, drifting off to sleep eventually, she thought of Ed Wilson. She'd only been in Viet Nam for two days, and it felt as though she hadn't seen him in years . . . him, or Gabby, or San Francisco . . . or Peter.

# CHAPTER 13

∨

Ralph and Paxton drove back to Saigon the next day with their crew, and they were all quiet on the drive back. It was impossible to see death and pain and the loss of men and not feel it.

"It gets to you, doesn't it?" Ralph sat quietly, sitting next to her. He had let the sound man sit in the front with their driver.

"Yeah." She nodded. She was still thinking about the boy from Miami. What would his life be like with one arm? Or worse, what if he hadn't lived through it? And what were they fighting for over there? No one seemed sure anymore. It all seemed crazy.

"You're going to get an education here," Ralph said. "Most of the people who stay for a while are never the same again."

"Why?" She was still looking for the answers.

"I don't know . . . they see too much . . . they care too much while they're here . . . they get bitter and angry and disillusioned. They go back to the States and people hate them, and treat them like murderers. No one understands. Back in the States, people are listening to the radio, and hanging out in bars and buying cars and chasing women. They don't give a shit what's happening here. They never did. And they don't want to hear it. Viet Nam? Where's that? Who cares? It's just a bunch of gooks fighting with each other . . . fighting with each other, and killing us. But everyone forgets that. These boys over here are getting their asses shot off for nothing."

"Do you really believe that?" It hurt her hearing it, especially when she thought of Peter. It was easier to believe that he was a hero for dying here. But the truth was that, even to her, he wasn't.

"I do. And the sad thing is, so does everyone else. Nobody really cares what's happening here. I don't think they even understand it. I'm not sure I do. We're trying to save the South from the North, like we did in Korea. But this isn't the same thing. The people in the South are fighting us too. You can't even tell who's VC and who isn't. Shit, most of the time I think they all are. Christ, look at the kids. Most of them would blow your face off with a grenade just as soon as look at you. And knowing that makes people crazy. Nobody knows who to believe anymore, who to respect, who they're fighting. Half the grunts over here have more respect for Charlie than they do for their own COs, the VC fight harder than anyone. And the ARVN, the southern army, is a joke. See what I mean? It's all crazy. And if you stay long enough, you get crazy too. Keep that in mind when you start to think about staying. The day you stop wanting to catch the next plane home about ten times a day, that's the beginning of big trouble." He was teasing her a little bit, but he was sharing some important truths, too, and she knew it. There was something strangely seductive about Viet Nam, something that made you want to stay, something about the air and the smells and the sounds and the people, the odd contrast of Saigon and the incredible beauty of the countryside, the innocence of the faces, and the agonies of the people. You wanted to believe that they were pure, that it was all hurting them and you could help them. But that was the question now. Could we help them and save ourselves? Or was it all hopeless?

As they drove into Saigon at noon, Paxton had none of the answers.

Ralph dropped her off at the hotel, and went on to the AP office in the Eden Building. And as she walked across the lobby, she couldn't believe how filthy she was. Her fatigues were still covered with dried blood, and dirt and sweat, and she looked awful. She ran into Nigel on the way, and he looked at her with a raised eyebrow.

"My, my, you look like you've had a busy day, or did you cut yourself shaving?" His glibness irritated her, and she snapped at him as she pulled off her helmet.

"We were in Nha Trang. And there were a lot of wounded." They seemed a lot to her, and she felt tears sting her eyes as she said it.

"Should I be surprised? I believe that's why we're all here." He was a supercilious jackass, and his whole attitude annoyed her. "What are you doing for dinner tonight?"

"I don't know. I want to turn in my story." Because of her arrangement with the *Sun,* she had no real deadlines, she was just going to send material in when she had it. But she wanted to get something off to them soon, to show them that she had come here to work, and she was serious about what she was doing.

"Maybe we'll catch you later. Did Ralph go home or to the office?"

"I'm pretty sure he went to the office," she said, sounding exhausted.

"You'd better get some sleep. You look knackered."

"I am . . . see you later. . . ." And she had every intention of writing about what she'd seen, but as soon as she had a bath at her hotel, and lay down "just for a minute," she fell asleep and when she woke up, it was dark and she was starving.

She went downstairs to the dining room, and didn't see any-one she knew. And when she tried to eat, she found she couldn't. Even the pineapple froth she had developed a taste for when she first arrived tasted awful. All she could think of was what she'd seen at Nha Trang. And after a cup of bouillon, and some *chao tom,* little skewers of shrimp paste, she went back upstairs and sat down to write her story. She wrote until two a.m., and she cried when she tried to describe the boy from Miami, and the kid from Savannah. She realized that she didn't even know his name. But even that didn't matter. And when she was finished, she sat back in her seat, feeling drained, but relieved. Writing about them was almost like a catharsis.

She tried to describe the beauty of Viet Nam, the contrast of what she'd seen, even in so little time, the horror of those maimed, the sleaziness of the hookers, the noises in the streets, and the incredible beauty driving north, the brilliant green, the rich red earth, and yet the whole country silently ravaged and bleeding, and our boys bleeding with it. Bleeding for it. It was a powerful piece and she was pleased, and she wondered what they would think of it in San Francisco.

She went to bed at three a.m., and she was at the AP office the next day at nine o'clock, where she ran into Ralph, looking fresh and businesslike in a clean white shirt and khakis.

"What are you up to, Delta Delta?" She smiled in spite of herself and he looked happy to see her.

"Never mind that. I want to send off my story."

"Nha Trang?" he asked, and she nodded. "I inquired, by the way. All the boys they picked up the other day made it, except one"—her heart skipped a beat—"the one who didn't was a black kid from Mississippi. So your boy must be doing fine. I thought that might make you happy." She smiled in open relief and his eyes were gentle as he watched her. She was a good kid. She really was number one, top stuff. She had a lot to learn, but she was smart, and he liked her. "It doesn't always work out that way. Maybe you brought him luck. He'll be going home now." That was one way to do it, with one arm. But on the other hand, he wasn't going home in a body bag either. No "big PX in the sky" for him. "What are you doing today?" Ralph asked.

"Looking for trouble," she quipped, and he laughed.

"Watch out. In this town, you'll find it."

"So I've noticed." If nothing else, there was always Nigel Aucliffe, or the slightly married Jean-Pierre, who was meeting his wife in Hong Kong that weekend.

"*Time* magazine is giving a party in their offices tonight, at the Continental Palace. Want to go?"

"Sure." She wasn't sure if it was a date or just a friendly invitation, but she didn't care. She wasn't looking for romance, and every contact she made would be helpful.

"I'll meet you there." He glanced at his watch, and it was obvious he was in a hurry. "Six o'clock?"

"Fine." She spent the rest of the afternoon walking around Saigon again. And as she did, she was deeply affected by the children. They were so vulnerable and so young, and they looked so battered. And yet, if you sat at the cafés, they tried to sell you everything from heroin to cigarettes to stolen soft drinks. She knew she would write a story about them later. It was a strange world, a long way from the world she knew. But as she looked around her, she was glad that she had come here.

She went back to her hotel at five o'clock, and changed into a flowered print silk dress, and a new pair of sandals, and then she walked down the Tu Do to the Continental Palace. It was easy to believe that this had been a lovely city once, when it was French. It still was lovely, in many ways, but just beneath the surface, one sensed a constant tension. Even sitting in the cafés, people were constantly aware that the enemy was everywhere, and a bomb could be hurled into their midst at any moment.

When she got to the hotel, she walked past the action at the terrace bar, and as usual, she caught a glimpse of Nigel. He was entertaining two army nurses, one of them was sitting on his lap, and the other one was running her fingers through his hair and laughing. Paxton didn't say anything and went quietly upstairs to the Time Inc. office.

There was a nice crowd there, and Ralph was already waiting, engaged in animated conversation with the bureau chief, about the upcoming Democratic Convention in Chicago. There had been riots everywhere that year, ever since the murder of Martin Luther King, and the more recent killing of Robert Kennedy. And Ralph was making dire predictions.

"I think it's going to be a mess in Chicago." And as he said it, he noticed Paxton. He greeted her with a warm smile, introduced her to everyone, and eventually guided her around the room with a practiced hand, while treating her like his little sister. She was very touched, and she told him so over a glass of Scotch after she had met everyone he thought was important.

"I really mean it, Ralph. If it weren't for you, I'd still be sitting in my hotel room."

"Maybe you'd be better off." He took a long swig of bourbon. "I felt pretty guilty yesterday when we got back. Maybe Nha Trang was a little heavy for a first taste of what's going on here."

"I don't think so," she said quietly, looking into his eyes, "that's what I'm here for."

And then he grinned. "I was right, by the way. I did a little careful 'investigating' yesterday, when we got back. You're the one everyone is supposed to be watching out for and taking to parties at the embassy and the Golden Ghetto." It was once a fancy apartment building on Gia Long Street.

"I hope no one figures that out." She grinned.

"They won't." He smiled in answer. "No one has time to baby-sit here. Speaking of which," he looked at her cautiously, "are you interested in another mission? I'm going to Cu Chi, to do a story on the tunnels. I thought you might like it."

"I'd love it. Five o'clock again?"

He laughed. She looked so serious and so anxious. "I'll pick you up at eight. That should be plenty of time. And wear your combat gear again."

Paxton raised an eyebrow. "No tea parties at the officers' club? My friends in San Francisco will be very disappointed."

He winked at her. "Don't worry about it, Delta Delta, just send them some doughnuts." She pretended to swing at him, and he ducked and left a few minutes later.

She talked to a number of other reporters after that, and eventually she went back downstairs and avoided Nigel on the terrace. He was extremely drunk by then, and was looking very amorous with one of the nurses. Paxton went back quietly to her hotel, had dinner in her room, and was asleep by ten o'clock. She was waiting for Ralph Johnson in the lobby at eight o'clock sharp the next morning.

He had a different crew with him this time, a single photographer, and a different driver. And they had an army-issue jeep, and a young marine as their driver. He was a big friendly kid, with a redheaded crew cut and blue eyes, and a tattoo of a cowboy on his chest and he said he was from Montana. And Paxton tried not to smile when he said his name was Cowboy. He was nineteen years old and he'd been in Nam since the previous Christmas. He had six more months till he went home, but he said he was pretty happy there. He was temporarily assigned to the Information Agency, and he'd been driving reporters and visiting dignitaries all over the countryside. "And as long as we don't hit no mines, or get shot at by no gooks, I like it fine." He grinned at them, and Paxton decided he was a lucky kid. He could have been up north being shot at with the others.

The drive to Cu Chi took forty-five minutes, and they spent most of it talking about horses and riding, and growing up, and eventually Ralph and Paxton started to talk about the story they wanted. The photographer they had with them was French. His name was Yves and he was a friend of Jean-Pierre.

He kept to himself mostly, and spoke fairly limited English, which made him seem shy, but he really wasn't. Ralph had worked with him before, and liked him very much, and he was pleased to have him along for the day's mission. He was good and quiet and meticulous about his work, not unlike Paxton.

"Cu Chi Base is an interesting place," Ralph explained to Paxxie on the way. "It's the headquarters of the 25th 'Tropic Lightning' Infantry Division from Hawaii. They built the base more than two years ago, over the tunnels the VC had built there, and they figured they had them all sealed up. But they were wrong. The VC seem to keep right on operating right under their feet and they've had nothing but headaches with Cu Chi since they got there. It's a huge base, and it's right across the Saigon River from the Iron Triangle, where we've had some of the worst fighting all along."

"What are we doing there today?" She was grateful for every bit of information.

"They've uncovered a whole new network of tunnels out there. I thought it might make a good story. The guys who deal with that shit are called tunnel rats, and they're an amazing group. Tough as nails, with nerves of steel. You couldn't get me into one of those tunnels for anything in this world. The VCs have a whole subterranean world down there. They tried to clear most of it out when they cleared the Iron Triangle last year. But that still didn't do it.

"They even found a whole hospital complex down there last year in Thank Dien Forest, just north of the Iron Triangle. The VC are amazing little people." There was a lot more to what the GIs referred to as the "gooks" and "dinks" than met the eye, and Ralph knew it. They were a sharp, wily, hardy, incredibly courageous people who would fight to the death against the ARVN, the army of the South, and the Americans who helped them.

"Do you think I could go down into the tunnels?" Paxton

asked with fascination, and Ralph shook his head with a look of horror.

"Don't do anything like that, Pax. It's too dangerous and it makes me claustrophobic thinking about it." He almost shuddered but she disagreed.

"I think it would be fascinating."

"I think you're crazy." They rode the rest of the way in silence. She was impressed by how big Cu Chi Base was when they got there, and how well organized. It was a lot different than their trip to the firebase near Nha Trang two days before, until they were directed to a region well behind the base, still overgrown with vegetation. The heat seemed to rise from the brush, and there were troops everywhere, with bulldozers cutting down trees and bushes.

"Put your flak jacket back on," Ralph instructed her absentmindedly while saying something to Yves, and waving to someone in the distance.

"Why?" The heat was stifling, and no one else had one on. Most of the men were working bare-chested with just their fatigue pants and combat boots. A number of them had even taken off their helmets. "No one else is wearing them."

"Do what I tell you to do," he snapped, "they should be wearing them too. Cu Chi is famous for snipers." She made a face and put the heavy vest back on, and then started to take off her helmet, but another glance from him stopped her. Like the troops, she had started carrying her suntan lotion and bug repellent in her helmet straps. And most of them carried their cigarettes there too, playing cards, and whatever other odds and ends they needed. She noticed that everyone kept their M-16's nearby, and most of the men kept their standard issue .45's tucked into their belts or in holsters. She had been warned when she arrived, not to carry arms, but in the past few days she had learned that many people did carry guns. You could buy almost anything on the black market. But she had no desire whatsoever to have one.

And as Paxton rearranged her gear, a tall thin man walked up to them. He was the man Ralph had been waving to. He had sandy hair and light eyes, and an easygoing smile, but the tension in his eyes, and a constant wary air belied his casual manner.

"Hello, Quinn. Looks like you're keeping your boys busy."

Captain William Quinn, of the 25th Infantry shook hands with Ralph and Yves, and extended a friendly hand to Paxton. "Nice to have you all here." And then he turned back to Ralph. "We found a beauty here this week, after I saw you. Christ, this mother must go clear back to Kansas." He looked apologetically at Paxton, and as he gestured toward an area they had cleared, she noticed his wedding band. He was a good-looking man. He was thirty-two, had gone to West Point, and was career army.

He looked at Paxton then, with a shy smile. "Do you work for the Associated Press too?" His eyes seemed to look deep into hers and for a moment she forgot what he had asked her. He was a very handsome man, and there was an aura of quiet power about him, an air of total control, and yet there was something more too, something faintly wild and maybe even a little crazy.

"I . . . no, I'm from the *Morning Sun* in San Francisco."

"Nice town. I was based in the Presidio for a while before I came here." And that was where he had left his wife, but he didn't say that.

"She's my new protégée," Ralph explained with a smile. "Kind of reminds me of myself when I went to Korea. Although I think I was a lot less ballsy than she is," he said by way of a compliment, and she thanked him.

"Anytime, Delta Delta," he teased as they followed Captain Quinn to the clearing. There were tools and equipment and men everywhere, and if you looked down at the ground, here and there you saw small holes, which barely looked big enough for a child to enter.

"Christ, is that it?" Ralph looked amazed as he got down on the ground and peeked into one. Normally they were totally hidden and you could see no entrance at all, but Quinn and his men had uncovered all the openings they could find, so now you could see the tunnels more clearly. And you could even see the bamboo tubes they used for breathing when they were down there. "I assume they widen after a while."

But Bill Quinn shook his head. "Not always. They're amazing little folks." He said it almost with respect and humor. "It took us six days to blast the little buggers out of here. They're a tenacious lot."

"Yeah." Ralph nodded. "They always have been."

Bill Quinn showed them around, and Paxton asked if she could go in a few feet just to see what she could. Most of the Americans were even too big to fit, with their large bodies and broad shoulders. But she was lithe and supple and she wanted to see what was underground. She borrowed Yves' camera and a light and followed one of the small, wiry tunnel rats, one of Quinn's men, and after a few minutes she was breathless. She was pale and covered with dirt when she emerged, gasping a little, and more than a little frightened. There was still a smell of death down there, and the man who had gone with her explained that they hadn't "pulled them all out yet." It was a horrifying thought to think of the dead VC decaying somewhere down there. But everything around them was like that. Nha Trang had been just as frightening in its own way, more so with the open firing and the desperately wounded. This was subtler and more ominous, even though the lieutenant assured them that all the tunnels were clear now, and the only VC down there were dead ones.

"Do you use dogs?" she asked, still impressed by the experience, and he was impressed with her. She was the first American woman who had been willing to go down there. Even Yves, Ralph's photographer, had been less than enthusiastic. But she was young and smart and interested, and that made a difference. And she was also very pretty, the captain had noted, when she freed her cascade of blond hair from her helmet. Very pretty. And he felt as though he'd been at Cu Chi forever.

"We do use dogs," he explained. "But we lose so damn many of them, we try not to. We'd rather use men, they can fire into the tunnels, the dogs can't. At least our guys have a chance." But admittedly, not a great one. It was a frightening thought, and she felt a chill run up her spine as they moved on, and came to another opening, this one surrounded by bamboo air tubes. "This was a good one here," Quinn went on. "There were seven men and a woman. We figure they've been here all year, maybe longer." Right under their noses. They came out at night, he explained, and did whatever damage they could at the base, sabotage, plastic bombs, hand grenades, sniping. "We've had a hell of a problem."

It was quite an understatement, and for the first time, Paxton started to make notes, as a sergeant approached Quinn and told him there was a report of a sniper up ahead. He glanced at Paxton, and at Quinn again.

"Do you want them to go back to the base?" He seemed irritated to have the press there at all, and the glance he shot at them was neither warm nor friendly. But Bill Quinn seemed unconcerned. He checked his watch, and said something to the RTO, to find out if he had radio contact with the boys who were searching the brush areas they hadn't cleared yet.

"No, they're fine here," Bill Quinn told the sergeant, and then went on talking to the RTO before he explained to Ralph that there was one sniper, possibly two, and they had reason to believe there might be another tunnel up ahead. "You might even get a chance to see how we clear them," he said easily, with a smile at Paxton. She didn't know it yet, but he was famous in Viet Nam. He and his men had found and cleared more tunnels than anyone in the history of the war, and several times, he had gone down himself, been wounded four times, decorated twice, and all his men adored him. "You have to be a little crazy to be a tunnel rat," he always said, and it was something he looked for in his men. Something terribly brave and wild, and yet controlled enough to do what they were told. They had to be willing to die in a space barely big enough to move in. And it was Paxton's willingness to go down for a look that had intrigued him. But his sergeant was much less intrigued with her. He was clearly annoyed when they got the confirmation of the second sniper.

"Shall I take them back now, sir?"

"I don't think so, Sergeant," Quinn said firmly. "I don't think they came all the way out here for lunch. I think this is what they came for." Like Cowboy, their driver, he was from the Northwest, and he had an easygoing, seemingly slow-moving style, but his men knew he could change to the speed of a rattlesnake about to strike in a single instant. "Would you like something to drink?" he asked as he turned to Paxton. She was dying of thirst, and grateful for the icy Coke that miraculously materialized from an ice chest. He found some for Ralph and Yves, too, and a little while later they removed to a tent in a small clearing, which he called his "office." He answered all their questions for them, and stayed in contact with his RTO, and after two more calls, he frowned and said he thought he'd better get back outside. He didn't like the sound of the reports about the snipers.

He looked serious when they moved forward again, and this time he told Paxton and Ralph to fall back. Yves was crouching low in the brush and taking pictures with a long lens of something that had struck his interest. And then, barely more than an instant after they'd moved forward again, there was sudden movement in the brush, and an explosion of artillery fire just ahead, as everyone dove to the ground, including Paxton.

Bill Quinn crept ahead, and the boy on the radio was frantically trying to make contact with someone. "Come in, Lone Ranger, this is Tonto . . . Lone Ranger, do you hear me? What you got there?"

The voice that came back was staccato. And the RTO reported in rapid order to the sergeant. They had two snipers, and six VC, who had appeared seemingly from nowhere. Quinn was right. They had another tunnel.

Ralph looked at her as they crouched close to the ground, and she was suddenly grateful that she had kept on her flak jacket and her helmet. "We picked a nice day to come here," Ralph said ruefully.

"At least it's not dull." She smiled, trying not to appear frightened.

"You've been here too long," he said above the noise. "You're becoming a hardened case." And as he said it, the sergeant reappeared at their side, with an irritated look at Paxton.

"The captain wants you to fall back, please," he said, sounding like an elevator operator in a department store, and his manner instantly annoyed both Ralph and Paxton.

"Any reason why members of the press are being excluded?" Ralph asked brusquely, checking around for Yves, who was still taking pictures with his long lens and seemed satisfied with what he was getting.

"Yeah, I'd say there's a good reason, mister," the young sergeant snapped. "You've got a woman with you, and we'd prefer it if neither of you got shot, if you don't have any objection." His accent was pure New York, and so were his manners. "Sound reasonable to you?"

"No, as a matter of fact." Ralph looked him straight in the eye as Paxton watched. "I don't think sex has anything to do with press. If she's willing to take her chances, buddy, let her."

He wasn't being unkind, he was treating her with respect, and Paxton liked it. He figured that if she was in Viet Nam, she was there to do a job, and she was. And she was grateful to him.

"And you're willing to take the responsibility if she gets killed?" the sergeant from New York almost snarled. The name tag on his fatigues said "Campobello."

"No, I'm not," Ralph said fairly. "She took that responsibility herself when she took this job, just like I did . . . just like you did, Sergeant."

"Be my guest." He turned around and crawled through the brush, and a moment later, she followed Ralph a little closer to the action. They had moved ahead now, and the radio operator had called in a couple of choppers to take a closer look, and now the VC were firing at the chopper.

"Lone Ranger . . ." He was calling him again. "What you got?"

There was a yell of pleasure at the other end. "Hello there, Tonto, I got two Indians down, and one wounded . . . very nice . . . thank you for the assistance, and keep those cards and letters coming." And then suddenly a more ferocious sound. The M-60 machine gun had exploded into action . . . two hand grenades . . . and then suddenly before she knew it, somebody had grabbed her. A powerful arm had come up and around her shoulders, and she was being dragged backward by a force so strong, she didn't know what had hit her. And as she hit the ground, she felt the shudder of what seemed like an enormous explosion. The VC were throwing hand grenades now, too, and one had just missed her. The radio operator had deserted his post, and Ralph dove into the bush almost into the arms of the sergeant. But she would have been hit, if Bill Quinn hadn't grabbed her and run like hell, risking his life with hers. And as she lay facedown in the dirt, with his long limbs sprawled across hers, it took a moment to realize what had happened.

"Did I hurt you?" He looked concerned as she shook her head, and moved around a little stiffly, but he told her to keep her head down, even though the ground troops had advanced on the Viet Cong and the sounds of gunfire were a little farther in the distance.

"No, I'm fine." But he had knocked the wind out of her, and he dusted her face off, and then he smiled.

"You look like a kid who just took a fall in the dirt."

"I feel like a kid whose life has just been saved." She looked at him seriously. "Thank you."

He seemed unimpressed and unruffled, but it was what he was famous for, and why people liked him. He would have done anything for his men, at any cost to himself, and he never asked anyone to do anything he wouldn't do himself. Which was why he was so deeply loved and trusted.

"I guess Tony's right . . . I should have waited a few days before I had you all come out here. I didn't realize Ralph would bring a friend." He looked at her apologetically and then helped her up slowly.

"I'm glad we came. The tunnels are amazing."

He smiled in answer, impressed by her pluck, and pleased by her fascination with the tunnels. It was a job he had come to love, as long as he had to be there. There was a real challenge to it, some mystery, a lot of danger, and you had to think the way they did to catch them. "I like what I do." He smiled quietly and she found herself anxious to write a story about him, but she was afraid to ask. This was Ralph's turf, not hers, and she didn't want to annoy Quinn, or step on anyone's toes by being pushy. The sergeant had already made it clear enough that they were all intruders. And now that things had gotten more complicated, she didn't want to annoy him. "You'll have to come back again, after we clear this one. You wouldn't believe what you find down there." She still remembered the stench of the tunnel she'd barely entered. "I mean, weapons. Most of the weapons the VC use are stolen or captured from the GIs," he explained, "artillery, Soviet goods, Chinese tools, medical supplies, textbooks . . . it really teaches you something." He seemed to regard tunnel warfare as the ultimate challenge. But she was almost more interested in him than in what he was doing. What kind of man pursued an entire subterranean world, looking for an enemy no one else could find, but everyone knew was there? What kind of man could win a war like that, or was willing to die trying?

"How long are you in Viet Nam for?" he asked quietly as they went to look for Ralph and Yves. The action had moved far ahead now, and the sergeant was keeping close tabs on things, along with the choppers. "A few weeks?"

"Six months." She smiled. She already felt as though she'd been there for that long, and it had been less than a week since her arrival.

"You're pretty young to come this far, to cover a war like this one." She was a brave girl and he liked that. The truth was, he liked everything about her. Her looks, her balls, her guts, the way she'd gone unhesitatingly into the tunnel. He'd never met another woman like her. "Are you sorry you've come yet?"

"No." She looked him in the eye. "I'm glad." Glad and sad and scared, and sometimes happy. She knew she was in the right place at the right time, and that was at least something.

He'd been about to tell her how much he admired her when suddenly Sergeant Campobello reappeared and told him he was needed. Both snipers had been wounded and caught, two of the others were dead, and four had fled, presumably back into their tunnel. But if the snipers talked, they might get the exact location of the tunnel.

"I'd better get back to work," he said with a quiet smile. "I'll see you before you leave." And then he was gone with Sergeant Campobello, and she went to find Ralph and Yves. She was covered with dirt, and almost looked like one of the men now.

"You had a close call." Ralph looked at her disapprovingly. "You damn well better pay attention or you're going to get your brains blown out." He hadn't liked her going down into the tunnel either. "Pay attention, Delta Delta. These people aren't shooting blanks out there."

"I'm being perfectly careful," she snapped at him. "They threw a fucking hand grenade my way. They almost got the radio operator too. What do you expect me to do, wait in the parking lot while you get the stories?" she blazed at him, and suddenly he laughed. She was just like he had been at her age, anxious to get out there and stick her neck out, and get the biggest and the best and the most dangerous story.

"Okay, kiddo, go for it. But don't come crying to me if you get wounded."

"I won't," she grumbled as she dusted herself off again and he continued to laugh at her.

"You look like shit, you know that?" And with that, she started to laugh too. It had been an interesting day, and she liked Bill Quinn, maybe even a little more than she should have.

He came back after a while, when they were ready to leave, and thanked them for coming to Cu Chi, and he offered Paxton a tour of the base next time. In the meantime, he had to leave them pretty quickly. They were busy interrogating the prisoners.

"See you in Saigon, Ralph. Maybe we can have dinner next week." Ralph nodded, and Quinn waved to them as they drove off. They didn't see the sergeant again, which was probably just as well, Paxton decided. He obviously hated them, and had no desire to cooperate with the press. Not that it mattered. They'd done a good day's work, and both she and Ralph had gotten good stories. Yves said he'd gotten some good shots too. He'd gotten a great one when they shot one of the snipers. It was sick what constituted greatness here. Two dead men and a wounded girl made a "great" story here, a great shot, maybe even an award for brilliant journalism. It was strange how you won the prize for watching people die here.

But as they drove toward Saigon, all she could think of was Bill Quinn and his body covering hers as the grenade went off, the sheer power of him as he protected her, and the look in his eyes when she rolled over. She felt guilty thinking about it. He was a married man, and Peter had only been dead for a little over two months, and yet there was something, a raw energy about the man that was undeniable, an electric current that drew her to him and that she found irresistibly exciting.

# CHAPTER 14

∨

For the next week, Paxton stayed close to Saigon. She wrote the story of the incident at Cu Chi, and a separate story just describing the tunnels. The paper was running her articles under the caption "Message from Nam, by Paxton Andrews." And so far they had printed them all, and the *Sun* was syndicating them, which meant they might even turn up in Savannah, which she knew might impress her mother and brother. But it was Ed Wilson who called her himself and praised her for her insights and her obvious courage.

"You didn't go down in one of those tunnels yourself, did you, Pax?" She smiled as she listened to him. And tears came to her eyes. He was so far away now.

"I'm fine" was all she said in answer to his questions. She asked him to let her mother know that she was alright too. She hadn't had time to write to her yet and she knew she should have. She sent her love to Gabby and Matt and Mrs. Wilson, and after she spoke to him, she felt homesick for a day. But she got busy writing another story. She rented a car and drove herself to Bien Hoa, and she felt incredibly brave and independent. At twenty-two she was halfway around the world, discovering things she had never even dreamt of.

She was also fascinated with the black market, so one afternoon she went to Tan Son Nhut Base, where she'd arrived, to talk to some people there about the mass theft from the PX, of items that filtered directly into the black market, including uniforms and weapons. And as she walked slowly across Tan Son Nhut Base at sunset, she found herself watching a tall man in combat uniform far ahead. He had a rolling gait and a stride that seemed somehow familiar. But the sun was in her eyes, and she couldn't see who he was. She knew so few people in Saigon anyway, that she couldn't imagine it was anyone she really knew. And a minute later, he stopped and turned around to talk to someone. And as he did, he glanced at her, and then he walked slowly toward her. It was Captain William Quinn, from Cu Chi, and he looked incredibly handsome as he approached her, and in spite of herself, she could feel her heart pounding.

"Hi there," he said, looking down at her as though he'd been waiting for her there. He had a slow smile that said he was seldom in a hurry. He always seemed to be relaxed and at ease, and yet from somewhere deep inside him you could sense an almost electrical tension. "What brings you here?" And then he grinned. "You look a hell of a lot cleaner than the last time I saw you." She'd had dirt all over her face after she dived into the ground, covered by him, to avoid the hand grenade. And now she was wearing a white linen dress and flowers in her hair, and bright red sandals.

"Thank you. I'm doing a story on the thefts at the PX, of items that mysteriously reappear in the black market."

"Oh, that." He looked intrigued. "If you can solve that one, you get the Congressional Medal of Honor. But I think a lot of people here have a pretty big investment in seeing that you don't. You're talking some mighty big money."

"So I gather. Are you down from Cu Chi for a while?"

He shrugged nonchalantly. "Just a quick meeting with the general. I was going to drive back tonight." He paused and she didn't know why, but she held her breath, waiting for him. She didn't want to care, but she did. She was so drawn to him, she could hardly make sense in his presence. He made her feel terribly young, and in other circumstances than these, she would have felt almost silly. "I know it's short notice," he said quietly, "but is there any chance you'd want to grab a bite to eat before I drive back? I'm in no particular hurry." He looked deep into her eyes and the sheer power of him almost made her tremble. He was an odd combination of strength and gentleness that was difficult not to find appealing.

Her heart skipped a beat. "I'd love that."

He seemed pleased and then thought about it for a moment. "How foolish would it seem to you if we went to the officers' club here on the base for a hamburger and a milkshake? I've had a hankering for one all week," he confessed, looking like a kid, and she laughed.

He walked her across the base as they chatted easily about Saigon, and the hotel where she stayed, and where she'd gone to school. He had played football at West Point, he explained, which was easy to believe after the save he'd made the other day, rescuing her from the hand grenade. And when they walked into the club, the Beatles were on the jukebox, and lots of people were dancing. There was an easy, down-home American feeling in the air, and for the second time since she'd arrived, she felt suddenly homesick. The first time was when she talked to Peter's father in San Francisco.

They ordered hamburgers and fries, and she had a Coke, and he had a beer, and they watched the people dancing and listening to the music. The Beatles were followed by "(I Can't Get No) Satisfaction," everyone's favorite, and "Proud Mary," which Paxton had liked when she was at Berkeley.

"So when did you graduate?" he asked comfortably as they listened to the music and chatted. He seemed somehow younger here, as though the pressure was off him and he could relax, and she no longer sensed his underlying tension. And she laughed at his question.

"I didn't." She grinned sheepishly. "I should've graduated in June, but I dropped out."

"That's perfect," he smiled, "perfectly in tune with your whole generation." He was teasing her and he didn't seem to care, and it no longer seemed so dramatic as they sat there. Whether she had her degree or not was of absolutely no importance.

"Things kind of piled up on me last spring, and I got . . . I don't know . . . disillusioned. . . ."

"And now?" He looked her straight in the eye. He didn't really care what she'd done in school. He was interested in her as a grown-up. This was a grown-up world filled with real life and urgency, and people who died suddenly, whether or not they had gone to college.

"It no longer seems very important."

"Viet Nam does that to you," he said cryptically, sipping at his beer, and Paxton tried not to focus on how handsome he was. After all, he was married. "The things you used to care about don't matter much anymore, the house, the car, all the little bullshit stuff that used to seem so important. And the things you took for granted matter a lot . . . it's the people you care about here . . . that you stay alive for." His eyes never left her. "Home seems a long way away sometimes, and yet supposedly, that's what we all fight for."

"And is home what you're fighting for?" she asked softly.

"I'm not sure anymore. I'm not sure what the hell we're fighting for here, if you want to know the truth. This is my fourth tour here, and I swear I don't know why I do it. We're supposed to be winning the hearts and minds of the people, but that's crap, Paxton. We're not winning shit. All they can see is that we're killing their people and destroying their country. And they're right, we are."

227

"So why do you stay?" she asked sadly. She kept wanting to know why people volunteered to be there. No one really knew why they were there, except the boys who'd been drafted. The others didn't seem to know, and if they had known once, they had long since forgotten.

"I stay because they're killing American boys over here. And if I stay, maybe I can protect them. Maybe I've been doing what I do long enough to know how to do it just a little better. Or maybe not," he said with a sigh, finishing his beer, "maybe it doesn't make a fucking bit of difference." It was a disheartening thought, but something everyone had said at one point or another. Everyone felt, at some time, that what they were doing was futile. "You're a brave girl," he said then, remembering her willingness to go down into the tunnel. "No one else who's visited the base has ever done that, no woman anyway. And most of the men are scared to death, too, but they won't admit it." His eyes shone bright with admiration.

"Thank you. Maybe I'm just stupid."

"Maybe we all are," he said gently. He had lost two more men the day after she left, including the young radiotelephone operator whose call name was Tonto. But he didn't tell her that. This wasn't the time or the place for that, and it didn't really matter.

They walked out into the warm night air afterward and strolled for a little while. At least on the base, they were relatively safe. Except, even there, from time to time, there were bombs or snipers.

"I'd like to show you some of this country sometime. It's a beautiful place, even now." There were times when he really loved it.

"I'd like that. I went to Bien Hoa last week. I want to see more, but I'm not quite sure where to go yet."

"I could show you," he said softly, and then he turned to her. "I'm not quite sure what to do about you," he said with a look

of confusion. "I . . . I've never met anyone quite like you."
She was flattered and she was drawn to him and she didn't
know what to say either.

"What about your wife?" She decided to be open with him,
and she wanted him to be honest with her, and he looked as
though he would be.

"We've been married for ten years, since I graduated from the
Point. We have three kids. Three girls, funnily enough." He
smiled. "Somehow I always thought I'd have sons. And she's
fed up to the gills with the army. She was an army brat, too, just
like I was, and I thought she knew what she was getting into,
but she didn't. Or maybe she did, and she just didn't figure
she'd get so tired of it. She wants me to come home now, and
I'm just not ready."

"Do you love her?" Paxton looked him squarely in the eye,
she wanted to know what this man was about, and he wanted to
tell her.

"I did. I don't know anymore. I meet her in Tokyo a couple
of times a year, or Hong Kong, and we fight about the future.
She wants me to get a job, and I'm not sure I could anymore.
I'm thirty-two, and what the hell do you sell? The fact that
you've been crawling around in VC tunnels for four years? The
fact that you haven't stepped on a land mine? That you take
pretty good care of your men? What would that make me? A
good director at a Boy Scout camp? I don't know. I was trained
for this. I guess that's it," he said sadly, "I'm a trained killer."

"How many men have you saved since you've been here?"
Paxton asked quietly. "Isn't that really what you do best? Saving your men from being killed by the others?"

"Maybe." She was very perceptive, and he liked that. He
liked how smart she was, and how honest, and how gutsy, and
how pretty. She was everything Debbie wasn't. His wife complained all the time, and whined, about the kids, and the house
where they lived, and her parents, and his, and Viet Nam, and

their pay, and the PX, until he just couldn't stand it. He wanted something more than that. But he didn't know what yet. Or he hadn't. Until the week before, when he'd seen Paxton. "I want you to know something." He wanted to be straight with her. "I've gone out with a couple of other women before. Nothing important. A couple of nurses . . . a Wac in Long Binh . . . a girl in San Francisco once, but it was always on the up-and-up. They knew I was married and it was just a quick, straight thing. But . . . I don't even know if you like me . . . but this is different . . . I've never met a woman like you. . . ." And he wanted her to know that.

She smiled in the light where they stood, and without thinking, she reached up and touched his cheek. "Thank you." And the gesture brought tears to his eyes. No one had touched him like that in so long that he had forgotten what it felt like.

"I think I'm in love with you. Is it possible for a grown man to fall in love with a girl in a place like this and have anything good come of it?" He didn't see how, and yet there was an intensity to their situation here, a sense that life was only for the moment.

"I don't know." She looked sad for a moment, thinking of Peter. And this was so different. This was only for now, with no promise of anything more, no tomorrow, and very probably no future.

"I never thought I'd leave my wife," he said honestly, as they walked along, "and I'm not sure I would. We've been married for a long time and I love my children."

"How often do you see them?" Paxton asked.

"Not very often. She brought them to Honolulu last time, but it was tough. We're practically strangers now. This thing over here has been hard on them, and on her, I guess. At least I'm not in a hell of a lot of danger."

"That's not what it looked like the other day."

He shrugged it off. To him, it was nothing. "You know what I mean. Hell, the fly boys go up and they get shot down by Charlie and the next thing you know they're POWs. I'm pretty much behind the lines most of the time." Except that they both knew there were no clearly defined lines here.

She turned to him then, there was something she had to say to him. "I don't want anything. You don't have to make me any promises, say anything. I don't expect you to tell me you'll get a divorce so I'll go out with you. We don't even know each other yet. Why don't we just see what happens."

"Do you mean that? No promises? No deals? No 'I'll love you till the day I die?' " he said, as he gently put an arm around her shoulders. But she stopped walking then and looked up at him.

"Just don't die. That's all I ask of you. Is that a deal?" She looked earnestly up at him with his great height and broad shoulders.

"I promise."

"Good. Then that's settled." And they walked on, and they talked and laughed, and passed other couples doing the same thing, and she wondered if he was concerned if other people saw him, but he didn't seem to be, and after a while he stopped and laughed as he looked at her.

"Where the hell are we going? We've walked halfway to the DMZ tonight. I swear we've walked this base from one end to the other."

She laughed too. She was just enjoying being with him and it all seemed a little crazy. "I guess I should go back to my hotel."

"I'll follow you back," he said regretfully, he hated to leave her. "Where are you staying?"

"The Caravelle."

"How about a drink at the penthouse?" They both felt as though they had something to celebrate, but she wasn't sure what yet.

She smiled, she liked the idea, and wondered if they'd run

into any of the other journalists there, but she didn't really care. She had no secrets.

He followed her back in her rented car, an ancient Renault that barely made it, and he parked outside the hotel and followed her inside, and put an arm around her as they went up to the penthouse. It had been an amazing evening for both of them, and Paxton felt as though she had come a long way in a short time. And it was more than just from San Francisco to Saigon. She felt as though she had been hurled from another life to this one, and she was not quite sure what she felt yet. She knew she was drawn to Bill Quinn, and she couldn't have torn herself away now, there was an urgency to what she felt, and yet there was fear, too, and from a strange distant place in her heart, there was also sadness. There were other people in their lives, he had his wife, and she was still struggling with the memory of Peter. And yet, they were here now, and suddenly she knew she needed him, just as he needed her, and maybe that was more important.

"Paxton?" He said her name carefully, because it was new to him, and she turned toward him with a shy smile.

"Yes?"

"You were looking very serious there for a minute. You okay?"

She nodded. "Yeah. I was just thinking."

"Don't." He smiled, and then brushed the top of her head with his lips as they reached the penthouse. Tom Hardgood was there, and Jean-Pierre fresh from Hong Kong, but he was with a girl, and then in a corner, Paxton noticed Ralph sitting quietly, deep in conversation with a beautiful Eurasian. She was startled to see him there. She hadn't seen him all week, and she had just left him a message at the AP office that morning.

Bill Quinn had seen him too, and he guided Paxton over to him, and Ralph introduced her to the lady.

"France Tran . . . Paxton Andrews." She was incredibly

beautiful, and when she spoke, Paxton noticed that she had a French accent. She looked to be about Paxton's age, and she was wearing a white *ao dai,* and seemed perfectly at ease at the penthouse.

"Hi, France," Bill said, "how's An?"

"He's fine." She smiled, glancing at Ralph warmly. "He's a little monster."

"He sure is," Ralph agreed. "He put a frog in my boots last week. Fortunately, I checked before I put them on." Ralph laughed, and Paxton was surprised to see a side of him that she had never even suspected. She wasn't quite sure whom they were speaking of, but she assumed they were talking about a child, and this woman's son obviously. But suddenly she wondered if she and Ralph were married.

They chatted a few minutes longer and then she and Bill sat down, and she was trying not to look confused, but she leaned over and asked him, "Who is that?"

"France?" He was surprised she didn't know her. She and Ralph seemed so close. "She lives with Ralph. She married a boy in the forty-fifth cav, and An is their baby." He seemed to hesitate, and Paxton stared at him, wanting to know the rest of the story. "He was killed before the baby was born. Now he must be about two, something like that. And she and Ralph have been together for about a year. They live together, I think, but he keeps it pretty quiet. In Gia Dinh." All she knew was that it was a suburb of Saigon.

"Are they married?"

"No. Her mother was French and her father was Vietnamese, and I've only talked to her a few times, but she seems to have some pretty strong feelings about mixed marriage. The army gave her a terrible time when Haggerty died. I'm not sure they've given her widow's benefits yet, and they tried to accuse her of being a whore and An not being his baby."

"What about his family?"

"He never told them he'd married her, and I think his family was pretty uptight. From some hick town in Indiana. They won't acknowledge her or the baby."

Paxton looked horrified. "And what about Ralph? Won't he marry her and adopt the child?"

Bill smiled at her naiveté. She wanted everything all neatly tied up. But things didn't always work out here. "Maybe you should ask him."

"She's beautiful." Paxton had been impressed by her obvious gentility and education.

"Yes," he acknowledged. "And smart. But if he tries to take her home, back home they'll call her a gook, just like they will the whores who hang out at the Pink Nightclub. Back home, no one knows the difference."

"All you have to do is look at her, Bill." She sounded exasperated, but she was naive, and he knew it.

"That's all *you* have to do, maybe, Pax. Other people don't see it that way. To them, a gook is a gook is a gook is a dink is a slanteye, is the same person who killed their son or their fiancé or their brother. It's not going to be easy taking these girls home."

"But she's different." Paxton pleaded her cause for no reason.

"Not to them." She wanted it not to be true, but suspected it was, and it made her sad for this woman she barely knew. But she knew he was right. Back in the States, the beautiful Eurasian girl would be a "gook" just like the others.

They talked for a long time that night, about the war at first, and then about other things, and he never mentioned his wife again, or his children. He had been in Viet Nam for so long that he had begun to feel alienated from everyone. And he was fascinated to hear all that she had to tell him about Berkeley.

He escorted her back to her room when they closed the bar, and he left her at the door, without pressing further.

"I should be back in Saigon in a few days," he said quietly,

"I'll call you before I come." And then without another word, he bent and kissed her gently on the lips, and then he was gone, and when he left, she wanted to beg him to stay alive. But she didn't even dare think now of the danger lurking in the Cu Chi tunnels.

# CHAPTER 15

∨

Bill Quinn came back to Saigon three days after that, and he called Paxton before he came, and when he arrived, he looked handsome and clean in a starched dress uniform, and she was waiting for him in the lobby. This was an "official date," he had said, and she smiled when she saw him walk into the lobby, looking tall and young and very handsome.

"Wow!" he said when he caught sight of her. She was wearing her hair down, and she was wearing a pink silk dress she had brought from home. It was very short and it showed off her legs and she tried not to remember that Peter had always liked it.

Bill had made reservations at a restaurant near the embassy, and she felt very grown up as he ushered her in, and they showed them to a corner table. The room looked very French, and was romantically lit, and there were fragrant bouquets of flowers on all the tables. And here, finally, they escaped the smell of fuel. And there were Americans at almost every table around them.

She told him about another mission she'd been on with Ralph, near Long Binh, and he frowned while he listened to her.

"It sounds dangerous." He looked frankly worried, and wondered if he should say something to Ralph now.

236

"So is being here. Don't be silly, Bill. I'm safer than you are in Cu Chi."

"Like hell you are," he said quietly, feeling strangely protective of her, which even struck him as odd. He never worried about what Debbie did, back in the States. But Debbie was in San Francisco, and Paxton was ten years younger and running around Saigon, looking for trouble.

"Looking for Viet Cong in tunnels isn't exactly what I'd call safe." In fact, she had forced herself not to think about it all week. And when she'd gone to Long Binh with Ralph, he had given her a somewhat stern lecture, about "not fraternizing with the troops," which at first had amused her. But then she realized that he was serious, and she had turned to him in amazement.

"How can you say a thing like that?" She was referring to France, and he knew it, but that didn't sway him.

"It's different for me, Pax. I'm a man. And Bill Quinn is married."

"So what? What difference does it make? His wife is halfway around the world and so are we. What if we're all dead next week? What difference will it make then?" In a matter of weeks, she had come to think like everyone in Saigon.

"And when he goes back to her?" Ralph had said quietly. "How will you feel then? You've had one heartbreak in your life, isn't that enough?"

"I can't help that." She had looked away from him. She didn't want to justify her love life to Ralph Johnson. He was her friend, but he had no right to tell her who she could go out with and who she couldn't.

"It's not too late to stop it now. But Viet Nam is a strange place. Things get serious very fast, or sometimes they don't get serious at all when they should, because half the time we're all scared shitless we're going to be dead by this afternoon, and the other half of the time we've watched so many people die that we don't give a damn about anyone or anything. Don't get involved with a soldier here, Paxton . . . or even a correspondent. You'll get hurt. We're all a little bit crazy." He was trying to warn her and he meant it.

"And what am I for being here with you? I'm a correspondent too," she defended herself, and he smiled. But she was still young, and untouched by the horrors the rest of them took for granted.

"You're still new, Pax. It's not too late for you. I'm telling you . . . don't get mixed up with Bill. He's a great guy, and I like him. But whatever happens, you'll get hurt. Why put yourself through that?"

"And France?" she said, wanting to get back at him, but the look on his face told her that she had touched a forbidden subject.

"She has nothing to do with this," he'd said, and he'd gone off in a helicopter, with a medevac team for the next three hours. And when he came back, neither of them brought up the subject again, and she didn't mention it to Bill that night. It was too late for them anyway. As they sat and talked, he held her hand, and they talked about the kind of things people talk about when all is new and love is dawning.

They had almost finished their chocolate mousse for dessert, when a pretty Vietnamese girl in an *ao dai* walked into the restaurant, and set down an armful of flowers. Paxton watched her thinking how pretty they were, and at the same moment, Bill turned and saw her. He watched her for a split second and then saw her leave, and then without a moment's thought, he grabbed Paxton, dragged her off her chair, and pulled her under the table. He pressed his body on top of hers, hard against the banquette, and at that exact moment, there was a tremendous explosion. All the windows at the front of the restaurant blew out, and bodies seemed to be hurled everywhere around them. For a moment after that there was silence, and then screams, and Paxton could see a wall of flame explode to their right, as Bill grabbed her and pulled her along the floor to where they could see light in the darkness. He pulled her to safety in the street as the sirens began, and everywhere around them people seemed to be shouting. There were still screams, and cries of pain, and he started to leave her on the street and hurried back inside to help, but she was right behind him. Her arm was bleeding from where a piece of glass had sliced through her dress, but other than that she was unhurt by the explosion. Her legs were scratched, her body bruised from the force of it, but she went back inside and helped carry a woman out. She was screaming and she couldn't see. Her face and arms were covered with blood, and all Paxton could do was comfort her as they waited for the ambulance to come. And she saw Bill help another man carry two men out, but both were dead. And then finally, the police and the medics took over. It was an ugly sight and there was blood and broken glass everywhere, and she was shaking violently as they walked back to his car, and he stopped and pulled her into his arms. They were both covered with blood and she started to cry as he kissed her.

It was a terrible way to fall in love, a terrible place to be, a terrible war that had brought them together.

"What are we doing here?" he asked, his voice sounding shaken. It was not so much because of what he'd seen, but because if things had happened differently, she might have been killed, and suddenly more than anything, he didn't want to lose her. "Why aren't we someplace ordinary like New York or Maryland or Texas?"

"Because," she smiled through her tears, "if we were, you probably wouldn't know I'm alive, and you'd be with your wife." She laughed and dried her eyes, trying to forget what they'd seen and just been through. "Or something like that."

He smiled too. "You have a way with words, Miss Paxton Andrews."

"I speak the truth. It's one of my biggest failings."

"And virtues. I don't think I'd love you as much if you didn't. One thing this place does to you is makes you develop an absolute hatred for bullshit. That's what happens when I go back to the States between tours," he explained as they got into his car. "I can't listen to the lies anymore, the explanations, the things no one believes and everyone says. In some ways, it's easier being here," and then he thought about what had just happened. "At least I used to think so."

"That happens a lot here, doesn't it?" she asked, meaning the bombing, and he nodded. And then she smiled sadly. "Why is it, every time I'm with you, I come out looking like I've been dragged through a trench somewhere."

"Because you're crazy to be here." He kissed her then, hard, and in a way that told her he was glad they were both alive and nothing had happened.

He took her back to her hotel then, and without saying a word they went upstairs. He had stopped at the bar and picked up a bottle of Scotch, and when she unlocked her room he laid it on the table, and then he turned to look at her, with sad eyes that said he loved her. "Pax, do you want me to go?" He had made arrangements to stay at the Rex, but he wanted to be here with her while he could, but only if it was also what she wanted. "I'll go if you want me to."

She shook her head and smiled and walked slowly toward him. She wasn't sure what to do. Peter had been dead for four months, and she had thought she would be bonded to him forever. And yet suddenly he seemed part of another lifetime, another world, a place she would never be again, and Bill Quinn was all that mattered.

"I don't want you to go," she said softly.

He leaned down and took her in his arms, and she reached out to him with the passion born of loss and fear and sorrow, and he touched her with the strength of a man who puts his life on the line every morning. They had almost died that night and perhaps they would die the next day, but for now, for this single moment in time, they were alive, and belonged only to each other.

He lay down on the bed with her and gently stripped her clothes off. The dress had been reduced to shreds of silk by the explosion and there was blood on his uniform, and all they wanted to do was shed the past, and the pain, and the loneliness that had brought them together. He felt the satin of her skin as he lay with her, and he moaned softly.

"Oh, God, Pax, you're so beautiful . . ." He couldn't stop touching her and holding her and kissing her, and then she reached up and brought him to her, and as he entered her, there were tears in her eyes, not for the past and what they'd lost, but for what they'd found together.

# CHAPTER 16

∨

Paxton managed another trip to Cu Chi with Ralph three weeks later. By then the Democratic Convention had exploded into an orgy of madness in Chicago, and Harriman was still overseeing the Viet Nam peace talks in Paris. The irony of it all seemed like a bad joke to Paxton when she read it on the teletype at the AP office when she went there to meet Ralph before the continuing Five O'Clock Follies. Nothing seemed to make sense anymore, except what was happening right there, and the life she now shared with Bill. All that mattered was that he was safe, and nothing happened to either of them. It seemed a miracle each time he came to her at the hotel, and spent the night, which he was able to do fairly often.

Ralph refrained from making comments on it most of the way to Cu Chi base, and then finally just before they arrived, he turned toward her and asked a question.

"It's serious with you two, isn't it?" She nodded, not wanting to say too much in front of the driver. Ralph hadn't mentioned any names, but gossip circulated quickly from Saigon to all the bases. Who was sleeping with whom and why always seemed to be a popular subject of conversation. And there was a lot of it going around, like VD and a host of tropical diseases.

"Yes," she said seriously, "it might be. It's kind of new, and we haven't figured it all out yet. There are some things that would have to be worked out, if . . . if . . ." If it lasted. Ralph knew what she meant, and he shook his head disapprovingly and looked out the window.

"You're both fools. But surely you know that."

"Why?" She was still so naive, so hopeful, as he turned back to look at her.

"Because you'll get hurt, Pax. Everyone does here. You have to. I don't have to spell it out to you. You're a big girl. You know what the options are, and most of them aren't pretty." He meant that either Bill would go back to his wife when he got shipped home eventually, or he could get killed. He could survive of course, he could even leave Debbie. But Ralph didn't think it very likely.

"You've been here too long. You're too cynical."

"Maybe so," he said, lighting a cigarette. The worst of it was he had actually come to like Ruby Queens, the local brand. "I've seen the movie."

"Maybe you didn't watch the right ending. Maybe you didn't stay long enough. You don't know everything."

"Look," he tried again, because he liked her, "you're smart, smarter than most. You're doing a terrific job. You write great stuff. You could even win a Pulitzer one day."

"Yeah, sure." She laughed, amused.

"All right. So not a Pulitzer. But you're good and you know it. What do you need this headache for? You're only here for six months. Save it till you go home and meet Prince Charming behind a desk somewhere in some nice safe city like Milwaukee."

She turned to him determinedly. "Look, I can't help what happened. It did. It's there. I can't pretend it isn't. And why should I? This is where we are right now. This is real. The rest is all bullshit."

"What if the rest is real, and this is bullshit?"

"Then I was wrong. Haven't you ever been wrong, Ralph?" She didn't want to mention France again, but he had gotten involved with her for the same reasons. Because they were there, and it was hard, and everyone was scared, and all around them people were dying. What better antidote to all that than to fall in love with someone, whether one meant to or not. How could he of all people not understand that? "Look." She turned to him again as he stubbed out his cigarette. "Just get off my back. I know you mean well. But you don't understand."

"Maybe not," he said sadly. And when he saw them together later that afternoon, he wondered if she was right and he was wrong. There was undeniably something very strong and tender and beautiful between them. They tried to keep it hidden from everyone, but it was difficult. Their feelings for each other were so strong, so physical in some ways, and at the same time so honest, so pure, so built on mutual admiration and tenderness and love that it was very difficult to hide them.

Bill's sergeant, Tony Campobello, saw it too, and he was furious over it, which even she had noticed. He was barely civil to her, and when she was around that afternoon, his tone to his superior officer was icy. And all Bill did was raise an eyebrow in amusement. But when they ran into him at Tan Son Nhut one afternoon, at the PX, Paxton couldn't resist saying something to him, while Bill was paying.

"I'm sorry . . ." she started to say to Tony, but he cut her off.

"For what?"

"The way you feel," she said honestly, since he made it no secret.

"The way I feel has nothing to do with this," he said coldly.

"Then what are you angry about?" She looked him straight in the eye, which was easier than it was with Bill because Tony was almost the same height she was. "Or is it just that you don't like me?"

"I don't give a shit about you." He was out of line and he knew it, but he didn't care. He hated her and he wanted her to know it. "It's him I care about. He's saved my ass more times than you'll ever know. He's saved more men in this godforsaken country than you can count, and you're out there risking his ass, and you don't even know it." She was shocked at what he said and she didn't understand.

"How can you say that?" She had done nothing to risk his life, on the contrary, she wanted him to stay alive, even if that meant he went home to Debbie. But she didn't want him to die. This guy was crazy.

"Lady, do you know what it takes to stay alive here? You gotta crawl on your belly every day, and think of only one thing, yourself. You think about the next guy too much, you watch your buddy and not yourself, and you're a dead man. In one second, it's all over. You know what he thinks about out there now? Not us, not himself, not what he's doing, not who's in the tunnel, or is there a guy out there in the bushes just waiting for us . . . he thinks about you, and he sits around smiling. And you know what that's going to do to him? It's going to get his ass blown off by a land mine, or his brains blown out by a sniper. And do you know who's fault it'll be, lady? Yours. You think about that next time he reaches out to touch you." And as he said that, Bill walked over to them with his purchases and he was smiling.

"Hi, Tony . . . you know Paxton, don't you?" He did and he didn't want to. And something disturbed Bill about the way Paxton looked as the sergeant said, "Yeah, sure," saluted, and left them. She didn't say a word to Bill about what he had just said to her, but she was frightened all night as she lay beside Bill and thought of the sergeant's warning. Were they all right? Was she wrong to love him? Would it destroy them both? Was there no room for love here? It seemed hard to believe, and everyone had someone, even if it was only for a moment. And all the while Ralph was telling her that she had no right to love Bill, he was living with the Eurasian girl in Gia Dinh . . . he went home to her at night, didn't he? But why was it that no one wanted her to be with Bill? Especially not the angry young sergeant.

"You were awfully quiet last night," Bill said the next day. He had three days off, and he had noticed it, but she still wouldn't tell him what Tony had said. She just told him she was worried about a story.

They went to Vung Tau that weekend, for three days R and R, in the lovely coastal town that was still a beautiful resort with exquisite beaches. Paxton thought she had never been happier in her life. They talked about the future sometimes, but as infrequently as they could. There was nothing to talk about now, except the time they shared. And when he went back to the States, he would have to decide what he wanted to do about Debbie. They were both due to go back at almost the same time. She had promised to go back by Christmas, and his DEROS was a month later. He was due back in San Francisco at the end of January, and he and Paxton agreed, he had spent enough time in Viet Nam. Four tours were sufficient. He was going home to figure out the business of living.

"Do you really think you could stand being an army bride?" he asked her in bed one night in Vung Tau, and the scary thing was that he meant it.

"I think so." She smiled. "I could write for *Stars and Stripes*."

"You're too good for them." Even though they were informative and everyone read them.

"Baloney." She rolled over in bed and he kissed her. They had a wonderful time in Vung Tau, and they went back again in October. And shortly after that, he went to Hong Kong for a week's R and R with Debbie. It was something he and Paxton had talked about at length, and he was tempted to cancel. But

Paxton thought he should go, even if it was hard on her. She felt he owed that to Debbie. This was no time for a confrontation. But when he came back, he was in a bad mood for weeks. Debbie had put a lot of pressure on him about his attitudes, and the war. She had recently gotten involved in an antiwar group, and she told him he was a killer. She also told him she wanted a new car, and she was sick to death of the army.

Nixon had been elected by then, and Paxton's news from home was pretty good. Her mother seemed fine, although anxious to see her at Christmas. And Gabby wrote and told her she was having another baby. Their lives seemed to go on, but Paxton could no longer imagine what it would be like to be there with them. After five months in Viet Nam, she felt as though she'd been living on another planet.

And she said as much to Bill one night when they were out for dinner. "You know, I feel guilty even saying it. But I don't want to go home for Christmas." She wanted to stay in Viet Nam with him. It meant more to her than going home, and being with her family in Savannah. She had hated that for years, and now it would be worse. She had grown up too much this year. And it was just too different. Besides, Christmas at home without Queenie would be truly awful. And being in the States would bring back a flood of painful memories of Peter. And although she thought less about it now, she felt that a part of her would always love him. Things were just different now, but even Bill understood that.

"Why don't you stay here for Christmas then?" He knew he should have encouraged her to go home, but he was feeling selfish and he didn't want to. It would be their last peaceful time before he went home himself the following month and tried to figure out what he was going to do about Debbie.

"Do you really mean it?" Paxton looked at him mischievously.

"Sure."

"Then it's done." She leaned over and kissed him and they went back to the hotel and made love for the rest of the evening. And in the morning she sent a telex to the *Sun.* "Cannot be home December as planned. Big stories breaking here. Home by January 15. Please advise family in Savannah. Paxton Andrews." She knew it would cause a little stir, but she didn't really care. She wanted to be with Bill, and maybe this would be their first and last Christmas. If he decided to end their affair, at least they would have had this. She was very philosophical about it. But one had to be in any case, when one lived with constant danger.

They went to church together on Christmas Eve, and they woke up in each other's arms the next morning. He'd bought her a sweater at the PX, and a beautiful gold bangle bracelet in Hong Kong, when he was there with Debbie in October. It had a single tiny diamond in it, and he put it on her arm and kissed her. She had bought him a handsome watch at the PX, some books she knew he wanted that she'd ordered from the States, and some funny underwear she'd found on the black market. It was all silly stuff, and the best they could do under the circumstances. But the bracelet he gave her was really special, and inside, delicately engraved, were their initials, and *Xmas '68.*

"The first of many," he said cryptically as he kissed her.

They went to Martha Raye's Christmas show that afternoon, and everyone enjoyed it. Bob Hope was in Da Nang that day, being applauded by ten thousand servicemen and women. Ann-Margret was the hit of the show even though Paxton felt that showcasing sex symbols only teased the men. But they loved it anyway. And at the end of the show, General Abrams pinned the Outstanding Civilian Service Medal to Hope's shirt and the audience gave him a standing ovation.

Paxton and Bill ran into Tony Campobello at Martha Raye's show and Ralph was covering it for the Associated Press. He had even brought France and her little boy, An, who was ador-

able and looked just like her. Bill and Paxton chatted with
Ralph and France for a little while, and then they moved on.
And they didn't see them again after that. The crowd was enormous. And they didn't see Tony or any of Bill's men after that
either. And he had been pointedly cool when he ran into his
captain with Paxton. He still hadn't gotten over his feelings
about her, and he made no effort whatsoever to be pleasant.
And it didn't really matter anymore. She and Bill would be
going home in a month. They talked frequently now about how
strange it would be to be in the same city and not be together.

"It won't be for long," he kept saying, but Paxton kept wondering what would happen when he saw his children again, and
was really home. She had a strange feeling that he wouldn't be
quite so ready to leave them, no matter what he said now in the
heat of passion.

They spent a quiet New Year's Eve at the officers' club and
then finished it off with a drink at the penthouse. And then they
made love in her room and saw the new year in with tenderness
and passion. And they were still lying in each other's arms and
kissing and whispering the next morning. They slept most of the
afternoon, and at nightfall he had to go back to Cu Chi to
report for duty. He was due back in Saigon again in two days,
and she had a story to write for the *Sun* again. Her column,
"Message from Nam," was doing extremely well and was bringing in a lot of favorable letters, some of which they sent her in
Saigon. She was giving people honest reporting of what was
happening over there. And her honesty and integrity seemed to
shine through her writing. Ed Wilson was especially pleased,
and he now took full credit for sending her to Viet Nam in the
first place. In an odd way, he felt what she said had avenged his
son, and Peter hadn't died for nothing. She had gone there to
tell his story, and that of half a million boys like him. And she
was touched by the letters she got in answer to her column.

Sometimes she tried to answer them, but most of the time she was just too busy.

The story she had to write the next day was about street beggars in Saigon, and another piece she had done about Hue. And then there was the one about Martha Raye, and the Bob Hope show. She had a busy couple of days, and she was still at her typewriter at eight o'clock the night Bill was due to arrive. He was late, but she knew that sometimes it was hard to get away. And if Tony Campobello knew he was meeting her, he would often do everything he could to delay him. It was a game he liked to play, and Bill was patient about it, but his constantly hostile attitude still irritated Paxton.

She glanced at her watch again at ten o'clock, and she was mildly worried about it, but she still knew that as the officer in charge, he often couldn't totally plan his departures. Especially lately. There was so much to do before he left in three weeks, and he was trying to break in a new CO fresh from the States, and Paxxie knew it wasn't easy.

At eleven o'clock she looked at her watch again, and began to pace the room. And by midnight, she was seriously worried. She decided to go down to the lobby then, and she told the operator where she would be in case Bill called her. She thought maybe he'd been waylaid by someone he knew on the way in, and she might find him at the bar, which had happened once or twice. But she didn't see anyone she knew there tonight, not even Nigel. And she knew Ralph had gone away with France and An, to relatives of hers in Hau Bon over the New Year weekend.

She wandered aimlessly around the lobby for a long while, and he didn't show up. And there was nothing more she could do. It was too late to try to call the unit. She went back to her room, and sat up most of the night, wondering if some problem had come up that made it impossible for him to leave but it hardly seemed likely.

She finally fell asleep at four o'clock, and she woke up again with the dawn. And there was still no sign of him. She had somehow hoped he might turn up during the night while she was asleep, and slide into bed beside her, since he had the key and had done that more than once, when he was able to get away unexpectedly and surprised her.

But there was no surprise that night. The other half of the bed was empty when she awoke, and she went to the AP office at seven-thirty. She checked the Teletypes to see if anything had come up during the night, but other than a plastique bomb in a bar, and a street fight in Cholon, everything had been peaceful.

And she knew Ralph was due back late the night before, so she called him at home, from the AP office, an hour later.

"I know this sounds crazy . . ." She felt foolish calling him but she didn't know who else to call. "But Bill didn't show up last night. I'm sure nothing's wrong, but I just thought . . ."

"Oh, Christ, Pax," he said, turning over in bed with a groan, "and you want me to call them out there?"

"Yeah."

"Why don't you call them yourself? Hell, you've got the same credentials I do."

"Bullshit. Everyone knows I'm involved with Bill." In spite of the initial caution, it had become one of the worst-kept secrets in Saigon.

"So what?"

"So it looks like I'm playing nosy girlfriend. I just want to know he's okay, and then whenever he shows up is fine." It hadn't even dawned on her that he might be out with someone else. Their relationship was nothing like that, and they were so much in love that the issue of anyone else had never arisen between them.

"Okay, okay, I'll call. What do you want to know?"

"That Cu Chi Base is still standing, hasn't been attacked during the night, and Bill's okay."

251

"Listen, kid," he said, sitting up in bed and smiling at France. He was both happy and worried about her. She had just told him the night before that she was pregnant, and she wanted to have his baby. "If Cu Chi base has been blown away, we're all in deep shit. That place is bigger than New York, for chrissake."

"Never mind the wiseass cracks, Johnson, just call them."

"Okay, okay, I'll call." He hung up and leaned over to kiss France, still lying beside him.

"Is she all right?" France asked. She liked Paxton too. And although she didn't know her well, she had always felt a silent kinship with her.

"She's fine. She's just getting short and she's getting nervous. Everyone gets like that before they go home. They all drive me crazy."

"And you?" she said, looking at him almost sadly after her news of the night before, "when will you go home, my love?"

"Never. Unless you come with me." But she said she never would. And she meant it. She was too proud to be treated like a whore in the States. She was going to stay in Saigon, and she would love him forever.

He sat on the edge of the bed and called Cu Chi. He had a contact or two there, but the most important one was Bill, and he asked directly for his unit. He got a young guy he didn't know, who stalled him when he asked for Bill, and then he went through the other names and got nowhere. And suddenly he wondered if Paxton's instincts were right, and there was something wrong. He had a thought then, and asked for Sergeant Campobello. There was a long pause, he was told to hold on, and then he was left there, hanging. And it was almost ten minutes later when Tony came on the line. And Ralph had been smart enough not to hang up. By then he was convinced that she was right and there was a problem.

"Tony?" Ralph said, as though they were old friends, but they weren't. Tony didn't like him because he'd introduced Paxton to Bill, and Campobello was a guy who could hold a grudge forever. "Ralph Johnson, AP in Saigon."

"I know who you are, man." The voice was coarse and cold, and he wasn't interested in the call. "What do you want?"

"I . . . we . . . unofficially, we were wondering if anything happened yesterday . . . I mean . . ." Shit, if it had been any-one else, he could have asked him straight if Bill was okay. But he didn't want Campobello to know he was calling for Paxton. And he felt like a kid now, playing games. "Look, we just heard some rumors that you might have had some trouble out there. Everything A-okay?"

There was an endless pause. "I guess you could call it that. We only had one casualty all weekend. Just one. Pretty good, huh?" But he sounded brittle and bitter.

"That's great." Ralph wasn't quite sure where to go from there, but Tony solved the problem for him.

"Only problem, of course, is that it was . . ." He almost snapped as he said the words "our commander. Remember him? Great big tall guy. Real nice-looking. Bill Quinn." Oh my God. Ralph's blood ran cold. What the fuck was he going to tell her?

"I . . . oh my God . . . how did that happen?" Ralph's voice was faint at his end, and Tony sounded like he was crying.

"How did that happen? Real simple. He fell in love with this fucking bitch a few months ago and stopped paying attention. He started to fall in love with the whole fucking world, and wanted to play Prince Charming . . . Sir Galahad . . . you want to know how it happened, mister? Our guys were too fucking afraid to go down a hole yesterday, and you know who went? That's right, the captain. He thought he could outshoot the guy at the other end because he always had before. And you know what, mister? After four tours, he was wrong this time, he was too big for the hole, he was too slow, too old, his head was too full of other shit because he was going home with her in a few days to tell his wife to go fuck herself probably, and his kids, and little old Charlie at the other end of the hole, he blew his head off." Ralph felt sick as he listened to him, sick from the anger and the sorrow and the bitterness and the irony of what had happened. He had less than two weeks to go, and they'd killed him. And it had happened to thousands of others. But not this one. Bill Quinn was such a nice guy. And he was so much in love with Paxton. "Did you get your story, Mr. Johnson?" Tony asked him bitterly, making no secret now of the fact that he was crying. "Did you take notes, or would you like to come out and view the body? He won't be going home till tomorrow afternoon. And I guess now he won't be going home with his girlfriend." He wasn't the first man who had fallen in love while he was there, nor the first man who had cheated on his wife, but somehow all along the sergeant had been outraged. And he had predicted this all along. Again and again, he had seen men get involved with the women there and get so taken with them, they got careless. He was convinced that Bill had died because of that and nothing would ever change his mind. In his mind, Paxton Andrews had killed Bill Quinn, and that was the end of the story.

"This is going to kill her," Ralph said more to himself than to Campobello. And at his end, Tony wiped his eyes with his sleeve.

"Good. I hope it does. She deserves it."

"You don't really believe that, do you?"

"Yes, I do," he said frigidly. "She fucking killed my captain."

"He was a grown man." Ralph felt honor bound to defend her to this man, and he was getting angry. She hadn't killed anyone. If anything, she'd hurt herself. And she'd taken a chance on him. And she'd lost. Just as she had once before. But that was the way the war was. If you gave a damn about anyone there, a dog, a soldier, a child, you ran the risk of losing. "He made his choices, Campobello, just like she did. And he knew what he was doing. If he bought it yesterday, the guy at the other end must have been pretty goddamn slick. I don't believe Bill Quinn would ever get careless." He was too fast, too sharp, and he knew too much about what he was doing. And there was a lot of truth to that, but Tony Campobello didn't want to hear it.

"Bullshit. He should never have been down that hole."

"Then why did he go?" Ralph pressed him.

"Maybe to prove something . . . maybe because he was thinking of her . . ."

"He wasn't that sloppy, or that dumb, or even that brave." Even though all the generals said, and Bill had even said himself, that to be a tunnel rat you had to be a little bit crazy.

"He was crazy nuts in love with her."

"Yes, he was," Ralph agreed in deference to both of them, "but that was his business, and I don't think he'd let that interfere with anything. I just don't believe that. And if you've got an attitude about it, Campobello, I suggest you bury it right now. If you cared about him at all, why don't you just shut up your fucking opinions and keep them to yourself. That girl is going to be devastated over this and she doesn't need you mouthing off at her if your paths should happen to cross sometime, which I sure as hell hope they don't."

"So do I."

"For his sake, do me a favor, if you do run across her, be a gentleman, keep your mouth shut."

"Go fuck yourself, mister," Tony Campobello spat into the phone, tears welling up in his eyes again. "That bitch killed my captain." He was like a child standing beside his dead mother, wanting to kill everyone who came near her. And when he slammed the phone down a few minutes later, Ralph sat for a long moment, staring unhappily out the window. What the hell was he going to tell her?

France had been listening to him all the while, and when he

255

stood up to get dressed, she came and put a gentle hand on his shoulder. "I'm sorry about your friend." She had a wonderful French accent, and a gentle touch, and a wise heart, and he turned around and held her. "I'm sorry for both of them."

"So am I. I tried to warn them a long time ago."

"Why?" she asked softly.

"Because I thought they were wrong. The price is too high if you lose over here. I tried to tell them that. But they didn't listen."

"Perhaps they couldn't." She was wiser than he was in the end. And she watched while he dressed. And an hour later he was at the Caravelle, knocking on the door of Paxton's room with a grim look in his eyes. But when she opened the door, she was dressed in jeans, a shirt of Bill's, and her combat boots, and she looked painfully pretty.

"Did they tell you anything?" she asked nervously, and stepped back so he could come in. She had made the bed herself and after not eating dinner the night before, she hadn't eaten breakfast that morning.

"Yeah," he said noncommittally as he stepped in and looked around. He wanted desperately to avoid this moment.

"Well?" she asked, and he sat down heavily in a chair. The same chair Bill had so often sat in. "What the hell did they tell you?"

What did you say? How did you tell her? He had done this a thousand times before, and suddenly he couldn't do it one more time, he just couldn't do it anymore, or he thought it might kill him. He was thirty-nine years old and he had seen and heard and smelled and written about more death than he ever wanted to see in a hundred lifetimes. He dropped his face into his hands and then looked at her. There was nothing left to do but tell her. "He was killed yesterday, Pax." His voice was a drumbeat in the room and for a minute she thought she was going to faint. And all she could see was Ed Wilson's face when he came to tell her about Peter, and the sound of her heart crashing to the floor and breaking. She sank slowly onto the bed this time and stared at him, refusing to believe it.

"He wasn't."

"He was." Ralph nodded. "He went down into one of the tunnels, and Charlie got him. It was quick. He didn't suffer. The rest doesn't make any difference." And he didn't know if it was true or not, but he felt he owed her that much. He reached out a hand to her from where he sat, but she just sat there staring at him and didn't take it.

"Can I see him?"

He hesitated while he thought about what Tony had said about Bill having his head blown off by Charlie. "I don't think you should. They're sending him home tomorrow."

"Two weeks early," she said, almost without thinking. She was sitting there, staring into space, deathly pale, in his shirt, feeling as though there was nothing left in the world for her. She was nearly twenty-three years old and she had lost the only two men she'd ever loved to this miserable war, and now she felt as though her own life was over.

"I told you this could happen, Pax. You knew it yourself. It's the chance we all take just being here. It could be me this afternoon, or you . . . it was him. It could have been anyone."

"But it wasn't." And then slowly, the tears began to run down her cheeks, and Ralph moved over to the bed and sat next to her and held her in his arms while she cried for what seemed like hours, grief that rolled on relentlessly like thunder.

"I'm sorry . . . I'm so sorry . . ." But she was beyond words, beyond thinking, beyond consolation. She had nothing left. She had nothing. She had lost him. Gone. Like a memory. And all she had left from him was the bracelet he'd given her for Christmas. She looked down at it emptily, and then suddenly she realized that the army would send all his personal effects to Debbie in San Francisco. The books she'd given him, inscribed by her, the trinkets, the photographs they'd taken of each other in Vung Tau, the letters.

"Oh my God . . . they can't do that . . ." Ralph thought she was still grieving for him, but then she explained what she was thinking. "We have to stop them."

"It's happened before, Pax, to other guys. She'll just have to understand that he was in a war zone. He'd been here for a long time. People change."

"But that's not fair. Why should she have to live with that now?" She thought of her mother, when her father had died with the other woman. "And the kids. Can't we stop them?"

"I don't know." He thought about it for a while, and he admired her for thinking like that, but he wasn't sure how to do it. The army was pretty circumspect about sending home a man's effects. They sent home everything right down to his underwear and his postcards, which proved she had good reason to worry.

"Who can we talk to?"

They both thought of the same man at once, and Ralph almost groaned at the thought of him, but Paxton said his name first. "Campobello."

"Jesus. I'm not sure he'd do fuck all for me, Pax."

"Then I'll call . . . no . . . I'll go see him. He must be pretty broken up too." It was a mild understatement, and Ralph didn't want to tell her now that the guy hated her guts and held her responsible for Bill's death.

"Look, why don't you let me take care of it?"

She blew her nose and her voice quavered again when she answered. "I owe it to Bill to do it myself. I'm going to drive out there."

"Shit. I'll come with you." She had no idea what she was walking into, but all his efforts to dissuade her were useless. And the mission of saving Debbie from the knowledge of their affair seemed to have given her new life and slightly better control over her grief, as he drove her to Cu Chi. But when they got there he hadn't been prepared for the shock of running into Campobello almost as soon as they arrived and having him almost attack Paxton physically, while Ralph finally grabbed him by the shoulders and shook him.

"For God's sake, man, stop! Can't you see the state she's already in!"

"She fucking well should be," he shouted, tears streaming down his face, as she stood trembling near the car, trembling uncontrollably at what he'd just told her. It was more of what he'd said to Ralph earlier on the phone, but delivered with even greater venom. "Would you like to see the condition he's in?"

"Please . . ." She sank to her knees as she sobbed and began to retch as Campobello grew pale and watched her. "Please stop . . . I loved him . . ." And then suddenly, in the place where they stood, with recruits standing in the distance, watching them, only guessing at what it was about, there was silence. Campobello stood trembling and pale in Ralph's hands, and Paxton stood staring up at him with open hatred. "I loved him. Don't you understand that?" she said quietly, and now he was sobbing too.

"So did I. I would have died for him. He saved my life in one of those fucking holes . . . and this time I couldn't help him."

"No one could, man," Ralph said to him, letting go of him then, "no one can help anyone here. It happens or it doesn't. Look at all the guys you know who're so fucking careful they squeak, and they buy it the day before they go home, and the others who're sloppy and drunk all the time and they don't get a scratch. It's destiny. Fate. God. Call it whatever you want. But hating anyone over it isn't going to change it." Campobello knew it too, but that was what was driving him crazy. He wanted someone to blame, someone to take it out on. Too many of his men had died, and now the captain he loved, the man who had saved his life, been his friend, laughed with him, drank with him, been his pal, was gone, and it had to be someone's fault. And he wanted desperately to blame Paxton.

Ralph explained to him quietly what they had come there for, and Campobello looked startled. "Can you help us, man? She's right. That stuff shouldn't go home to his wife." The sergeant looked at her angrily then, the venom coming back to him, but she was back on her feet then, looking shaken but determined.

"You afraid of getting caught? Is that it?" he asked her.

"No." She shook her head. "I'm afraid of hurting her, and their girls. He loved her, too, and them. There's no reason to hurt them. We were talking about getting married. There's no reason now for anyone to know that." And then, although she didn't owe him anything, she told him about her father. "He died with another woman in his plane, and my mother has had to live with that for the rest of her life, and one day my brother told me, and I always wondered why. We all did. In my parents' case, I kind of knew, but it still wasn't right. We didn't need that. Neither do they. It's enough to deal with the fact that he died . . . I'd like my things back."

"Like what?" He looked suspicious of her, and it was clear that he still wanted to hate her.

"Three books of poetry, that I wrote some things in, and a bunch of photographs and letters. The rest won't make any difference." She looked embarrassed then. "I bought him some funny underwear for Christmas, and he had a lock of my hair somewhere. I think those are the only things that would matter."

"Why are you really doing this?" he asked her, walking closer to her now, unable to believe that she had no ulterior motive.

"I told you why. What happened is painful enough for all of us. She doesn't need to know about us." And for an instant, just an instant, he believed she was a good person, and that hurt him even more. It hurt him even more to think that Bill Quinn had really loved her, that maybe he had died for her, or if he hadn't, he might have. They were all tired and confused and over-wrought, and they had all been there too long, Quinn and Campobello, and Ralph, and even Paxton.

"Are you going home after this?" he asked her, almost forgetting that Ralph was there, and tears filled her eyes again as she answered.

"I don't know." She shrugged emptily. "I guess so."

He nodded. "I'll go through his stuff. Wait here."

He did, and was gone for half an hour while she cried and Ralph smoked Ruby Queens, and finally the sergeant came back with a small package.

"I've got the books and the photographs and letters and the underwear. I couldn't find the hair, but it's not there anyway, so it doesn't matter." She wondered if he'd been carrying it when he died, but she didn't say it for fear of enraging Campobello further.

"Thank you," she said softly, trying to control herself, and taking the small package from him. It looked so pathetic now. There was so little left of the enormous love she'd had for him. So little left of their hopes and dreams. Like the towns the army had to burn to smoke out the VC, they left nothing behind them but rubble and ashes.

He stood watching her as they walked back to Ralph's jeep, and then he turned and called out to her. "Hey . . ." He didn't want to say her name and she stopped, looking at him, the man who had hated her so much, who thought she had killed Bill.

"I'm sorry," he said, with his lips trembling. She wasn't sure if he was sorry he had been so hard on her, or sorry Bill was gone, but either way, so was she.

"Me too," she said as she got in the car, and he was still watching them as they left the base and drove back to Saigon.

# CHAPTER 17

∨

"You gotta go home, kid." Ralph was standing in her room at the Caravelle, and she was sitting on her bed again, with a belligerent look on her face this time and her arms crossed. Nixon had been sworn in the week before, and Bill had been dead for a month, and she was a month late going home now. "There's nothing left for you here. Your six months are up. Your paper wants you home. Bill's not coming back. And the Teletypes in my office are gonna drive me fucking crazy. They want you back, Pax. You've been here for seven months. You've got to go now."

"Why? You've been here for years."

"That's different. I'm assigned here, and I have no one to go home to. No one who gives a damn. My parents are dead, I haven't seen my sister in ten years, and I live here with the woman I love who's having my baby. I have reasons to stay, you don't. And you're starting to go nuts here. You're like those guys who've been down in the tunnels too long. Go home, get some air, get some R and R and if you love it here so fucking much, let them send you back or find someone else who will. But if you don't get the hell out now, you're going to do something stupid." She had already gone on two missions with Nigel and Jean-Pierre, and Ralph could tell from the stuff she was writing that she was too overwrought to do herself or anyone else any good. "Get out, before I call them to come and get you." He also knew that she'd stopped watching what she ate and she had dysentery so bad, she'd been running a low-grade fever. And she'd looked awful since Bill died. She was grieving, but she was trying not to let it show. It was like being dead on her feet and not willing to admit it.

"Are you willing to make sense? Can I send you home? Or do I have to call them to come and get you? They will, you know. Your guy in San Francisco is getting pretty freaky. He wants us to call the ambassador and have you expelled if you don't agree to get your ass home."

"Okay, okay, I'll go home. You win."

"Christ." He heaved a sigh of relief. He'd been desperately worried about her. And he had run into Campobello at the PX once, too, and he didn't look so hot either. It had taken a toll on all of them. "Okay, when? Tomorrow sound okay?"

"Why so soon?" She wanted more time. She didn't want to go. Maybe because Bill had died there. Staying in Saigon was like staying with him, in the room they'd shared, near the restaurants they'd gone to.

"Why not?" Ralph answered her. "I'll get you a ticket for tomorrow morning. There's a Freedom Bird out of here sometime before noon. And I want you on it."

"You just want to get rid of me." She smiled through her tears. She hated to leave him, and the people she'd met, and even the noise and the fumes and the craziness of Saigon. In an odd way, she'd come to love it.

"I'm jealous of the shit you write," he teased. "I'm never going to get my Pulitzer, if you stick around here."

"Will you come and see me in San Francisco?" she asked sadly.

"Is that where you're gonna be?" He'd relaxed now that she'd agreed to leave the following morning.

"I guess so. I don't know. I will if they give me a job on the paper."

He smiled admiringly at her. He had come to love her like a kid sister in the past seven months, and he was going to miss her very badly. "They'd be stupid if they didn't give you a job. Lady, you're one hell of a good reporter."

"From you," she said with awe and love in her voice, "that means a lot. Christ, I'm going to miss you. Do you want to have dinner tonight?"

"Sure."

He came alone, he left France at home with An, as he often did. Most of the time he didn't like her hanging out with the other reporters. And tonight he just wanted to be with Paxton.

"You gonna be all right?" he asked her seriously after their second Scotch.

"I guess so," she said, looking into the glass as though it had all the answers. "I don't know." She looked up at him. "Is anyone ever the same again when they leave here?"

"No," he said honestly, "they aren't. Some of them just hide it better. But maybe you haven't been here that long, maybe it hasn't really changed you."

"I think it has." He was afraid of that too. For her sake.

"Maybe you just think that because of Bill," he said hopefully. He'd seen people ruined by Viet Nam. The drugs, the VD, the danger, the disease, the wounds, and the strange things it did to one's spirit. It was so beautiful, and our being there was so wrong. For most people, it was desperately confusing. But he hoped she hadn't been there long enough to be poisoned by it, or to fall so in love with it that she couldn't forget it. "It'll do you good to go home. There is life after immersion foot." He smiled, but she didn't.

"It would do everyone good to go home. Maybe you too one day," she said gently. "God, I'd love to see you there. It's going to be so hard going back. How do you begin to tell people what you've seen here?"

"Does your family know about Bill?" She shook her head. She hadn't told anyone. She'd been waiting to see what he decided to do about Debbie. And maybe he would never have left her after all. That had always been a possibility between them.

"I don't think I'll tell them now. There's no point."

He nodded. There was a lot one could never tell anyone about Saigon.

They stayed up drinking until four o'clock in the morning, and he came back later to take her to the airport. She had the same small tote bag she'd had when she arrived, the same small valise, the same ache in her heart, except now it was considerably bigger. She had lost two men in Viet Nam. And yet, in spite of everything, she had come to love it.

"Do yourself a favor, Pax," he said with a sad smile as they said good-bye. "Forget this place as fast as you can. If you don't, it'll kill you." Some part of her suspected he was right, but another part of her told her not to let go of it. Because she didn't want to.

"Take care of yourself, Ralph." She hugged him tight. "You know, I really love you."

And when he pulled away from her there were tears in his eyes, and the last thing he said to her before she boarded the plane was "I love you too, Delta Delta."

# CHAPTER 18

∨

She landed at Oakland Airport after a seventeen-hour flight, on a plane that had been chartered by World Airways. She had talked to a few returning GIs on the flight, but almost everyone was so exhausted and burned out and scared to be going back that they didn't want to talk to anyone, not even a pretty blonde like Paxxie. They had all hoped and dreamed of this day for so long that now it was terrifying to be going home. And what were they going to say? How did you explain to someone what it felt like killing a man? How did you tell someone what it was like killing a man hand to hand, running a bayonet through his guts, or shooting a sniper in the face who turned out to be a woman. How did you explain the nine-year-old boy who had thrown a hand grenade and killed your friend, and then you rushed into the bushes and dragged him out and killed him? How did you tell them what it was like? Or about the sunsets on the mountains, or the green of Viet Nam, or the sounds and the smells, and the people, the girl who couldn't even say your name, but you knew you loved her. There was nothing any of them could say. So most of them rode home in silence.

And when Paxton got off the plane in a skirt and a blouse, her hair pulled back in a bun, wearing the red sandals that were battered now, it was hard to believe that she was home. This didn't feel like home anymore. Home was Saigon and a room at the Caravelle. Or was it here in the house she had once shared with Peter in Berkeley? Or the Wilsons' home? Or her mother's house in Savannah? It was only when she got off the plane that she realized she didn't have a home anymore, and a young boy standing next to her, looked at her, shook his head, and whispered, "Man, it feels weird to be home from Nam," and she knew what he meant, because she had been there with him.

Ed Wilson had sent a limousine for her, and she rode sedately in the back of it, on her way to the paper. But she wasn't prepared for the reception she got. She felt like a hero in a foreign land, when editors and people she had never met shook her hand and told her what a terrific job she had done in Saigon. She was stunned, and she had no idea what they meant, and there were tears rolling down her cheeks as she thanked them. And then finally, she was alone with Ed Wilson, and he looked long and hard at her and he knew that it had taken a terrible toll on her. She had changed. She had grown thin and gaunt, but more than that, there was something in her eyes now that scared him. Something sad and old and wise. She had seen men die. She had been in battle.

"You've had a rough time," he said without asking her anything, and she tried to smile as she nodded.

"I'm glad I went." And she really meant it. Because of Bill, and Ralph, and herself. And because in an odd way, she'd felt she owed it to Peter, and her country.

"I'd like you to go home and rest for a while, and then come back, Paxton, and write about anything you'd like to. You've done a beautiful job, and we'd like to keep you on, with your own byline." She was touched and pleased and she wanted to do that, but there was still a little tug at her heart when she thought of the column she'd written from Saigon.

"And 'Message from Nam'? Will someone else be taking it on?"

He shook his head and smiled at her, knowing that all journalists were like that. Their columns were their babies. "Nixon is promising to de-escalate the war. And for the time being, I think we can get by getting our reports from Saigon from the AP office there."

"They've got some great people," Paxton said, thinking of Ralph, but Ed Wilson was smiling proudly at her.

"And you were one of them. Paxton," he said honestly, "you surprised the hell out of me. I never knew you had it in you. I thought you'd be back here in a month, horrified at what you'd seen there."

"I was pretty horrified at first, but at least I felt I was doing something useful."

"You certainly were. And for the last few weeks, I never thought we'd get you back to San Francisco." He frowned. "What was the delay anyway?" For a minute, she didn't know what to tell him. *The man I fell in love with was killed . . . another one . . .*

"I . . . you get pretty involved over there. It's not easy to just up and leave."

"I guess it isn't. Well, get a good rest now, and come back here in a few weeks, whenever you feel ready." She wondered how soon that would be, and she looked at her watch, remembering that she still had to get a hotel room. But his office had already taken care of that too. "We booked a suite for you at the Fairmont. Marjorie wanted you to stay at the house, but I thought you'd need the rest, and by now you must be pretty independent." And he'd also told Marjorie that if she was carrying any diseases from Viet Nam, they didn't want that in their guest room.

They had also provided a car and driver for her, and the Wilsons were expecting her for dinner. But by dinnertime it was fifteen hours later for her, and Paxton could hardly keep her eyes open at the table. It was an emotional meeting for all of them, and she felt almost as though they all expected her to tell them why Peter had died, and she had no new answers for them now, only more questions.

Gabby chatted endlessly all through the meal about how cute Marjie was, how active little Peter was, and how wonderful their new house was. They had Fortuny fabric on the walls, Brunschwig wallpaper everywhere, and blue curtains in the bedroom, she explained, and twice during dinner, Paxton was so exhausted and got so confused, she accidentally called her Debbie. It was as though she couldn't cope with it all. It was all too much, and their lives for the past seven months had been just too different from hers. And more than once she had to fight back tears and the urge to tell them she just couldn't stand it. She missed the sounds, the smells, her room at the Caravelle, Peter . . . Bill . . . she felt as though her head were spinning when she left them. And when she got back to the hotel, she lay there awake for hours, feeling vulnerable and tired and shaken. She finally fell asleep as the sun came up, and two hours later the hotel operator woke her up. And she had to get up and shower and change to catch her plane to Savannah.

And there things were even worse. She had brought all the wrong clothes. She had nothing to say to anyone. And she couldn't deal with the Junior League, or her mother's bridge club, or the luncheon given for her by the Daughters of the Civil War. Everyone said they wanted to know about Viet Nam, but they didn't really. They didn't want to know about the stench of death, or the boy from Miami with his arm blown off, or the beggars with no limbs crawling around the terrace of the Continental Palace Hotel at sunset. They didn't want to know about VD, or drugs, or boys dying at the hands of the VC, or how old people and children were being shot. They didn't want to know how it broke your heart, and yet how you came to love it.

And all she could say to anyone was how sorry she was that

she was so tired, so ill, so thin, so totally unable to tell them. What they wanted was a nice clean war movie, with popcorn, no bones, no blood, no shrapnel, no flying flesh that splattered all over you, no boys who were lost, no country that was dying.

Paxton had never felt lonelier than she did in Savannah. And she had never looked worse, and she had never missed Queenie so much. But she knew she couldn't have told Queenie about it either. She had come of age, and she was alone. And she was a stranger. It was impossible to tell anyone, except someone who'd been there. She was out with some friends she was sorry she'd called when she ran into a boy in a bar one night. They began to talk, and finally there was someone she could relate to. They talked about Ben Suc and Cu Chi, and Nha Trang, Bien Hoa, Long Binh, Hue, and Vung Tau where she and Bill had spent their first weekend. It was like a secret language among old friends and it was the only good evening she had during her two weeks in Savannah. They firmly shook hands, and she went home that night feeling a little less lonely.

She had a hard time talking to her mother too. She thought Paxton was still grieving over Peter. But there was so much more than that. If anything, she was grieving for her lost youth, and a country she would never see again, two men she had loved, and a part of herself they had taken with them.

And her brother put it down simply to exhaustion. And finally, with some new clothes that seemed more suitable than her combat boots, which she took with her anyway, in mid-February, Paxton flew back to San Francisco.

And she began working at the *Sun* in earnest. They put her up at a hotel for several weeks until she found a small apartment. And every night she promised herself she would call Gabby, and found she couldn't. She had nothing to say to her, didn't want to see her new house or her new curtains, and somehow now Matt seemed so stuffy and so stilted and they all seemed so artificial. And so totally unimportant. The days when they'd all seemed so close were somehow over. And the people she had come to love since then were gone. There was no one left. And she even hated what she was writing for the paper.

Because of what she'd seen in Viet Nam, they had her covering local political events, and she found it unbelievably boring. And Mr. Wilson urged her to go back at night, if possible, and get her degree at Berkeley. She couldn't imagine doing it, and it all seemed so tiresome, and so incredibly pointless. She was exhausted all the time, and she hated to go home at night. She was twenty-three years old, and she felt as though her life were over, and the only people she could talk to were the people who had been there.

Every now and then she came across someone who had been to Nam, and suddenly they exploded into each other's lives and talked for hours, and then they were gone and everything was silence. And all the while she knew that in Viet Nam people were fighting and winning and losing and dying. And she felt as though she were missing everything because she wasn't there. And until it was over, she didn't want to be anywhere but Saigon. She tried to explain it to the editor one day, and he just smiled and told her what a good job she was doing on her current assignments.

And Paxton kept reading the news of what was happening in Viet Nam, and wondering what Ralph and the others were doing. Why were they still there? Why had she had to come home? What had she done wrong to deserve this?

And contrary to the promises she'd heard, along with the American public, the attacks seemed to be stepping up, the casualties getting even greater.

And by May, after four months at home, she couldn't stand it. Peter had been dead for more than a year by then, and she had gone to the ceremony at his tombstone. But the worst of all was that she felt as dead as he was. At least he and Bill had lived and died, and come and gone, but she was vegetating, writing about things she couldn't care about, and feeling that her life was wasted.

And finally, on the first of June, just before Nixon went to Midway to meet Thieu, to agree to withdraw twenty-five thousand troops from Viet Nam, she made her decision. She walked into Ed Wilson's office feeling better than she had in months, and sure of herself at last. She asked him for her column back, and told him gently that if they wouldn't send her to Saigon again, someone else would.

He was horrified. And for a moment he wondered if the time over there had been too much for her, and she was secretly a little crazy.

"For heaven's sake, why would you want to go back again? My God, Paxton, our boys would do anything to avoid it today." It was a far cry from his earlier position until it cost him his son. "Why would you want to go there?"

"Because I need to be there," she tried desperately to explain, "because I'm useless here. Because no one really understands what's happening there except the people who know it."

"And you understand it so much better?" He sounded skeptical as he listened.

"No, but I've seen it. I know what it's all about. No one has to explain it to me. And I can't sit here talking about people's cars and curtains and babies and barbecues while I know what's happening over there. Mr. Wilson, I *have* to be there." It sounded crazy to him, but she was old enough to make her own decisions and there was no doubt about it, her column had been good for the paper. They'd had a lot of complaints when it stopped, but none of their other people had wanted to go to Saigon.

"How does your family feel about this?"

"I haven't said anything to them yet."

"What if you're killed?" he asked her bluntly.

"Then it was fate," she said quietly, "just like Peter."

272

He nodded. He had come to terms with that in the same way as she had, although he knew Marjorie still hadn't. She was still railing at the Fates over their injustice. And he knew it wasn't fair. But . . . it had happened . . .

"How long do you want to stay in Saigon this time, Paxton?"

"I don't know. . . ." She gave it some thought as she sat there. "A year maybe. Something like that. Actually, I'd rather leave it open-ended." She smiled at him, at ease for the first time in four months. "I'll let you know when I can't stand it anymore. Or when the war is over."

"Paxton." He looked at her long and hard. "Are you sure you want to do this?" and as she nodded, he decided he had to satisfy his own curiosity. He couldn't imagine her wanting to be in Viet Nam again. "Is there someone you're involved with?" She knew what he meant, but she only shook her head.

"Just friends, some other lunatics like me," she said, thinking of Ralph, and the others, "who need to see it through till the bitter end, like I do."

"I hope it ends soon," he said sadly. And then he named a salary which surprised her. "You can stay at the same hotel, or a better one, if there is one. Do anything you want while you're there, Paxton. You have carte blanche." He stood up then and kissed her and she thanked him, and when she left his office, she was beaming.

"Someone got a raise," one of the editors said as she walked by them.

"You bet." She turned with a grin. "They gave me back my column and I'm off to Saigon."

"Shit," the girl said, shaking her head. For the others, it was impossible to understand.

And when she went back to her desk, Paxton composed a telegram to Ralph Johnson at the AP bureau in the Eden Building, Saigon. "Coming home as soon as I can get a flight. Get ready. Love, Delta Delta." She sent the telegram and went home to pack, and call her mother and Gabby. Her mother was appalled, but secretly not surprised. And Gabby cried because her third baby was due any minute. But Paxton had her own life now. And two days later she was on a plane to Saigon.

# CHAPTER 19

⌄

Paxton's arrival at Tan Son Nhut this time felt like a home-coming to her, and she looked around the familiar base with more warmth than she had felt when she went back to Savannah. She felt immediately at home here, and she knew she had done the right thing as a cab drove her down the Tu Do, to the Caravelle, where she'd lived the year before. It was strange to think she'd been gone for five months, and now finally she felt as though she were home again. She'd been numb when she left, but now she felt alive coming back here.

She dropped her bags at the hotel, and directed the driver to take her to the Eden Building in the square, and as they drove past the Marines Statue she smiled. She could hardly wait to see Ralph. And when she walked in he was there, looking harassed and complaining, just returned from covering a combat mission. He had his back to her and he was complaining about the stinking driver they'd had, and she walked up behind him slowly and tapped him on the shoulder. And when he saw her, he broke into a broad grin, and threw his arms around her.

"Delta Delta . . . I don't believe it . . . you crazy bitch! What the hell are you doing here when you could be sitting on your ass in San Francisco?"

"Oh, really, who said so? I've covered every stinking boring event they had, and if I ever have to go to another political meeting, or sit-in, I'm going to puke."

"Welcome back," he said quietly, looking genuinely pleased to see her.

"Thank you." Their eyes met and held. They had been through some rough times, and she owed him everything she knew about Viet Nam.

"Too tired for a drink? When did you get in, by the way?"

"About two hours ago. And no, I'm not. I don't know what the hell time it is for me, but I don't give a damn." She was ecstatic to see him.

"The terrace at the Continental Palace?" he asked, laughing. He still remembered how horrified she'd been by it when she first arrived and Jean-Pierre had taken her there, and she asked Ralph about him as they drove toward the Tu Do again.

"How is he, by the way?"

"Drinking too much, as usual. His wife finally walked out on him. She got sick and tired of waiting for him to come home from the war. But I think he kind of expected it." He glanced at her from time to time as they drove. He was so happy to see her. She was almost like family to him now, and she felt the same way about him.

"How's France?"

"Fine." He sounded strange for a moment. "The baby's due in September." She looked at him long and hard, wondering how he felt about it now. He'd been upset about it at first. He didn't think, given the uncertainties they lived with, that they should have a baby out of wedlock. "I tried to talk her out of it, for the baby's sake. But she wants it desperately, so . . . *voilà*." He shrugged with a smile, in spite of himself. "I guess I'm going to be a father." He still hadn't married her, but he was thinking seriously about it now, with the baby coming, and he was still trying to convince her to get married. "How was it in the States?" He hadn't been back in so long, it was beginning to seem like a foreign country.

"Strange." She was honest with him. "It was really weird at first. I hated it. All the people are so different now, or at least they seemed that way to me. They're all involved in themselves, and no one gives a damn about all this. It's like it doesn't exist, except to the people who've been here. They don't want it to exist, so it doesn't."

"I wondered about that." They had arrived at the Continental Palace by then, and Paxton realized she had forgotten the unbearable heat of Saigon. It was a far cry from chilly San Francisco. But she didn't even mind that now. She was just glad to be here, with the endless noise and the familiar smell of flowers and fruit and gas fumes.

They walked slowly up the stairs and Paxton wondered if they'd run into Nigel. She said as much to Ralph, and for a moment he looked vague and then he looked at her strangely.

"He was killed at Bien Hoa two months ago. Some stupidity. A car blew up . . . it was a small bomb planted by the VC . . . it was a stupid thing, and it killed him." A lot of them died for stupid things, like Peter, and countless others. And even the ones who died in battle, that seemed stupid afterward too . . . like Bill. But she tried not to think about that now and just enjoy being with Ralph.

"That's too bad about Nigel." She was sorry, although she had never really liked him. "Are you working a lot?"

"Too much," he smiled happily, "but I love it. It's going to be fun working together again. How soon do you want to start? I've been saving a trip to Da Nang until I could find someone to go with me."

"I'd love it." She had never been to Da Nang before, and she had always hesitated because of Peter. She was never sure how she'd feel being where he'd been killed. But this time, she was ready.

"Good. I'll set it up. How about if I drag you along with me day after tomorrow?"

"I'll be there." She smiled at him, and then he looked at his watch. He had to get back to France, he didn't like to leave her alone as much now. She hadn't been feeling well lately, and An was a handful.

"Do you want me to take you back to the Caravelle?" he asked as he stood up, but she smiled and shook her head.

"If I can stay awake long enough, I'll walk. And if I'm lazy, I can always catch a pedicab. No problem."

He leaned over and kissed her on the cheek then. "Welcome back. I'm glad you made it."

"So am I." She gave him a warm hug in return. "And give my love to France. I'll see you tomorrow at the Five O'Clock Follies. Are they still on?" She laughed at the thought of it, and all the familiar correspondents she would see again. This really was home now, but that said something about her, too, something a little scary. She was one of them now, no longer a Greenseed. She was one of the hard core, one of the people who belonged here until the war was over.

She waved at Ralph as he left, and closed her eyes as she sipped her drink on the terrace. There was a Green Beret sitting with a Vietnamese girl at the next table. And he was wearing the elite tiger-striped camouflage and red, white, and blue scarf they were all so proud of. Only the Green Berets wore the camouflage mixed with brown, "the Tiger Stripes."

Paxton was drinking a *thom xay,* the pineapple froth she'd become addicted to before, because she knew if she'd had anything alcoholic, she'd have dropped in her tracks, and as she put the drink down and looked up, she had a start. It was like a dream. She had come back, and suddenly all the same familiar faces were there around her. But this part of the dream wasn't quite as easy.

She didn't know what to say at first, she wasn't going to say anything, but he had stopped and he was staring at her and he looked awkward and nervous. It was Bill Quinn's first sergeant, Tony Campobello.

"I thought you left," he said strangely, as though he was confused by the dream too.

"I did," she said hesitantly, wondering if he'd attack her again verbally, and this time Ralph wasn't there to protect her. "I just got back. Today, as a matter of fact."

"Oh." He nodded. "How was it stateside?" He stood there, awkwardly, talking to her, in his uniform, and she wasn't sure what to make of it, but seeing him again reminded her of Bill, and it was painful for her, and for him too. Somehow the three of them were still linked together, even though Bill had been gone for six months now.

"It was strange going home," she told him honestly. "No one really understands there."

"That's what everyone says. We leave here as heroes and when you go home, they treat you like convicts."

"These are strange times," she said quietly, wondering if she should ask him to sit down and join her. He looked nervous and wiry. He wasn't a tall man, but he exuded strength and a quiet force that had always impressed her. And she knew Bill had liked and respected him, although her relationship with him had certainly never been pleasant. "Are you still at Cu Chi?" She didn't know what else to ask him.

"I re-upped," he said, looking half proud, half sheepish, as they all did, "for my fourth tour. Bill always said you had to be crazy to be a tunnel rat, and I guess he was right."

"Or very brave, or both," she said softly, thinking of Bill again, and as she did, her eyes met Tony's, and she didn't say anything, but Tony knew what she was thinking.

"He was something," he said with admiration, and then, looking awkward again, "I owe you an apology."

"No, you don't." She didn't want to go back to that again. It was such a terrible time, she didn't want to think of it . . . when Bill had died, and Ralph had come to tell her . . . she knew she could never go through that again, and she looked up at Tony sadly. "I understand. We were both upset."

"Yeah . . . but you did something pretty special. I thought about it for a long time, and I always wanted to tell you what I thought. It made me realize why he must have loved you. He did, you know." She smiled sadly at the memory, and wondered what had impressed him.

"I loved him too. And I guess you did. That's why we both went a little nuts when . . ."

"Yeah. But when you came back for the stuff you'd given him, so it didn't go back to his wife, I was impressed by that. Most women wouldn't have done that. They would have figured to hell with it, or just let her find out, and figure it didn't matter anymore anyway. Lots of guys have other women over here, but no woman I've ever known has ever come back to get the evidence so his wife didn't have to get it. He would have liked that. Those kids meant the world to him." There were tears in his eyes, and she had to fight back her own again. "And that thing you told me about your father that day . . . you didn't have to tell me that." He took a step closer to her as she set down her empty glass. "I just wanted to tell you how sorry I was. I asked the AP guy about you once, but he said you'd gone back to San Francisco." He stuck his hand out to her. "I'm surprised you'll even speak to me after the things I said to you."

"We were all under a lot of pressure. But thank you, Tony." She shook his hand then, and it was cool and firm and strong, just the way he looked, and his dark eyes bore into hers like bullets. "Thank you." She was beginning to understand why Bill liked him. He was straightforward and sincere, even if he did have one hell of a temper. "Do you want to sit down?" She motioned to the chair Ralph had vacated earlier, but Tony shook his head, he still felt ill at ease with her.

"No, I'm okay. I have to meet someone in a few minutes."
His eyes seemed to take her in and ask ten thousand questions.
"What made you come back to Saigon?"

She smiled at him. "I re-upped. Second tour." And he
laughed.

"You've got guts. Most people can't wait to get the hell out of
here."

"That's how I felt about San Francisco."

"Is that where you're from?" he asked with obvious curiosity.
Bill Quinn had told him very little about her.

"That's where the paper is that I work for, and where I went
to school for four years, in Berkeley. But I'm from Savannah
before that."

"Shit," he said, looking impressed. "I spent a weekend there
once years ago, after I did basic training in Georgia. Those
people are about as straight as you get. I thought they were
going to run my ass out of town for going dancing. I'm from
New York. Things are a little livelier up north." She laughed at
his description of Savannah.

"You hit the nail right on the head. That's why I don't live in
Savannah . . . more or less . . . I have a hard time explaining it to my mother."

"She must really be thrilled you're in Saigon," he said, looking wise for his years as she tried to figure out how old he was.
In point of fact, Tony was thirty.

"Not exactly," Paxton admitted, referring to her mother,
"but she didn't have much choice. I just couldn't take it anymore. I had to get out of San Francisco, and come back to Viet
Nam."

"Why?" In some ways, he couldn't understand it. She was a
pretty girl, she was young, she obviously had a good job and she
was smart, she could have gone anywhere other than Viet Nam.
What the hell was she here for?

"I don't know yet," she answered him honestly. "I haven't

figured it out. Unfinished business, I guess, I just knew I belonged here. I couldn't stand the trivia at home anymore. The new cars, the old jobs, the new curtains people talk about, while people are being killed by the VC," as they both knew only too well. "I just couldn't stand it."

He touched his forehead in what she thought was a salute. "Where I come from, they call it *pazza.* Crazy. Nuts." He made a very New York face and she laughed, and then she stood up. She was getting tired. There was a nine-hour time difference for her and all of a sudden she could hardly see straight. "You look bushed," he said as she got up, almost weaving.

"I am. I just got in."

He was watching her, as though trying to decide something about her, and she was trying not to let him make her nervous. She kept thinking of when he'd been screaming at her six months before, and how much he'd hated her then, and all the time she went out with Bill, but that was all over now and there was no point thinking about it anymore. And he seemed to want to make some kind of truce with her. There was no point having a vendetta with anyone. And she knew Bill would have liked them to be friends, even if the sergeant was a little strange, she was willing to overlook it. Not strange so much as intense, and occasionally very nervous. But in Saigon, who wasn't?

"Can I give you a lift to your hotel? I have a stolen jeep outside. I picked it up at the airport," he said coolly, and she laughed.

"That's reassuring. Actually, I was going to walk." But thinking about it now exhausted her. "Would you mind?" He shook his head. "I'm at the Caravelle, just down the street."

"That's a nice place," he said by way of conversation. "I had dinner at the penthouse once. The food is very fresh." And he laughed when she looked at him strangely after he made the comment. "I know. That sounds ridiculous. My family are wholesale grocers. All my life I've been hearing about whether or not the vegetables are fresh, every place we eat. I hated hearing it as a kid, fuck the vegetables, I used to think. Then I discovered when I grew up, it's a family curse, it becomes an obsession." She was laughing with him, and she was so tired, she almost wanted to be friends. It was so strange to come back and run into him again, and to be chatting with him after all his hostility and anger the whole time she went out with Bill. Maybe he'd just been jealous. She'd been told that some noncoms got strangely possessive about their captains.

"I'll remember that, about the vegetables, if I have dinner there again." She smiled tiredly at him.

"You do that." They had pulled up in front of the Caravelle by then, and he helped her get out. "Christ, you're half asleep." She could hardly keep her eyes open. "You gonna be all right?"

"As long as I make it to my bed, I'll be fine. Thanks for the ride, Sergeant."

"Anytime, Miss Andrews." He saluted her smartly, and she remembered thinking that she was surprised he remembered her name after all this time. And then she picked her bags up at the desk, walked into her room, and collapsed on the bed with her clothes on, and it was twenty hours later when she woke up with the afternoon sun streaming in through the windows. And she could remember talking to the sergeant on the terrace the night before. And for a minute, as she lay there, she thought she must have been dreaming.

# CHAPTER 20

$\vee$

Paxton stayed awake for two hours, unpacked her things, bathed, went downstairs to eat, and then went back to bed and slept until morning. Ralph had left a note for her at the desk, telling her he'd pick her up downstairs at seven the next morning. And the next day, at six, she smiled as she watched the sun come up. It was beautiful and hot as hell as she put on fatigues and a khaki undershirt and laced up her boots. They were the same ones Ralph had given her when she first arrived in Saigon a year earlier. She didn't feel afraid to be here this time. Somehow everything felt right now. And as she walked downstairs she looked totally at ease in her own skin, and confident that she knew what she was doing.

As usual, Ralph was on time, and he had Bertie, an old British photographer with him, a terrific guy Paxton had worked with and liked. He cracked bad jokes as they drove out of town, and Paxton smiled as she looked at Ralph and poured herself a cup of coffee from the thermos. The sun was well up by then, and the streets were almost steaming, and there was still the same pervasive smell of fuel and flowers and fruit everywhere, the same smoke that seemed to hang low over them, and the same green on the hills as they left the city, the same red earth that made you want to reach out and press it through your fingers . . . the same beggars, the same orphans, the same wounded and maimed. The same country she had come to love so much, she could no longer leave it. Ralph had left a message at the hotel the night before that his assignment to Da Nang had been changed, but he wanted to pick her up at the same time the next morning to go to a different location.

"Do you realize I don't even know where we're going today?" Paxton said. "Talk about trusting. So what are we doing?" she asked Ralph, as the photographer chatted with their driver.

Ralph had wondered about the wisdom of taking her, and he'd wanted to call it off late the night before, but by then it had been too late to call her. He'd meant to give her a choice before they left, but then in the excitement of going out on a story with her, he'd forgotten to tell her.

"We're going to Cu Chi today." He glanced at his watch, nervously. "But listen . . . it's no sweat, if you want we'll turn back. You don't have to come on this one. The stupid thing is, I haven't even been here for six months. And now suddenly yesterday, they came up with a hot story." The last time they had been there had been anything but easy. And if that lunatic was still around . . . "I feel bad about this, Pax," he started to explain. "I should have just canceled you out of it, when they switched me from Da Nang to Cu Chi."

"No, you shouldn't. Maybe I need to face this."

"Do you want to go back to town, Pax?" he asked gently.

She shook her head silently and for a long time she stared out the window. Bill had been dead for six months, Peter for fifteen. That was just the way it was here. You couldn't stay away from the places where they'd gotten hurt or out of the places they'd been. There were too many painful memories. Peter had been killed in Da Nang, Bill at Cu Chi. She couldn't hide from them forever. You just had to keep on going, go on living.

"I'll be okay," she said quietly. She remembered all too clearly the last time they'd been there, to pick up the letters she'd written him, the day before they sent his body back to Debbie in San Francisco. And that reminded her of running into Tony Campobello on the terrace. She took a deep breath and another swig of the black coffee and looked at Ralph again. "You'll never believe who I ran into yesterday, on the terrace of the Continental Palace after you left."

"Ho Chi Minh," he said easily. He was so damn happy that Paxton was back in Saigon and covering a story with him. As much as he had wanted her to leave Saigon for her own sake, he was thrilled she'd chosen to return. And he could see for himself that the time in the States had done her good, and she was ready to do her job again, the job they all loved so passionately and couldn't leave till the war in Viet Nam was over.

"I saw Tony Campobello," she filled in for him. "You know, Bill's first sergeant." She was able to talk about Bill again. For five months in the States she hadn't talked about him to anyone, because no one knew him.

"That lunatic? What did he do? Throw his drink in your face?" He remembered all too well their final meeting in Cu Chi, and it had been anything but pleasant, as he shouted at her, and Paxton grieved for Bill, and clutched the small bundle of letters.

"Actually, you won't believe this," she said with a look of disbelief herself, "he was almost pleasant. Kind of uptight and nervous, but he . . ." She hesitated, thinking back to the last time she'd seen him six months before. ". . . he apologized for the last time we saw him."

Ralph looked at her long and hard for a moment before he answered. "There's a change. I thought the son of a bitch was going to try to kill you. I'd have kicked his ass if he tried anything, but for a while there I thought the bastard had slipped his moorings."

She stared out the window as she thought about it. "I think we all did." But there had been nothing crazy about her. She had just been heartbroken over losing Bill. It was Campobello who'd been out of order. But they were all like that, the tunnel rats, Ralph commented, they lived too much on edge, with too goddamn much stress and too much danger. And eventually, it happened to all of them. They snapped. And who could blame them?

They arrived at the base, and came through the main gate, and Ralph told them he wanted to see the new commander of the 25th, and Paxton followed him inside. He was a pleasant man, and he explained that they had recently uncovered an entire new network of tunnels. There had been an arsenal of bombs, living quarters, "offices." They hadn't known it, but once again the men at Cu Chi had been living over an entire subterranean village. He showed them photographs and diagrams, and then called on an aide to show them around, and he invited them to come back and see him again if they had any further questions. And he looked appreciatively at Paxton when he said it. He didn't know who she was when they met, but he knew she was one hell of a pretty girl in combat gear or not, and he thought Ralph was pretty damn lucky.

They drove out to the back of the base after that, and Paxton felt her heart ache as she looked around at the place where Bill had lived and worked. Coming here was turning out to be very painful. And Ralph could see it on her face as they drove to the same place they had gone with Bill, and Ralph was suddenly sorry he had brought her.

"I'm sorry, Pax. I shouldn't have done this to you. I just wasn't thinking."

"It's okay." She patted his arm, and readjusted her backpack. She kept some notes in it, and a few things, like her canteen and a first aid kit. Like the troops, she still carried her suntan cream and her insect repellent in her helmet. "I'm fine," she said, but she was lying, as they got out of the jeep again. She was sad, and she was thinking of him as she suddenly collided with someone who almost knocked her off her feet and then caught her before she fell.

"Shit . . ." the voice said as she stumbled in midair, and then he caught her. And as she turned, she saw that it was Tony Campobello.

"Hi," she said shyly, trying to regain her composure. Ralph was already talking to someone else, and the photographer was reloading his camera.

"I didn't mean to knock you down just now . . . sorry . . ." And then, with a slow smile that lit his dark eyes like embers, "I seem to be saying that to you a lot these days. You get home okay the other night? You looked so tired, I thought you weren't going to make it." His New York accent was familiar to her now, and she could almost see why Bill had liked him. He was nervous and tense, but he was also smart, and quick, and sharp, and he cared intensely about the people around him, and everything that happened to them.

"I slept for about twenty hours after I left you," she explained. "I didn't even bother to take my clothes off."

"That's about how you looked." He smiled, watching the pain in her eyes. It was rough for her coming back here and he knew it. It was hard for him too. Everywhere he went, he was reminded of the men he had loved and lost. There were ghosts everywhere for him, and for most of them if they stayed in Nam for long enough. There were good memories, too, but there were so many sad ones.

"How are the vegetables here today?" She smiled back at him, lightening the moment. A look had passed between them that said they both missed Bill, and for a crazy instant she wanted to reach out and touch him.

"Pretty fresh," he laughed, and was surprised that she'd remembered the details of their conversation, and then he sobered again. "So are the snipers. We've got to look out to the east. We've been getting some pretty lively action. One of my boys

288

got hit in the arm a few hours ago. Nothing much, fortunately, he was pretty lucky. We've been keeping down ever since then. Keep well back when you go out to look at the tunnels." He had heard why they were there, and his CO had told him to give them every cooperation.

"I'll watch it, thanks." And with that, Ralph turned to her with a look of irritation. The heat was getting to him, and he wasn't pleased to hear that the VC were so tight in that day. He hadn't wanted to drag her out on a difficult mission. He had just wanted to start her off again with some new information.

"You with me, Delta Delta, or you gonna talk all day?"

"Keep your shirt on, I'm coming."

"Keep your ass down. Charlie's out there."

"So I've been told." She glanced at Tony, and then went off with Ralph. She was introduced to the lieutenant who had taken Bill's place, and felt a tug at her heart again, but she tried to concentrate on what they were doing. Ralph explained about the shots he wanted the photographer to get, and told Paxton the angle of his story, and all around them there were men, and there was activity as people came and went, and some of them went out into the brush to tangle with the VC they knew were out there.

"Christ, you'd think when they turned the Iron Triangle into a parking lot just across the river that that would have done it," Ralph muttered to one of the men, but the guy only shrugged. He already knew there was no way to stop them.

"There's no way you can get rid of these guys. You can burn 'em, you can dig 'em out, you can kill the little fuckers, but Charlie keeps on coming. They just got bokoo boys to send down here to see us."

"Yeah." Ralph nodded, and Paxton crouched as she followed Bertie into some tall grass beyond the clearing. He wanted to get some shots of the exchange with the sniper before he went back to look at the tunnel, and for some reason, Paxton followed him, sensing that she was hot on the tail of a story. Ralph was doing something else by then, and there were half a dozen troops all around them, and a point man out front trying to see what he could find. And as Paxton knelt in the brush, a radio man came up behind her.

"Lady, you okay?"

"I'm fine."

"You sure you're supposed to be out here?"

"I didn't know they had special seats for the press." But as she said the words, a burst of fire whistled past her. Without saying another word, she and the radio operator dropped flat on the ground, his arms covering hers, their helmets touching as they ate the dust they lay in. "Come to think of it," she said softly as they waited, "maybe they should have special seats. That was close."

It reminded her of the time Bill had saved her from the grenade in almost the same location. But the bullets had been closer than they knew. As they got to their knees again, the RTO saw that Bertie had been shot clean through the heart and was lying beside them. "Oh fuck . . ." He checked for a pulse and there was none, as fresh fire erupted nearby, and a dozen GIs ran past them waving their M-16's and opening fire at what they thought were two more snipers. "Get your ass out of here," the RTO shouted at Paxton, "go back." But as she moved, they opened fire on them again from a different angle, and he lay on top of her as he frantically called for help. There were more than two snipers out there. "Mother Goose . . . Mother Goose . . . this is Peter Pan . . . come in . . . we're out in the clearing and they're taking pot shots at us, I've got one visitor down, and a Delta Delta on my hands out here . . . draw them off and I'll bring her in. . . ."

"We read you, Peter Pan . . . this is Mother Goose. . . ." It was the operator at the base, and they would instruct some of the troops to try to draw off the snipers, but it wasn't going to be easy.

"We've got two choices," the RTO explained as he almost smothered Paxton. "We can run like hell, back the way we came, or we can go ahead into the trees, which is shorter." But it was also where the snipers were, and a lot more dangerous for them, and he didn't know what the hell to do with Paxton. He was a boy about her own age, from Maine, and the last thing he wanted was to get her killed and have to bear the blame for making the wrong move in the heat of the moment.

"I vote for the trees," she said calmly as another round exploded near her knees. "In fact"—she pulled away from him and rolled over—"I think we ought to move fast." And as she said it, she lunged ahead, and he followed and as they ran, the spot where they had been lying took a direct hit from a grenade. The VC were definitely not kidding. She didn't even think as she ran. And as they approached the trees, she dove into them and lay on the ground, panting, as the RTO slid in beside her, and at that exact moment the M-60 opened fire, and beyond it there was a huge explosion.

"There goes the pig," the RTO explained, and then made contact with the base again.

"This is Mother Goose," the base answered. "Peter Pan, where the hell is your Delta Delta?"

"I got her." He smiled at Paxton, and she wanted to laugh. It was crazy. The VC were trying to kill her, and her own people were still calling her a Doughnut Dollie.

"Any injuries?" The voice at the other end sounded worried.

"She looks fine." As best he could, the RTO looked her over and confirmed it. "Can you get us out of here?"

"We're trying. There are more of them than we thought." There always were, and at Cu Chi they always seemed to infiltrate in numbers. They knew the old tunnel system too well, and the recent discovery of the new network proved that there were always more. Somehow, no matter what you did, Charlie was always one step ahead, and he always seemed to be winning. "We should have you out of there in a few minutes, Peter Pan. Just sit tight." There was another round of fire, and Mother Goose announced that one of the snipers was wounded and had been captured. The RTO told Paxton to stay where she was, he was going to go up front and see if he could help them.

"I'll be right back." But as soon as he left she heard shots behind her, and she didn't know which way to move. There seemed to be no choice, except to follow the RTO, and suddenly before she knew it she was in the midst of the fire again, and there was a boy lying on the ground beside her. His whole back had been blown open and his head was thrown back, and as Paxton looked, she saw that it was the boy from Maine, with his radio beside him. She was sure he was dead as she approached, but as she lay next to him, she saw that he was still breathing. He was unconscious, and so were two boys next to him, and then the fighting moved away again. But she could hear the grenades and the M-16's, and the M-60. And without thinking she grabbed the radio from the boy's hands, and did what she had seen him do before, to rouse the base.

"Come in, Mother Goose." She spoke into the mike cautiously.

"I hear you . . . this is Mother Goose . . . who is this?"

She hesitated for only the flicker of an eyelash. "This is Delta Delta. The RTO is badly wounded. I've got two other boys hurt here too."

"Where are you?" Mother Goose sounded panicked.

"I'm not sure. We're in the bushes, and the fighting's not too far from us. There must be more than just snipers out there. Can you get us out?" Her voice sounded strong, but as she held the radio, she could feel her hands shaking. One of the boys had stirred and let out a moan, and she kept telling herself silently not to panic.

"We're trying to get you out, Delta Delta . . . have you got a flare?"

She started to say no, and then remembered that she had one in her backpack. "Yes."

"I want to know exactly where you are, Delta Delta. Just wait a minute. Don't do anything till I tell you." And when he stepped away from the phone, he shouted across the room to anyone who could hear him. "Get me the lieutenant, someone. I've got a woman out there with three wounded guys, and we don't know where the fuck they are, they're out there somewhere in the bushes." The lieutenant came running within seconds, and a few minutes later someone got Ralph, and he came back to the base and stood nervously listening to the radio with the others. They were still trying to draw the sniper fire off out in the brush, but someone had seen more VC by then, and it had become obvious that they were dealing with an NVA unit from somewhere up north.

"Great," the lieutenant groaned. "Just what I needed. Regular army from Hanoi, and a female journalist from San Francisco." He closed his eyes for a minute while he thought, and looked like he was praying.

"Can you get her out of there, Mack?" Ralph looked terrified.

"For chrissake, Ralph, I'm trying. I don't know what the hell we've got up there, and I don't know how she wandered into it. But it's beginning to sound like the whole fucking North Vietnamese Army."

"On the edge of the base like that?" It seemed hard to believe, but nonetheless it had happened. It happened everywhere, they tiptoed right through your midst while you were sleeping. And they slit your throats, or stole your rifles, or didn't. But their presence was no secret today, and where Paxton was lying, she could see the action. They were tossing grenades at each other now, and the M-60 machine gun was in full action.

"This is Mother Goose," the RTO at the base spoke into the phone. "Delta Delta, can you still hear me?"

"I hear you fine, Mother Goose. Could you send a cab please?"

Ralph shook his head, wishing he had never asked her to come to Cu Chi with him on the story.

"We'll have a cab out your way any minute." And almost as he said the words, the fighting seemed to move away from them, and deeper into the brush and away from the base. It was finally working. "How are your wounded?"

She had just checked everyone. One of them was conscious now, and the other two were still breathing. "We're okay," she said to the base, "but barely. Can you make it quick?"

"Give us two more minutes and we'll have a Dustoff out your way. You got your flare?"

"I've got it."

"We'll tell you when, Delta Delta." And in the next five minutes, the fighting moved farther away, and almost at the same moment, she heard the whirring of a chopper, and saw the Dustoff in the distance. "Can you see the cab, Delta Delta?" The voice was calm, and she felt tears sting her eyes when she saw him. It had been quick, but it had been very, very scary. And it reminded her that she was back in Viet Nam. This was not San Francisco or Savannah. People were dying here, and going home without legs or arms, or blind, or deaf or without faces. And for a minute there she had thought they were going to get her. But she didn't have time to think about it now, all she could think about was getting the wounded boys into the chopper.

"I see the cab, Mother Goose," she confirmed.

"Show us your flare, Delta Delta." There was sweat running down Ralph's face as he listened from the control room. Dear God, don't let those assholes kill her. . . .

And in between transmissions to her, the RTO at the base

was talking alternately to the guys in the brush, and the medevac unit.

"We see you, Delta Delta. They're coming in to pick you up." And after that, the men in the control room stood and waited, while Paxton lay where she was, as the helicopter came down, right where Bertie had been killed. She saw them put his body in the chopper and then two men with a stretcher ran into the trees where she lay with the three men who'd been wounded.

"You okay?" They glanced at her as she nodded, and they rapidly put the first man on the stretcher and then ran back for the two others, and then beckoned to her. "Come on, quick . . ." She ran through the enormous dust cloud they had caused, and the wind from their chopper blades, and without saying a word, they dragged her into the chopper and took off, and flew the short distance to the 159th MDHA unit on the base where they had a helipad all set up, and a cluster of nurses and corpsmen waiting.

"This is Mother Goose . . . come in Two One Alpha Bravo, you got her?"

"We got her," the pilot said calmly. "She looks okay. How are they doing downstairs?"

"Fine so far. You've got all their wounded."

"Over and out, Mother Goose. We're coming in now."

Paxton was still clutching the radio to her as they came down, and her whole body had started shaking. The radio still had the RTO's blood on it, but he was doing fine in the hands of the medics. Paxton let them unload the wounded first, and then she thanked the pilot again, and climbed gingerly out of the chopper. And almost as soon as she did, she felt herself grabbed and swung around so hard, her helmet fell off her head, as her golden hair spun around her.

"What the fuck were you doing out there?" She didn't even understand who it was at first. He was shaking her like a child, and for a minute she thought he was going to hit her. "Don't you know you could have been killed? Why the fuck did you go out there? The whole fucking area is restricted!"

"I . . ." And then she saw him, his black eyes blazing at her in fear. It was Tony Campobello.

"Don't you follow rules? Or do you think you're too important for that? You could have gotten yourself killed, and everyone with you!" But all of a sudden she couldn't take any more, and she wasn't going to take it from him. She'd been through this before, and he wasn't going to make her feel guilty again. It hadn't been her fault this time, and maybe it wasn't her fault when Bill died either.

"Don't give me that shit!" she shouted back at him, her green eyes blazing into his like M-16 rifles. "I didn't do anything! And no one got hurt because of me! You've got the whole goddamn NVA out there, mister. And if you guys aren't smart enough to keep them out of your own goddamn base, don't yell at me! All I did was walk ten feet past where I was supposed to be, and I got shot at!"

"What the fuck do you expect out here? Ladies serving tea? This is a goddamn war zone!" The two of them were standing there screaming at each other, and the wounded were long gone, and the chopper had taken off again, and they were still screaming, and the men around them figured it was a personal gripe, so they didn't interfere. And it was. It went back a long time, and now the air needed clearing.

But as she shouted at him, her eyes filled with tears suddenly. They were tears of anger and frustration. *"Don't shout at me!"* she railed back at him. "It wasn't my fault those boys got hurt!"

"No, but it could have been!" he shouted back as Ralph and the lieutenant drove up in a jeep and watched the two yelling and waving their fists, and Ralph groaned in irritation.

Tony backed off when he saw his lieutenant arrive, and Ralph glared at him in totally unconcealed fury.

"You at it again?" he asked with open anger.

But he wasn't afraid to tackle Ralph either. "She could have gotten her ass blown off," he said to him by way of explanation.

"Thank God she didn't," the lieutenant said. He was older than Bill, and he looked shaken by the events of the morning. "Maybe I was a little premature inviting the press in to look at that tunnel." Their photographer was dead, Paxton could have been, and Ralph looked gray as he contemplated what had happened.

Ralph looked at her pointedly as he spoke. "Maybe we need to be a little more careful. What in God's name made you walk out there?"

"I don't know. Bertie said he wanted to get a few quick shots, and I wanted to see what he was doing. I guess I was just following him, and the next thing I knew, someone opened fire on me."

"If you hadn't taken the radio, young lady, you'd still be in there," the lieutenant said with respect. "You kept your head, and you probably saved those boys' lives." She glanced angrily at Tony, still fuming as he said it.

"The sergeant here thinks I tried to kill them."

The lieutenant smiled at what she said. Campobello was one of his best men, although a little hot-blooded.

"I didn't say that," he growled. "I said you almost got yourself killed." . . . and he had accused her of killing Bill . . . but that was another time, another story.

"That's closer to the truth," Ralph said, and as Tony and Paxton got into the jeep with them, still glaring at each other, Ralph talked to the lieutenant about getting Bertie's body back to Saigon. Everyone had loved working with him, and it would be a real loss now that he was gone. Another man gone. Another death. It was hard to live with.

"I'd like to thank your RTO at the base," Paxton said quietly before they left. And the lieutenant introduced her to him. And there were suddenly tears in her eyes when she met him.

"I just wanted to thank you . . ." She didn't know what to say to him. He had saved her life with his transmissions and cool action.

"Anytime, Delta Delta," he drawled. He was also from the South, but she didn't ask from where. "Sorry we got you into a hot spot."

"You got me out of it. That's more important." She knew by then that the other guys were okay. Only their friend Bertie wasn't. And Ralph was very upset about it as they drove back to Saigon.

They hadn't seen Tony again before they left, but Ralph was still furious with him, and he vented some of his frustration by shouting at Paxton. It had been a tough day for all of them, an ugly day in an ugly war, and they hadn't even gotten the story they came for. Ralph said he'd come back another day, but he had to get back to Saigon and report back to the AP and make some arrangements.

"What is it with you? Every time I see you two together, you're screaming at each other like lunatics." He was annoyed at her, or appeared to be. But in truth, he'd been scared to death, and now he was so relieved she was all right that he was angry at her.

"He accused me of trying to kill those guys by being careless."

"You were careless with yourself, which is worse. You're here to write about this war, not get killed to prove a point. And I don't know what his problem is, but I think he's crazy."

"He is." She confirmed it with a venomous glance. She was filthy dirty again, and covered with the RTO's blood. It reminded her of other missions she'd been on, and why she had come back to Saigon. It wasn't that she loved it. But she knew she had an obligation to be here. But an obligation to whom? To herself? To her country? To the paper? Or Ralph? Or Peter? Or Bill? It was an interesting question. And as they drove back to

Saigon, they didn't speak again. It had been a stinking day for both of them. And even for Tony, who had gone for a long walk, fuming to himself, and trying to figure out just exactly what it was he felt for Paxton.

# CHAPTER 21

∨

Ralph was still annoyed with her when he saw her at the AP office the next day, but she took him to lunch, and after a couple of drinks he relented.

"You jerk, I thought you'd had it when you were lying out there in the brush with those guys. I figured they'd pick you off next. I could just see the story."

"So could I," she admitted, drinking a *café sua.* It was strong coffee sweetened with condensed milk from cans, and a year before, she'd thought they were disgusting. Now she loved them.

"Were you scared?" he asked in an undertone, and she smiled.

"Afterwards, I was. Right then, I'm not sure . . . for a minute I started to panic, wondering what would happen if they grabbed me and didn't kill me. That really scared me more." It had already happened more than once, journalists who were taken prisoner, but usually they were released. The North Vietnamese wanted to give them a little propaganda to write about, but there was always the possibility that next time they wouldn't be as friendly. And the stories of torture and beatings at the hands of the Vietnamese were legend. "Right then, all I could really think of was getting those boys out before they died."

Ralph nodded, thinking. "Poor Bertie."

"Was he married?" Paxton didn't know him that well, although she'd always liked him.

"No. He had a girlfriend here. A girl from Cholon, I think. Other than that, I don't think he had anyone. No wife, no kids. I called the embassy for him. They're sending him back to London tomorrow." She nodded, thinking of when Bill had been sent back to Debbie. And then Ralph looked at her, and for a moment he looked very tired. "Don't you get sick of this? The dying, I mean. Sometimes I wonder what it would be like to live in a place where people only die from things like cancer or falling off ski lifts." She smiled, knowing what he meant, although she'd been away from it for a while. But it was still hard. It still hurt you. And yet none of them seemed to be able to leave it. They couldn't go home and leave unfinished business. That was what had happened to her when she'd gone back. It all felt so wrong being home again, because in her heart, she knew it wasn't over.

"Yeah. I get sick of it. We all do."

"It worries me sometimes . . ." he said to her honestly. His third drink had taken a toll on him, which was rare. She didn't see him drunk very often. "I think about France having the baby here. It's a hell of a world to bring up a child in."

"You could go home, with them," Paxton said softly, but she wondered if he could. Maybe he'd been there too long to feel comfortable anywhere else again. There were journalists like that, who had lived in places like Turkey and Algeria and Viet Nam for so long that they could never go back to New York and Chicago and London. She wondered sometimes if he was one of them, or if she was.

"She doesn't want to go home with me. She wants to stay here. She knows what it was like when she was married to the

GI who was An's father. The army treated her like shit, his family hated her. She thinks that if she goes back to the States with me, people will stone her in the street, and you know what, Pax? I'm not all that sure they wouldn't. I'm not all that sure I have a right to take her away from here. And this is one hell of a sad place to grow up in. If we were in the States, there's so much I could do for An. But here, I'm just happy if I can keep him safe and decently fed and out of trouble." An was hardly more than a baby himself, but Paxton knew there were five-year-olds selling heroin on the street. Even though An was nothing like that. France took beautiful care of him, and kept him at home with her. He went to a French Catholic nursery school that had once been very exclusive, and his mother was every inch a lady. But they lived in a dying world, and into that world, they were going to bring their baby.

"How's she feeling, by the way?" Paxton asked.

"Fat," he laughed, "she's cute." And he was excited about the baby. He'd never had a child before, and he was going to be a father at thirty-nine, and despite the cool indifference he tried to portray to his friends, he was very excited.

He went back to the office after that and Paxton went to the Hotel Catinat on the Nguyen Hue for a swim, and then she went back to the Caravelle to write her story. She still hadn't composed her thoughts after what had happened at Cu Chi the day before, and she was lost in thought as she walked across the hotel lobby. She jumped when someone touched her arm, and she looked up in amazement to see Tony.

"I . . ." She didn't know what to say to him, and she wondered if he was going to start shouting at her again. It seemed to be his favorite form of conversation. "What brings you here?"

He blushed crimson as he looked at her this time. It was easier dealing with her when she was wearing an undershirt and combat boots and fatigues, and the remarkable golden hair was hidden in her helmet. But suddenly, here, she looked very beautiful and very womanly, and he felt foolish as he looked at her, and sorry he had come at all, but he'd felt he had to.

"I owe you an apology again." The dark brown eyes looked into her green, and for a moment he seemed almost boyish. "I shouldn't have shouted at you yesterday. I . . . I was scared for you, and relieved that you were okay, and . . . it was hard seeing you there again. It brought back memories." As he said it, his eyes were damp. He still missed Bill Quinn, more than he did a lot of men, but he was sure she did too. And he wasn't someone who could hide his feelings. "It must have been hard for you too."

She nodded, touched by the honesty of what he said. It made it easier for her to talk to him. "I hadn't realized that was where we were going. I just went along for the ride, and the story, and then suddenly there we were, and all I could think of was . . ." Tears filled her eyes and she shook her head and looked away. And then she looked back at him. "Maybe you were right a long time ago. Maybe when your head is too full of someone, you get hurt, or other people do . . ."

"I should never have said that to you. That's not why he died, even if I wanted to blame you. I wanted to blame you because I was so sick and tired of blaming Charlie. Charlie has killed so many good men I knew. And he did it again. It was Bill's fault too," he sighed. "He never should have gone down into that tunnel, and he knew it. But he was one of those people who always takes responsibility. It always had to be him, instead of someone else, and all the other times, he was just lucky. And yesterday, you just walked into it. We had a whole unit of VC just sitting there in our backyard and you walked into it. Someone would have no matter what, and we did pretty good, all things considered. But for a while there, I thought they were going to get you, and thinking about it just made me crazy."

"Thank you," she said with a slow smile, looking at him, "for caring." It was easy not to care anymore. To see so much death that you no longer felt anything for anyone. Because if you did, it would kill you. "I was pretty scared, too, when I thought about it on the way home. When I was out there, with those guys, I didn't have time to think about much before they came and got us."

"It was pretty close," he admitted to her. He and the lieutenant had talked about it afterward, and it could have turned into a pretty ugly story. "It could have gone either way." It made him sick when he thought about it.

"I was lucky. I was just going upstairs to write about it, as a matter of fact."

"Oh." He looked disappointed. "I had to pick up some papers at MacVee, and I thought maybe . . . that is . . . I didn't know . . . you wouldn't want to go somewhere for a cup of coffee?" She hesitated for a minute, not sure what he wanted from her, but the story could wait, and they had both been pretty shaken up by what had happened, maybe it wouldn't hurt anything to go have a cup of coffee and make peace with him. Despite the gruff exterior, she suspected he was harmless.

"Sure. I can write the story later." She followed him outside, and they walked a little way to a sidewalk café on the Tu Do. They had a front-row seat to watch all the chaos and the traffic and the street life, but they both took it for granted.

"Ralph says we shout at each other all the time," she said with a smile, sipping her *thom xay,* and he laughed when she said it.

"Yeah. We do, don't we?" And then he looked sheepish. "I guess it's my fault."

"You could say that." She laughed at him, and he relaxed.

"I can't help it. I have a very Italian temper."

"Oh, that's what it is." She was still laughing. "Ralph says it's because we're both crazy."

"That's possible too." He grinned at her, and she noticed that he had a great smile when he relaxed a little. "You get that way here."

"Is that a diagnosis, or a warning?"

"Maybe both."

Funnily enough, it was easy being with him, in spite of all the anguish they'd been through, and the pain that he had caused her.

"Are you married?" she asked conversationally. He was certainly old enough to be. In the bright sunlight, she guessed his age accurately. He was exactly seven years older than she was. He was thirty.

"No." He shook his head. "I used to be. I got divorced before I came here. In fact . . ." He sighed, and decided to be honest with her. She was that kind of a person. "That's pretty much why I came. My wife and I got married when we were eighteen. We were high school sweethearts. We had a little girl almost right away. You know, like a year later, I mean. We didn't get married because of that," he was careful to explain. "And she died of leukemia. It almost killed us. We just didn't understand. She was two years old, and how could she die? How could God do that to us? You know, stuff like that." He looked away, still pained by the memory as Paxton watched him. "And then we had a little boy." His eyes beamed as he looked up at her. "He's a great kid. Joey. Joe. We named him after my father. And the funny thing is, he looks just like him." He was a million miles away when he talked about his son. And Paxton was touched as she listened. "He's terrific. Anyway," his face clouded as he went on, "when Joey was two, Barbara, that's my wife, tells me she wants a divorce. That's it. After seven years of marriage, five years before that, one kid dead, and little Joey two years old now, it's over, she wants out. I almost died." He looked at Paxton honestly as he said it. "I didn't know if I wanted to kill her or myself."

"What happened? Why? Had she just gotten bored?"

305

"No," he looked at her bitterly, "or maybe the right answer is yes, she was bored with me. Whatever it was. She had fallen in love with my brother. He's two years older than I am, and he was always the star in the family. Tommy the Wonderful. Tommy the Fantastic. Tommy who did so great at school. Me, I worked my ass off with my father, and saved his business. Tommy became an accountant and went to work in the city and then went to law school. Now he's a lawyer. Anyway, she left me, and married him, and I decided to hell with it. Joey thought the world of him, and how do you explain to a kid that your uncle is now your father and your mother is a rotten cheat. And my parents told me not to make a big stink because it would destroy the family." He made a helpless Italian gesture. "So I left and came here. And I haven't been home since. And that's the story." He looked out at the traffic for a minute while she absorbed it.

"And you haven't seen Joey since?" She looked stunned by what he'd told her.

Tony shook his head as he looked at her. "No. What can I say to him? That I hate his mother?"

"Do you?" she asked him honestly.

"I used to. I don't know what I feel anymore. I used to lie in bed at night and get so pissed off I wanted to kill her. So instead I went out and killed Charlie. But the truth is . . . I don't even know if I'm mad at her anymore. Maybe she did the right thing. They've had three more kids, she's happy, Tommy loves her, Joey looks good in his pictures and he's crazy about him. So who's to say they were wrong? And you know, the truth is, sometimes I can't even remember what she looks like."

"It's a funny thing about hate," Paxton said quietly, "that's what happens. You get so busy hating, sometimes you forget how it even started." It had happened in Viet Nam, and other places, other lives.

"You're an interesting woman," he said quietly. "That was

what impressed me after you left. Barbara would never have done a thing like you did for Bill, picking up your letters and stuff so his wife didn't get them. She hit me right in the face with the fact that she was sleeping with my brother. But you came back, you went all the way out there to get those letters you'd written him, so she'd never know and you wouldn't hurt her. And you didn't even know her."

"I did it for him." But for them too. She had done it for the children.

"You loved him a lot, didn't you?" Tony had to ask her.

She nodded. "I did." And then, she had to ask him. "Why did you hate me so much, back then? I mean, at the beginning."

Tony took a deep breath and tried to explain it, to himself as much as to her. "I don't know . . . I think maybe I was afraid of you. That you would distract him and make him careless. I meant that. I've seen that happen to other guys, and they get killed because they're staring gooney-eyed into some broad's picture while they step on a mine and get their heads blown off. But to tell the truth, he wasn't like that. I don't know, maybe it just annoyed me . . . who knows?" He looked very Italian again. "Maybe I was jealous. Life is a lot simpler here sometimes without women." That was true. It was easier for women sometimes without men too. But on the other hand, sometimes it was better with them.

"He thought a lot of you," she told Tony, as a last gift to him from Bill.

"And he loved you very much," Tony told her quietly. "I could see it in his face whenever he talked about you. Do you think he would have left his wife in the end?" he couldn't help asking her. He had wondered about that afterward, and so had Paxton.

"Probably not," she said honestly, stirring her drink. "I don't think he'd really have wanted to leave his kids. It's easy to love someone here, in the heat of the moment. It's easier for all of us here. You don't know if you'll be alive next week. You don't have to worry about if the marriage will work, if you like his job, if he likes your folks, where you want to live. You just have to stay alive long enough to spend a weekend in Vung Tau. In some ways, it's very simple." There was a lot of truth to what she said, and he knew it.

"How long are you here for this time?" he asked, still curious about her. But the more he knew about her, the more he liked her, even though sometimes she drove him into a frenzy. She drove him nuts with her independence, her bravery, her refusal to do what she was told, and yet at the same time she touched his heart with her decency, her warmth, her honesty, her kindness.

"I'm here for as long as I can stand it," she smiled, "and as long as they keep printing my stuff."

"I hear you're good."

"I don't know." She shrugged. "I love writing."

He laughed. "I don't even like writing letters. I write to Joey when I can. But it's hard. It's been so long since I've seen him."

"Don't you think you should go back and see him one of these days?"

"Maybe," he answered her. But the truth was it scared him. "And maybe I should leave him alone. What do I have to give him now? Tommy is doing real good. And since Joey has the same name, everyone thinks he's Tommy's son anyway. What does he need me for?"

"You're still his real father. What does he call you when he writes?"

Tony's voice choked up when he answered. "Dad." And then, after a long pause, "Maybe after this tour, I'll go and see him."

She nodded approvingly. "And what happened to the family business? The vegetables." She smiled and he smiled in answer.

"My father died last year, and my mother sold the business.

She did okay. And Tommy takes care of her too. She split the money between me and Tommy. When I come out, I can do something with it. But I haven't figured that out yet. I used to think I'd go to California and buy a farm . . . or maybe go to the Napa Valley and buy a vineyard. Something like that. I want to do something with the earth . . . the land . . ." His eyes lit up as he said it. ". . . that's the only thing I really like about Viet Nam . . . that rich red earth . . . and that incredible lush green." He smiled at Paxton, feeling a little foolish. "I guess in my heart, I'm still a farmer. Maybe Joey would like to come out and visit if I bought a place like that one day."

"I'm sure he would." And something about him told her he could do it. He was a simple man in his heart, with simple ideals, and decent straightforward values. But he was bright too. He hadn't outsmarted the VC in the tunnels of Cu Chi because he didn't have brains. But she wondered what he was going to do with his life when he went home to the States. It was obvious that, for him, it wasn't going to be easy. And the story about Joey was very touching.

"Have you ever been married, Paxton?" He was curious about her too, and he had just told her his entire life story.

"No, I haven't."

"How old are you?"

"Twenty-three. I came here right after college."

"Why?" She told him about Peter then, and Gabby, and her mother and George. And how alienated she had felt from all of them when she went back after Bill died.

"I don't know what I'd do in the States anymore. And the only thing I do know is that I can't go back yet."

"Be careful," he warned her as he sat back in his chair and inhaled the fumes of Saigon. "This place is addictive. Just like all the GIs you see, hooked on smack, and smoking dope," and there were a lot of them these days, "there are people like us,

309

hooked just as bad in our own way, and they can't detox us."
She knew exactly what he meant, but so far she had no solution.

"I guess we just have to stay till we get it out of our system,"
she said, thinking of Ralph too.

"Yeah," Tony nodded, "or it kills us. There's that too. You
came damn close yesterday." And he didn't like that.

"And you haven't? You must have come close a thousand
times. I'm beginning to think the only thing that makes a difference is luck," and they both knew that was true too. How many
guys bought it the day before their DEROS, the day before they
were due to go home? A lot. It just happened.

"Maybe I'm just lucky." He shrugged. "So far anyway. I
didn't used to think so before I got here." He was referring to
his wife again, and then he pulled a snapshot out of his wallet
and showed a picture of Joey to Paxton. "He was six then, but
he's seven now."

Paxton smiled when she saw the picture. "He looks just like
you."

"Poor kid." Tony laughed. There was a picture of Barbara in
there, too, but he seldom took that out now. And there had
been other women since then. Nurses. Wacs, a couple of times
local girls near Cu Chi. There had been a beautiful girl when
they cleared Ben Suc two years before. But he never gave a
damn about any of them. He had never had what she had had
with Bill or Peter. Not since Barbara. And he could hardly
remember how that felt anymore. All he knew was what he saw
in Bill Quinn's eyes, a kind of light and peace there that for
years now, to Tony, had meant nothing.

They walked slowly back to her hotel on the Tu Do, listening
to the shouting, the bleating horns, the pedicabs race past, the
bicycles with their bells, the screaming and squawking and the
squealing that were Saigon, and when they reached the steps of
the Caravelle, he turned to look at her with serious eyes.

"Thank you for spending the afternoon with me today, Paxton. I'm surprised you did, I've been such an asshole everytime I've seen you." She laughed at his honesty and shook her head.

"Don't be silly."

He wanted to tell her how beautiful she was in case he never saw her again, but he didn't. There was something else he wanted to say to her instead, and as he asked her, he felt strangely nervous. "You wouldn't want to have dinner sometime, would you?"

She looked startled for a minute, and then nodded. She couldn't quite make head or tail of him, but maybe he just needed a friend, and she was willing. "Sure . . . I'd like that . . ."

"I'll call you sometime."

"Thanks, Tony." She shook his hand, and went back upstairs, to write the story of what had happened the day before. But after she wrote it, she sat staring into space for a long time, thinking of the little boy whose father had left him five years before to come to Viet Nam, and she didn't know why, but without even knowing him, her heart went out to Joey.

# CHAPTER 22

∨

Tony called her the following week when he came to Saigon again, and she was out on a story with Ralph and some other men, but when she came back, she called him at the number he'd left her. He was staying with friends at Tan Son Nhut Base, and he wondered if she wanted to go to dinner and maybe a movie on the base afterward. And she thought it sounded like fun. It had been ages since she'd seen a movie.

He picked her up at seven o'clock, and she'd just had time to shower and wash her hair and change, when he knocked on her door, and they went to Ramuntcho's on the ground floor of the Eden Building for dinner.

It was a good French restaurant, frequented by a lot of GIs, and no one paid any attention to them as they talked, and laughed and joked, and now that they knew each other a little better, the dinner was relaxed and easy. He had a good sense of humor, and much of the time his view of life in the army had her in hysterics.

"So why the hell do you keep reenlisting?" she asked.

"I've got nothing else to do. I did two years of college at night. I speak Spanish fluently. I used to change a diaper pretty good." He had been brilliant at caring for a dying child. "I supposedly have strong powers of leadership, and I've been a tunnel rat for four and a half years. So what's that going to get me? A job in the sewers of New York? What else can I do?"

"What about your farm, or the vineyard in the Napa Valley?"

"There's plenty of time for that. Besides," he confessed, "I hate walking out on unfinished business." Yet he had walked out on his son. But he had been twenty-five years old, and felt completely helpless. "What about you?" he asked her. "What are you going to be when you grow up?"

"Dorothy in *The Wizard of Oz*," she said without a moment's hesitation. "I have a thing about red shoes."

"Now I know why I like you." He grinned. "You're crazy." And then he got serious again. "Do you want to keep working for a newspaper when you go back?"

"I guess so. I always wanted to be a journalist, and actually, I like it a lot."

"You're lucky. It's also a nice clean way to earn a living." And then suddenly they both remembered what had almost happened to her in Cu Chi, and they laughed. "No, I guess I take that back. What have you been up to this week, by the way?" And when she told him, he was impressed by the stories she'd covered. She wasn't afraid to get dirty, get shot at, or see the ugly side of war, and although it frightened him for her, he also respected her for it.

And in the end, they decided to skip the movie. They went to the bar at her hotel instead and talked for hours, about themselves, Viet Nam, Bill, Tony's family, hers, and even Queenie.

"I feel as though I've known you all my life," he said admiringly as he left Paxton that night. There was something so warm and giving about her that it was easy to open up and get to know her.

"So do I," she confessed. "I don't usually do this," but it had done them both good. She had even told him about how awkward she had always felt with her mother. Only that one time, after Peter had died, was there something different between

313

them. Yet when she went back, after she'd been to Viet Nam, she couldn't seem to make contact with her again. They were just too different.

"I haven't had a friend like you since I was a kid," he laughed happily, "you know, the kind of buddy you can say anything to." It had been like that with Barbara when they were kids. But not in a long, long time since then.

"When are you coming back to Saigon?" she asked as they stood in the lobby, and it was after two o'clock, and way after curfew.

"I don't know yet. I'll call you." He seemed to hesitate, and then reached out and touched her shoulder.

And the call came two days later. He had traded time off with someone else, and made the offer of the movie again, and this time they almost made it as far as Tan Son Nhut Base, but someone had blown a car up in the road, and there was an enormous traffic jam, and finally they turned around and went back to Saigon.

"What do you want to do instead? Radio City Music Hall? A nice Broadway play? A hamburger and shake at Schrafft's?"

"Don't," she groaned. "You make me homesick."

"Want to go dancing at the Pink Nightclub?"

"Let's go back to your place and watch TV and eat popcorn," she teased, and now he groaned.

"Screw it. Let's go back to your hotel and talk." And they did it again, and this time, when he left her in the lobby, he pulled her into a dark corner and kissed her. He ran his hands through her hair and touched the satin of the creamy skin on her shoulders, and it almost made him moan, it hurt so much just to think about her. "This is getting difficult," he said in the voice of the Munchkins from *The Wizard of Oz,* readjusting his trousers, and she had to laugh at him.

"You're impossible," she said, kissing him again.

"I'm extremely possible, I promise you. Want to try me?" he whispered into her neck, and she chuckled.

"You're not supposed to make me laugh at a time like this," she whispered to him, and he kissed her hard on the lips.

"Excuse me . . ." And then out of nowhere, ". . . let's go upstairs, Paxxie . . ."

"I'm scared . . ." she whispered back.

"Don't be." But she was. Everyone she had loved had died, and what if it happened to him now? She didn't want to do that to him, or herself, she just couldn't. She tried to explain it to him as they stood there, and he looked down at her gently and pushed the silky blond hair gently back from her shoulders.

"We're not in control of anything, Pax. It's all in the stars, in God's hands. What happens happens . . . it's not your fault what happened to Bill . . . or Peter . . . no matter what I said back then. And what happens to me isn't up to you either. We just have to take what we can while we can get it. And love each other and be there for each other, for as long as we can, and if something happens, then we did the best we could. Paxton, you can't hide for the rest of your life because you're afraid of what will happen to someone."

"But I feel as though I killed them," she said sorrowfully with tears in her eyes, and he hated himself for what he had said to her when he didn't really know her.

"You didn't kill anyone, and you know that . . . you're just scared." He put his arms around her and held her tight. "But, baby, please don't be. I've never loved anyone like I love you . . . don't run away from me . . . please . . ." And then he looked at her as he had never looked at any woman before and said something he had never said to anyone, but it was true, and he dared to say it. "Baby, I need you." They needed each other, and they all needed someone. You couldn't face the brutality of what they were living through without having someone to get you through it.

He walked her up to her room then, thinking about what they had said and holding her close to him, and when they reached her door, he pulled her close to him and kissed her for a long, long time, and when he pulled away again he looked into her eyes with a gentle smile.

"Whatever happens to us, Paxton . . . whatever you decide . . . I'll always love you." And then he walked quickly down the stairs, without turning back, while she watched him.

# CHAPTER 23

$\vee$

The following week, she got a telegram from the Wilsons in San Francisco. Gabby had had another little girl, and mother and baby were doing well. And they had named her Mathilda. Paxton was happy for her, but it all seemed so far away, and so removed from the life Paxton was leading now. And for the rest of that week, the Teletypes were full of reports of an incredible gathering of youth for a concert in a place called Woodstock.

She had been out with Tony again, and they had finally gotten to the movies this time and seen *The Producers,* and they had both loved it. They'd also seen a fantastic special newsreel of the first men walking on the moon a few weeks before, and Tony had tears in his eyes as he watched it. And afterward they'd had milkshakes and hamburgers on the base and talked about their childhoods. Hers in Savannah and his in New York were like night and day and when she had tried to explain the Daughters of the Civil War to him, he refused to believe her.

"Paxton, please . . . don't tell me people still care about things like that. The Civil War? I don't believe it."

And she had told him about other things, her father, and the things she'd done with him, and her beloved Saturday mornings at his office. And he had told her about working for his father every summer in The Bronx, and his family slowly making it, and eventually having a little money. And how hard he had worked, feeling like a man when he was a kid, and how much he had loved it. And how he had felt when his first baby was born, their little girl, and how he had felt when she was sick, and when she died. He had thought it would kill him. And then little Joey coming along after that like a little miracle, but so healthy and so strong, and so different.

"You don't know what it was like." His eyes were alight from the memory of the day Joey was born, although he didn't allow himself to think about it often. "It's the greatest feeling in the world . . . having kids." And then, almost as an afterthought, "You want kids one day, Pax?" There were still a few things he didn't know about her, but not many. Being together in a place like that, you learned things about each other that in most cases, you didn't learn in an entire lifetime.

"I guess so. I've never thought about it much." And then, slowly, she remembered. "No, that's not true." She always wanted to be honest with him. It was just her nature. "I guess with Peter I used to think that eventually I wanted kids . . . with Bill it was different, because I never let myself think that he'd really marry me, so I wouldn't be too disappointed if he didn't. But the funny thing is, I always feel so remote with other people's children."

"It's not the same when they're your own," he reassured her. "It's so different. It's just a miracle, it's hard to explain, and you feel this incredible bond afterwards knowing that that child is a part of you forever."

She looked at him gently then over their milkshakes. "Is that how you feel about Joey, even now?"

He nodded, thinking about it, and then he looked at her. "Yes, it is." There seemed to be no doubt in his mind, in spite of what had happened.

"Then you should go back and see him sometime."

"Yeah, I guess I should," he said hoarsely. And then they

went dancing that night, and eventually they went back to her hotel, and he had his arm around her as he walked her upstairs, and he didn't expect her to ask him in, so when he kissed her good night, he started to leave, and she tugged gently at his sleeve, and when he turned to look at her again, he saw that the door to her room was open. He didn't dare ask her what it meant. He just followed her inside, and closed the door behind him, and pulled her into his arms and kissed her as he hadn't kissed anyone in years, if ever. And she responded to him as she never had to anyone. Everything was different with him. What she thought, what she did, what she felt. He made her feel young again, and old, and incredibly womanly, and totally at ease. It was as though she had been born for him, and had waited all her life for him, and he felt the same way about her, and as they lay in bed afterward, side by side, he said that.

"I've never loved anyone like I love you, Pax. You make me want to pack my bags tonight, and run like hell, with you at my side, till we're home safe and sound forever." But thinking like that was dangerous here and they both knew it.

He spent the night with her, and several nights after that. And in an odd way, by the end of the summer, it was almost as though they were married. They went everywhere together when he had time off, and she consulted him about things she had never talked to anyone about before, even about the missions she went on with Ralph.

And Tony told her everything, except about his own missions, when he thought they were too dangerous and might scare her.

Ralph even relented about him, and in early September, the four of them went to dinner together. Poor France was enormous by then, and Ralph teased her about the way she looked, but afterward Tony said he thought she looked beautiful, and Paxton was touched. She couldn't imagine being that way, or having a baby inside her. Once, she thought she saw the baby kick, and it fascinated her that France didn't seem to mind it.

"Doesn't that hurt?" she asked Tony later. "Everything looks so enormous and so stretched, it must be awful."

"It isn't awful, it's wonderful. I promise." He kissed her gently again. "Trust me." Neither of them had said anything about marriage, or having each other's children, except they both knew that that was the plan if they ever got out of Viet Nam alive, but that was something they didn't talk about either. Instead they talked about R and R in Bangkok, or buying Christmas presents for Joey. And finally in mid-September he got a five-day leave, and took her to Hong Kong and bought her a ring and put it on her finger without further explanation. It was a ruby band with a ruby and diamond heart in the center and Paxton loved it. It said everything. They had a fabulous time in Hong Kong and stayed at the Ambassador Hotel, like the other GIs and their wives and girlfriends.

And when they got back, Paxton found out that Ralph was in Da Nang, which she thought was really stupid. The baby was due any day and she had already told him once that she thought he ought to stick around, but he said he couldn't just sit there waiting for her to have the baby. France had a midwife lined up, and a doctor if something went wrong, and he had given her Paxton's phone number and in any case, he was sure he'd be back from Da Nang at least a week before she had the baby.

And Tony and Paxton were in bed at the Caravelle one night sleeping soundly after they'd made love, when the phone rang, and Paxton answered.

"Mmm . . . yes?" She couldn't imagine who it was at that hour. She glanced at the clock in the dark. And it was four o'clock in the morning.

"Paxton?" The voice sounded French, and for a minute Paxton didn't recognize her. "It's France." Oh, my God. She sat up in bed wondering where Ralph was.

"Are you okay?"

"I'm fine. . . ." Paxton could almost see her smiling politely in the darkness. She was the kind of person who never complained, never made things difficult, never wanted to impose. And yet, she was calling Paxton, whom she scarcely knew, at four o'clock in the morning. "I'm terribly sorry," she began politely, and then seemed to lapse into silence while Paxton wondered what was going on. It never dawned on her that the girl was in pain and having contractions. "Ralph is away," she began again, "and I have been unable to reach the midwife . . . and the doctor I was to call in the event that . . ." She suddenly lapsed into silence again and Paxton began to panic.

"France? . . . France! . . . are you there?" She jiggled the button on the phone, thinking it had gone dead, and by then she'd woken Tony.

"What's up?" He raised his head and Paxton started to explain when France began talking again, this time a little more brusquely.

"I cannot reach my doctor, or the midwife . . . and I have An here . . . I am so sorry to disturb you, but perhaps . . . if you could take me to the hospital, and keep An with you until Ralph comes home. . . ." She stopped talking again, and this time Paxton figured out what was going on, while Tony watched her.

"Of course. I'll be right there. But you're sure you're all right? Should I call an ambulance?"

"Oh, no. Of course not," she said politely. "But you will come soon?"

"Right now. And France . . . you're having the baby now?"

"Hopefully not until we reach the hospital. Thank you," she said again, and hung up abruptly. And what Paxton did not know was that she was in excruciating pain and could no longer walk as she set the phone down. She had waited too long, but the pains had come on her very quickly. And in her hotel room

321

at the Caravelle, Paxton was already pulling her clothes on, and Tony had jumped out of bed.

"I'll drive you to Gia Dinh. There shouldn't be too much traffic at this hour," Tony volunteered, already dressing.

"Where's the nearest hospital there?" She was trying to keep her mind straight, but she was terrified. This was much more frightening than being shot at.

"I think it's . . . I don't know. I'll check at the desk on the way out. How did she sound?" He had already climbed into his uniform, and Paxton was wearing a skirt and a blouse and a pair of sandals, and she was brushing her hair when he asked her.

"Weird, actually. She kept lapsing into silence, and I kept thinking the line had gone dead, but it hadn't."

"If my memory serves me correctly, that's the real thing."

Paxton reached for her toothbrush with a smile. "I don't think she'd have called if it wasn't."

It took them twenty minutes to get to Gia Dinh after that, and when they reached the building where Ralph and France lived, Paxton rang the bell to their apartment. There was no answer for the longest time, and Paxton wondered if she had gone on to the hospital without them, but Tony pointed out that there were lights on upstairs so they waited, and then finally she buzzed them in, and they hurried up the stairs, and found her crouched at her front door, with a trail of water behind her. She looked mortified when she saw that Paxton wasn't alone, but Tony acted as though everything was perfectly normal. He let the hugely swollen girl lean on him as he helped her back to her bedroom. She'd been wearing a dressing gown, and under it she was wearing a pink nightgown, and in the room next to theirs, Paxton had glimpsed her little boy, An, peacefully sleeping. She closed his door quietly, and asked France if she had tried to call the doctor again, but she only shook her head and clung to

Tony. She didn't seem to care who was holding her and she wasn't paying any attention to Paxton.

"France, you have to get dressed," Paxton tried to say calmly, but as she said the words, France let out a small scream in spite of herself, and clutched at Tony. He held her gently in his arms and laid her down on the bed again, until the contraction was over.

"France, we have to get you out of here," he said calmly. "I'm going to carry you," he said soothingly, but she started to cry and with a terrible sound, clutched at him again. She was half out of her mind with the pains that had begun just before midnight. And it was five o'clock by then, and suddenly Paxton saw that there was blood in the bed and it scared her. She tried to motion to Tony, but he knew exactly what was going on, much better than Paxton did, as he looked at her calmly. "We're not going anywhere," he said quietly, "get me all the towels you can find, and some newspaper, lots of it." And as he said it, he started untying his shoes, and Paxton wondered if he had gone crazy.

He tried to leave France for just a moment after that, but she wouldn't let him leave her for a moment, and then between the pains she kept murmuring, "Oh I'm so sorry . . . so sorry. . . ." And then she would be racked with pain again as Paxton watched her. She couldn't imagine why Tony had ever thought that beautiful. It looked terrifying and terrible, and intolerably painful.

She came back with all the towels she could find, a pair of fresh sheets, and a stack of newspapers she'd found in the kitchen, and Tony told her to set them down and kneel beside him. And as she did, he got behind France, and held her, and this time when the pain ripped through her, she grabbed wildly for Paxton's hands, and Paxton held her tight, the two women holding hands as France began to push out her baby.

"Oh no . . . Oh no!" she screamed. "The baby's coming!"

"I know it is," Tony told her gently, telling her what to do, as he tied one of the sheets around him like an apron between the pains, and she continued to clutch Paxton's hands, and as she pushed again and again, Paxton cried with her, and then Tony told her to hold France's legs, as he held her shoulders, and she continued to push, and Paxton wanted to run away screaming. She couldn't bear to watch her in such pain. And then suddenly she gave an enormous push, and there was a tiny wail, and all three of them looked at the little red face that had sprung from France's soul, as she looked at it in amazement.

"There you go," Tony said, "now you have to push again, come on . . ." And this time the shoulders came, and Tony gently eased the baby out, holding it gently as the rest of France and Ralph's baby came. It was a little girl, and as Paxton looked at the miracle, she was crying, and for the merest instant, Tony bent and kissed her. France was smiling then. And Paxton watched in amazement while Tony tied the umbilical cord with his shoelaces. "Call an ambulance," he told her, as she looked at France with awe, and the man she loved with total admiration. She wanted to tell him how wonderful he was, but there would be time for that later.

Instead she went to call the ambulance, and before they came, she woke An. They had covered France up by then, and the little boy was pleased and amazed when he saw his baby sister.

"Did she come while Maman was asleep?" he asked, and the others smiled. "Did she wake you up?" he asked his mother. And he was very annoyed that they had to leave in the ambulance, but he was excited to go back to the hotel with Tony, while Paxton rode to the hospital with France and the baby. She was still overwhelmed by all that she had seen that night, the ghastly, searing pain, and then that tiny little face appearing, pushed from her hiding place into the world as her mother cheered her on. And now she lay peacefully sleeping in her mother's arms, and France looked totally content as she lay there.

"I'm sorry I was so much trouble for you," she said apologetically in the ambulance. And Paxton continued to hold her hand, totally in awe of what had happened. This all seemed so unreal to her. War was real. Death had almost become normal. But this miracle of birth, this part of her womanhood, took her by surprise and completely amazed her.

"You were so brave, France," Paxton said. "I'm sorry I wasn't more helpful . . . I had no idea what to do . . ." She thanked God for Tony.

"You were wonderful," France said sleepily, and closed her eyes, still clinging to Paxton's hand. And Paxton stayed with her at the hospital until late that morning. And when she went back to the hotel, Tony was playing with An, and both of them looked extremely happy. Fortunately, Tony was off for two days, so he had been able to stay and wait for Paxton.

"How is she?" Tony asked worriedly. "Everything okay?"

"Everything's great." Paxton smiled almost shyly at him. "The baby is beautiful, and she was nursing happily when I left them." She still couldn't quite believe all she'd seen, but somehow now she felt closer to him.

He looked at her for a long moment without saying anything, feeling it too, and then, still holding An's hand, he put his other arm around Paxton and kissed her. "You were very brave last night." It was a night they would both always remember.

"I've never been so scared in my life . . . my God, Tony . . . how do people do that?"

"It's worth it," he said without a moment's doubt, and she knew the truth of that now. That moment when the baby's head poked out and gave her first cry made it all worthwhile. Paxton knew she could never forget it.

"It really is a miracle, isn't it?" He nodded then, and reached down and put An on his shoulders.

And Ralph came to find them at five o'clock. He had gone home and found her note, and then raced to the hospital to see France and their baby. And in a way, Paxton was sorry for him, because she had seen his baby being born and he hadn't. He was beside himself by the time he got to the hotel, and he insisted on buying them champagne, and finally he left, with An in his arms, having thanked them both, and told them that they were naming the baby after Paxton, more or less. She was going to be Pax Tran Johnson. And Pax seemed an appropriate name for her. It meant "peace" in Latin.

And Paxton was still greatly moved by what she'd seen when they went to bed that night, still full of the thoughts of what had happened.

"I don't know, Tony," she said quietly as they lay in the dark. "I don't know if I'm ready for that." She was still impressed by the pain she'd seen. She still wondered how France had stood it.

But Tony only laughed softly in the darkness as he turned to her and kissed her. "I don't think you have to worry about it for a while. I'd say you've got a few other things to take care of first." Like surviving Viet Nam. They both did.

"You know what I mean. God, for a while there, it looked so awful."

"I think it must get pretty bad," he admitted. "But I don't know, women seem to forget . . . they must . . . or they wouldn't have more babies." It had really made him think seeing France's baby born, about the things that matter in life, the things one had left after a place like Viet Nam, and suddenly he longed for another life than this one. "I'd really love to have kids again," he confessed that night.

"You're good at it," she said sadly, thinking of how he'd been with An. But who knew if they would ever have the chance. Who knew if any of them would be alive to have children. But it was a bond between them, a special moment they had shared, and now held tightly between them.

"I love you, Pax," he whispered in the darkness.

"I love you too," she whispered, and fell asleep in his arms, dreaming of France's baby.

# CHAPTER 24

∨

In October, there was a nationwide moratorium in the States, with a huge demonstration to end the war. And there was another in November. And on November third, Nixon promised to end the war, and the people who listened to him, and believed him, were hopeful.

And on November sixteenth, the nation was rocked by the revelation of what had taken place at My Lai the year before, and suddenly there was a huge outcry in Viet Nam. In the States, Lieutenant Calley was being held, and in Viet Nam, the generals were questioning everyone about it. The responsible people in the military were outraged. And there had been so much cruelty in the Viet Nam war on all sides, that somehow this example of it seemed to drive everyone mad. There were photographs of babies and children who had been shot. And the AP office, like *Time* and CBS, ABC and NBC, were all being rocked by demands for investigative reporting. It kept everyone busy for quite a while, and was the source of some amazing stories. Ralph and Paxton were so busy, they hardly had time to catch their breath, and it was a fight for Paxton to find enough time to spend with Tony.

Tony pulled some strings and made some trades, and they managed to get to Bangkok over Thanksgiving for R and R.

They stayed at the Montien Hotel and spent four of the happiest days Paxton had ever had before they went back to Saigon. She was actually closer to Tony than she had ever been to anyone. They were as much friends as lovers, and seemed to be able to say anything to each other. And on the way back to Viet Nam on the plane, they talked about My Lai and Lieutenant Calley.

"Did you ever meet him?" She was curious about the man, and he was pleased to say he hadn't.

"No, but I've heard stories like that. Unofficially, of course. You get enough scared GIs pissed off at the gooks, and sometimes they get pretty crazy. There are no rules over here, Pax, you know that. And some of the men don't know what to do with that. Their buddies keep getting killed. They see no way out, their best friend just stepped on a mine, they can't take it anymore, and all of a sudden they go nuts and take it out on Charlie." It was pretty much what had happened at My Lai, but it sickened them anyway. The war had been too long, and much too ugly.

She went to the Bob Hope show with Tony at Christmas that year, and it was odd to think that only a year before, she'd gone to Martha Raye's show with Bill. But here a year wasn't the same time it was anywhere else. A year in Viet Nam was a lifetime. They spent a quiet evening afterward at her hotel and she had called her family in Savannah that morning. And the next day they went to visit France and Ralph, and they brought gifts for them and An, and the baby. Little Pax seemed to be thriving in France's care, and it was obvious that Ralph was totally nuts about her. She looked a little bit like Ralph, but like France as well. And he was still trying to convince France to marry him, but so far he hadn't convinced her.

He tried to talk Paxton into going out on a mission with him on New Year's Day, to the Mekong Delta, but she hadn't caught up on her work in days. Tony had to work that day, and she wanted to spend the time writing in her hotel room. And then she and Tony went to China Beach at Da Nang, for two days. When they returned she went to look for Ralph at the AP office, to find out if he'd heard anything about a firebase being overrun near An Loc over New Year's.

No one seemed to know where he was, and she went back again the next day, and by then they knew. And as Paxton walked in, there was total silence. It didn't register at first, and she stopped and checked the Teletypes and then she went back to see if Ralph was in his office, but he wasn't. It was empty, and she could see from the clean coffee cup that he hadn't come in yet. She tried to decide whether or not to wait, and as she glanced at her watch, she suddenly saw them. The others, watching her. They all knew, and everyone was afraid to tell her. They all knew her well, and knew how close she was to Ralph. And then finally, the assistant bureau chief walked slowly toward her. He beckoned to her without saying a word, and with a puzzled frown she followed him into his office.

"What's up? Where's Ralph?" She sounded young and bright, and as always, she was in a hurry. There were some stories she wanted to follow up on that day, and she hoped Ralph would turn up soon, and then he told her. Ralph had been killed on the way back from My Tho, a stupid thing, his jeep had run over a land mine. A "stupid thing" . . . a stupid thing . . . wasn't it always a stupid thing? Was there an intelligent way to die here? By friendly fire or plastic bomb in a restaurant or howitzer or land mine? What was smart about any of it? What difference did it make once it was all over? And as Paxton heard the words, she sat and stared at him, unable to believe what had happened. It couldn't have been. It couldn't happen to Ralph. He had been there for years. He was too smart to be killed, too shrewd, too good, too kind, too careful. And he was thirty-nine years old and he had just had his first baby. Didn't someone know that? Hadn't someone told the guy who'd planted the mine? Not him . . . he has a baby . . . not her . . . someone loves her back home . . . didn't anyone listen to those things? Didn't anyone give a damn? She couldn't understand what had gone wrong, as she got up and left his office without a sound, walked back to her hotel, rented a car, and drove straight to Cu Chi by herself, without thinking twice about the danger. All she wanted was to find Tony and tell him. And when he saw her walking across the base, he thought he had seen a vision. She didn't even have her combat clothes on. She was wearing a pink skirt and blouse and white sandals. And it was only by sheer coincidence that he saw her at all. He was about to leave to take some new recruits out on maneuvers when he saw her. He hopped out of the jeep and told his corporal to cool his heels for a minute, and then he ran across the field and stopped her.

"What are you doing here?" She had scared the hell out of him. For a minute, he thought something was wrong, but then when he saw the way she was dressed, he decided it wasn't. "Who drove you?"

"I did," she answered with a desperate air. She seemed to be glancing around him frantically as though looking for something.

"What's wrong with you, Pax? What's wrong?" Maybe something had happened. She wouldn't look at him, and she seemed so agitated and distracted. He had seen guys like that, right after their buddies were killed, half in shock, and about to go completely berserk. And then suddenly he knew, and he grabbed her. He held her fast against him and forced her to look at him. "Baby, what is it?" He was glad she had come to find him, but he couldn't believe the insanity of her driving out to Cu Chi alone. But she was insane at the moment. And then suddenly she looked at him and started to gulp air. There were great sobs in her throat and they were choking her, and she couldn't breathe as he held her. "Take it easy . . . breathe in slow . . . come on, that's right . . ." Another recruit was watching them and Tony didn't give a damn. All he could think about was Paxton, choking and hyperventilating in his arms. "Tell me what happened . . ."

"Ralph . . ." She could only say the one word for the first few minutes and he felt his guts grow taut.

"It's okay . . . take it slow . . . keep breathing . . ." He lowered her gently to the ground and sat down beside her. "You're okay . . . you're okay, Pax . . ." He'd been through this before, knew it too well, had seen it too often . . . and then she told him.

"He hit a land mine coming back from the Delta two days ago. No one told me." There was a blank look to her face and then suddenly she began to sob and she pummeled his chest in anguish and blind fury. "No . . . dammit . . . no! The fuckers got him! After all this time . . . they got him . . ." He felt sick listening to her, but to him, it was an old, old story.

"Does France know?"

"I don't know yet. I didn't call her."

Shit. With a GI kid, and now a brand-new baby. And what the hell was she going to do in Saigon with two Amerasian brats? Starve? Her parents couldn't help her anymore, they had nothing left, and no one else would help her either. This was just what she needed.

Tony pulled Paxton into his arms again and kissed her gently. "Look, I hate to do this, but I gotta go. I got a whole bunch of guys waiting to go on maneuvers. As soon as we come back in, I'll come back to the hotel. I'll take you out to see her then. And I want someone to drive you back now." She nodded, like an obedient child, barely seeing him, and he ran back to find a private who had nothing to do and told him to drive her back to Saigon.

"Be careful!" she shouted after him as she left, and he waved and was gone with the others. And all the way back to Saigon, she sat stiffly with the boy who drove her. She said not a word, didn't ask his name, or answer any of his questions. She just sat there and stared out the window, thinking about Ralph, and France, and An, and Baby Paxxie.

And when she got back to the hotel, she went to her room, and just lay there. And when the phone rang, she didn't answer it. When he got there at eight o'clock that night, Tony was hysterical, he thought maybe something had happened to her, because the kid he'd sent with her hadn't come back yet. The tension was beginning to wear on everyone. They had all been there too long. And when Tony let himself into her room, he found her where she had been all afternoon, lying on the bed and staring at the ceiling.

"Baby, come on." He lay on the bed next to her and talked to her gently. "Look . . . he knew the score. He knew what could happen. We all do. We take our chances. He was willing to do that."

"He was the best reporter I ever knew . . . the best friend I ever had . . ." she said, sounding like a kid kicking rocks into the riverbed with the toe of her sneaker. And then she looked up at Tony. "Until you . . . but he was special." He was the brother George never had been.

"I know he was. I liked him too. I've liked a lot of guys here. Some of them were lucky and went home okay, some weren't. If he was afraid of this, he'd have gone home a long time ago." She knew that was true, but it still didn't solve all the problems. And God, how she would miss him.

"What about France? What'll happen to her now?"

"That," he said grimly, "is another story." Her future was not going to be easy.

He showered and changed and they decided not to call her before they went, because she was so polite she would insist that everything was fine, even if it wasn't. And they used Tony's jeep to get there.

And just as had happened the night the baby was born, she

didn't answer the bell for a long time, but he could see the lights on. So finally they rang someone else, who yelled at them out the window, but buzzed them in anyway. And when they went up to her door, again there was no answer. They rang for a long time, and inside they could hear music. The radio was on, and the lights, but there was no sound at all, and finally Tony looked worriedly at Paxton.

"I hate to say this, but I get the feeling something's wrong in there. Maybe she's just too upset to see anyone." But the kids were quiet too. "Or maybe I'm wrong and she's out. Do you want to come back later?" But Paxton shook her head slowly, she had a strange feeling too.

"Can we get in?" she whispered.

"You mean break the door down?" He looked nervous. "We could get arrested for that."

"Do you think there's a landlord?"

"Yeah, maybe, and I don't know about you, but my Vietnamese doesn't cover 'excuse me, sir, but could you please let me into this apartment.' Wait, I'll try this," he said, pulling a knife out of his pocket. He played with the lock for a while, and just as he was about to give up, the door suddenly gave, and opened slowly inward. And then they both felt strange. They had wanted to get in, but now that the door was open they weren't sure they should do it. It seemed like such an intrusion.

He stepped in first, and Paxton was right behind him. Neither of them were sure what they were looking for and they both felt stupid as they looked around at how neat and clean and orderly everything was. Everything was obviously very much in order. And the music was still playing softly. The light in An's room was on, and Paxton looked in there first, but he wasn't there, and Tony glanced into the master bedroom, and then he stopped and instinctively put his arm out to stop Paxton.

"Don't!" he said too quickly, but she moved too fast for him, and then she stood there. But nothing seemed to be wrong.

They were only sleeping. France in her *ao dai,* with a gentle smile, and the baby in her arms in a beautiful little dress some-one must have made for her, and little An, looking like an angel beside them. His hair was combed and he had his best suit on. But Paxton hadn't understood yet. She wanted to tell Tony to be quiet so he wouldn't wake them, but nothing would ever wake them again. He knew it as he approached them, and then gently bent to touch their faces. They had been dead for quite a while by then. France had poisoned herself and the children, as soon as she heard about Ralph. There was a note in Vietnamese, and next to it a letter to Paxton. And as he knelt and looked at them, his eyes filled with tears and he began to sob, as Paxton came and stood beside them. She was crying, too, and she knelt down and touched each of them, as though in silent blessing.

"Oh, God, why . . ." she whispered to him . . . "Why? . . ." And An, and the baby. The baby they had deliv-ered only three and a half months before, and now she was dead . . . Pax . . . Peace . . . France had wanted to be with him, the note said in Vietnamese. She had wanted them all to be together again, and she knew how terrible their life would be in Saigon. "She could have gone to the States . . . she could have . . ." Paxton said, but Tony was shaking his head. He knew better. She couldn't have done anything in Saigon without Ralph's protection. So she had gone, to be with him, and had taken her babies with her. And all of them so beautiful, and so sweet . . . so gentle as they lay there.

Paxton and Tony stood there watching them for a long time, and then he went to call the police, and he explained what he believed had happened when they got there, and the note con-firmed it. The letter to Paxton said much the same thing, and she thanked her and Tony again for all they'd done for them, and then she said good-bye, and wished her well and a happy life, and then Paxton put the letter down and sobbed in Tony's arms. She had never seen, or felt, anything so awful. She watched as they took the three of them away. An wrapped in a little white cloth, and the baby bound to her mother. It was more than she could stand, and she was still sobbing as Tony led her away and drove her back to the hotel and ordered them both a brandy.

"Oh, God, Tony, why? Why did she do that?"

"She thought she had to."

Paxton felt a loss like none other she had felt before. A loss mixed with despair and sorrow, and loneliness now that her friend was gone. She wondered if she would ever be the same again. And Tony knew that even though she would seem to be one day, perhaps she really wouldn't. They were all like that now. Pieces of their hearts had fallen away long since, like lepers'.

And it was a long time before she felt even halfway human again. January passed like a blur. February with it. And finally, in March, when the monsoons came, she began slowly to feel human. She had been in Viet Nam, all told, for close to two years by then. And she and Tony had been together for eight months, which, these days, felt like a lifetime. She had a hard time talking about Ralph, or France, or the children. But she could talk about others she'd lost without feeling quite so totally destroyed. But Tony had been right. They were different.

They went out less frequently than they had before, and with the bad weather now, they seldom went away for the weekend even when he had a stand-down. Instead, they tucked themselves into her hotel room and talked and drank and made love, and tried to make some sense of what they were seeing. Her articles seemed stronger now. And the paper had written her a while back and told her she was being considered for an award, but she didn't really care. Those things didn't matter now. All that mattered was staying alive, and the end of the war, and maybe one day going home again, to see what was there, if anything. And now they talked about Joey a lot, and Paxton urged him to write to the boy more often.

Tony's tour was up in June, and he knew he wasn't going to re-up, but he didn't know what else he'd do either. He didn't want another tour in Viet Nam, but he didn't know if he was ready to go home yet. And Paxton had no idea what she was doing. She had told the paper she was staying another year last June, but that wasn't written in stone. She could always have gone home sooner or later. And she and Tony never talked about future plans. It seemed too dangerous to do that now, and both of them were getting superstitious.

But they were happier than they'd ever been, and closer and stronger. The death of Ralph and France and the children had shaken her to her very core and made her reach out and come closer to Tony. And he needed her more now too. The thought of going home frightened him, although he talked about it very little. All they knew, for now, was that they were going to make one more trip to Hong Kong in May, and after that they'd have to figure out what they were doing. And she still wore the ruby ring he'd given her the last time they'd been there, everyday and everywhere. It was her bond to him. A band of rubies and a heart, and it touched him that she always wore it. Like her, he made no promises, no demands, but his heart was hers. Forever.

Three weeks before they were to go to Hong Kong, with the monsoon in full swing, he set out on a mission to an area that was supposedly crawling with VC and had been for weeks. They loved infiltrating during the monsoon, and the grunts hated to go after them in the rains. They hated the constant wet, and had immersion foot from always having their feet wet.

It was hot and sticky and wet and miserable wherever they went, but they still had to go after the VC. So on a Tuesday morning they set out, and walked into a major ambush. Fifteen men were killed almost at once, and nine were wounded. The helicopters hovered but couldn't see a bloody thing, and the spotter planes couldn't take off at all in the weather. A second unit was sent in to help, more boys were killed. And the lieutenant himself took some shrapnel. It was a colossal mess, and it was two days before they could extricate themselves, and retreat back to Cu Chi with their dead, their wounded, and what amounted to tremendous losses. They came back wet and sick and scared and horrified by what they'd been through. And they came back without Tony. He was listed as missing in action.

# CHAPTER 25

∨

The lieutenant came to tell her the news himself at her hotel. But Paxton knew long before he arrived and knocked on her door that something had happened. She had sensed it for two days, and she had barely eaten or slept. She just knew that something was wrong, although she was not sure what yet. And oddly, she had the feeling that he wasn't dead, but maybe wounded. And then the lieutenant appeared at her door, and she backed into the room with a look of horror.

"No . . ." She held up her hand, wanting him to go away again. This couldn't be happening to her again. It couldn't. She wouldn't let it.

"Miss Andrews," he said uncomfortably, standing in the doorway, "I wanted to come and see you myself."

"Where's Tony?"

There was an endless pause as their eyes met and held and he shook his head unhappily. "I'm afraid he's missing in action. I can't tell you anything more than that. No one actually saw him take a hit, or go down . . . but it was a real mess out there. The monsoon, the VC, we were ambushed. We were fed erroneous information and we were attacked. We lost a lot of boys, and I'm afraid Sergeant Campobello just isn't accounted for. We combed the area before we left, and we didn't find his body, but that doesn't mean he's not dead. I just can't tell you more than that right now, except that he's missing in action."

"Could he have been taken prisoner?" The thought of it made her stomach turn over. She knew too many of those horror stories from Viet Cong who talked about the way they treated prisoners, and one GI who had escaped and talked to her several months before. But at least he wouldn't be dead. At least there would be hope. Maybe.

"It's possible." The lieutenant didn't want to raise false hopes. "But not likely. I don't think they were interested in taking prisoners, just in hitting us as hard as they could. And they did," he said sadly, still standing near the doorway, and she didn't invite him in any farther. He was like the angel of death standing there and she didn't want him in her life for another moment.

"Where were you?"

"We went through the Hobo Woods to Trang Bang, and then up to Tay Ninh, pretty close to Cambodia. And that's where we lost him."

She sat down in a chair as she listened, and put her face in her hands, trying to believe he was dead, but somehow she couldn't. She just couldn't go through it again. Not with him. It had been bad enough with the others. But with Tony, she'd had something she'd never had with anyone, a kind of trust, a strange symmetry, a kind of unspoken understanding. They always seemed to understand what the other was thinking. And now she was thinking that he wasn't dead, and she didn't know why, and she didn't know what to say to this man standing in her doorway. All she could do was look up at him and finally she just thanked him for coming to tell her. It would have been worse hearing it from someone else. But this was odd. The other times, she had known they were dead. She could grieve, she could mourn. And if she'd been brave enough, she could have seen them. But there was no question of what had happened.

But now, all they could tell her was that Tony had disappeared in a rainstorm, or something like that. It was crazy. And maybe he'd turn up in the morning. And after the lieutenant left, as she lay in the bed that she and Tony had shared for the past ten months, she had that same feeling that someone was going to come and tell her there'd been a mistake, and he was fine. Only this time she really did believe it.

And she felt like that for days. She couldn't even bring herself to cry, because she refused to believe that he was dead. And she went on moving, like a zombie. She wrote columns, she read Teletypes, she went to the AP office, she wrote a piece about Saigon, she even went on a brief mission. And when she was in town she went to the Five O'Clock Follies. And by now, after two years in Saigon, everyone knew her. She was certainly the prettiest correspondent there, and one of the youngest, and apparently one of the best, as the award they sent her from the State of California was supposed to attest. But she didn't really give a damn, and she brushed it off, as she did everything else, and those who knew her well knew why. Tony was missing, but she had died. In April. And as she went on moving, she could barely function. Everything she cared about was gone. The people she had loved had all left or died and taken the past with them. And without Tony, she had no present and no future. And it was May second when her brother called and told her their mother had died unexpectedly of a complication after a gallbladder operation Paxton hadn't even known about, and he thought she should come home to help Allison with the arrangements. She told him she'd call him back, and that night she drove to Cu Chi and went to see Tony's lieutenant to find out if they'd discovered anything, but they hadn't. No one knew anything more than they had in April. And Tony's family had been officially notified. First Sergeant Anthony Edward Campobello was missing in action.

"What the hell does that mean?" she railed at him, oblivious

341

to his rank or his good intentions. "Do I wait for him here? Do I look for him myself? Do I help you? Do I go home and wait? What the fuck do I do now?" she asked, as tears bulged in her eyes for the first time. She couldn't hide from it anymore. He wasn't coming back, maybe never, and she was beginning to understand that. And then, in a broken voice, "What if he's still wounded out there?"

"I don't think he is," the lieutenant said gently, "Paxton, I think he's gone. I think we just couldn't find him. I'm sorry." He reached over and touched her arm, and she moved away so he couldn't make the pain any worse with his kindness. "You know what I think? I think you should go home. We all have our limits here. All of us. The smarter ones go home when they reach it, the others wait too long. You've done the equivalent of two tours. Don't you think that's enough? Tony was going home in June, and he thought you were too. Why don't you hang it up, and go home now? If we find something, I swear to you, we'll call you." She nodded, and looked at him for a long time, and then she walked out of the room, and she knew that he was right. It was time for her to go home. Maybe for good this time. Without Tony. She had grown up in Viet Nam. She had come here as a girl, heartbroken over the boy she had lost, searching for answers. And she hadn't found them, she had found only questions. She was twenty-four years old, and she had lost three men to this war, four if you counted Ralph, and friends, and colleagues, and even people she didn't give a damn about, like Nigel. And a piece of herself that she knew she would never find again. But she had found something too. She had found a truth, and a country that was dying, a beautiful place that had once been lovely and was slowly being destroyed. But she had seen it before it had disappeared. And she had loved him before he'd gone. And wherever he was, dead or alive, he wasn't missing to her. Like Viet Nam, she knew she would always love him.

# CHAPTER 26

$\vee$

Her last day in Saigon passed like a dream before her eyes, and it was strange how little there really was to do, once she decided that she was leaving. She said good-bye to everyone at the AP office that afternoon, and she could hardly speak when she left, because all she kept thinking about as she walked across the square was Ralph, and France, and the two children. She went to the Five O'Clock Follies for the last time, and then just for the hell of it, she went to the terrace at the Continental Palace Hotel. And the beggars clamoring there no longer frightened her, they just depressed her. She ran into Jean-Pierre and said good-bye to him too. But there was no one she cared about anymore. The people she had loved were gone, for assorted reasons.

She sat down and had a drink with Jean-Pierre, but he was already pretty far gone, and for some reason, he kept talking to her about Nigel. He had been dead for a long time, and she was beginning to wonder if she had stayed, whether she would have wound up like Jean-Pierre, drunk, confused, aimless, bitter. Those who stayed too often did, and yet those who left were never quite the same again either. So who was left? Those who died? Who went unscathed after the time they spent there?

Maybe no one. Maybe that was the conclusion to all this. That no one won. And no one ever would.

"Will you come back?" He looked at her, almost sober for an instant between drinks, and she shook her head, and this time she knew she really meant it. No matter how difficult it was going to be going back, the answers were no longer here for her, nor were the questions. She had to go home and make a life of it now. And a part of her knew that she would continue prodding them about Tony. But maybe she could do it more effectively from there. There were other people in the States who cared about the men they'd lost, either as prisoners of war, or missing in action. "I should go home one of these days too," Jean-Pierre added, almost as an afterthought. But like her, he had nothing to go home to. The people she had loved had died there, except for Tony, and for now, he was gone too, or perhaps forever. And even in the States, nothing would be the same. Her mother was gone. And there was nothing to hold her to Savannah any longer.

She said good-bye to him then, and walked down the Tu Do to her hotel, and she felt a terrible tug at her heart at the sounds and the smells, and she laughed as she looked into the square and saw a GI trying to teach a bunch of street urchins how to play softball. There were softball games at Tan Son Nhut all the time, and she had gone a couple of times with Bill, but Tony had never really liked them. He was too nervous, too quick, he wanted to talk and think and argue and philosophize, he didn't want to sit around watching people play baseball. And he had taught her so much while they were here. About life, and people, and war, and doing what she had to do the best she could, but that was part of her too. She kept remembering things he had said to her . . . ideas they had shared . . . and the night they had delivered France's baby. And it all seemed like a dream now.

She walked through the lobby of the Caravelle, remembering

when he'd first come to see her there, how ill at ease they had been after their difficult beginnings. And how happy they had been in the end . . . how sweet the time in Hong Kong had been. She still wore the ruby ring with the heart, and she always would. Just as she still wore Bill's bracelet. And kept Peter's dog tags locked away with her papers. Just as others wore locks of hair, or pieces of string, or carried a tiny piece of someone's uniform or wore MIA bracelets with people's names. They were all relics of a time that had hurt so much and yet had brought them love, a time that had cost so much, and was not yet over.

There were ghosts around her everywhere as she packed her bags and put her books away. She was leaving them for a few friends. She was taking precious little with her, except for the memories, which no one could ever take away. And the next morning she took a cab to Tan Son Nhut Base, and waited with the others to go home again. There were Vietnamese girls crying for their GIs, and big, strapping, healthy-looking boys who could hardly wait to get on the plane, and a handful of wounded. But they were the easy ones, because you could see their wounds, a bandaged hand, a missing arm, a brand-new pair of crutches. The others who went back unmarked were more complicated. The wounds were there, like Paxton's, you just couldn't see them.

They circled once over Saigon, and she caught her breath as she looked down. *"Chao ong,"* she whispered as they headed home. So long . . . good-bye, Viet Nam . . . good-bye . . . I really loved you . . . and she could almost feel Tony sitting beside her as she closed her eyes. She felt like a traitor leaving him there, except that they kept insisting he was gone, and she had to make herself believe them.

And she had no choice now anyway. She had to go home for her mother's funeral. But it was strange. She didn't feel anything, for anyone. She felt absolutely nothing, except a rock in her heart that had once been the place where she'd loved Tony. She knew she still loved him, she always would, but he had taken a piece of him with her, they all had.

They flew from Saigon to Midway and from there to San Francisco. But she didn't call the paper or the Wilsons. They knew she was going home. But she had to change planes and go on to Savannah, and in a few days she would fly back to San Francisco to decide what she was going to do about her job on the paper. But "Message from Nam" had been written and closed, and now it was over forever.

It was four o'clock in the afternoon when she landed at Travis Field in Savannah, and she picked up her bags and hailed a cab, and gave the driver the address of the house she had grown up in. She still had her key, and there was no one there when she arrived. The new girl had been off since her mother died, there was no reason now for her to be there. And she called George almost as soon as she got in, and sat down with a groan of exhaustion in the familiar kitchen. There was nothing in the fridge, and surprisingly very little in the cupboards. But Paxton didn't care. She didn't care about anything. And coming back here turned out to be more painful than she had expected. Being there was a reminder of what had been and was no more, and some things that never had been.

She showered and changed and went to the funeral parlor downtown to meet George, and as she stood there, looking down at her mother, she felt absolutely nothing except pity. Pity for the unhappy woman she had been, unable to give love for most of her life, or receive it. At least her father had lived, and loved her so deeply, and maybe others as well. And Queenie had given everything she had to give . . . and Ralph had led a full life . . . and even France . . . and Peter and Bill . . . and Tony . . . but this woman had never done anything except go to her clubs and now it was all over.

"You look tired," George whispered to her. He was wearing a

dark suit, and Paxton noticed that there was a little gray in his hair, which made him look very distinguished.

"I've just been traveling for twenty-six hours." She looked at him ruefully. He was so much like her mother. He had barely kissed her hello, barely embraced her, never asked her how she was, and after all that she'd been through, he was surprised that she looked tired.

"You seem thinner."

She smiled at him. "I probably am. Things in Viet Nam can be a little dicey." Land mines, snipers, suicides, guys going missing in action, you know, just like downtown Savannah, she thought. They were speaking quietly near their mother's casket. "How are Allison and the kids?" They had had a second baby while she was gone, and Paxton felt totally distant from it.

"Fine. She'd have come tonight, but the kids are sick." It didn't matter. Her mother would never know the difference.

People came to pay their respects that night, mostly from the Daughters of the Civil War. And the next day, they held the funeral at St. John's Episcopal Church, with pomp and ceremony, and her pallbearers were the husbands of her friends. It was respectable and appropriate, and everything her mother would have wanted. And afterward, all Paxton wanted to do was get out of town. Just being there, in the empty house, depressed her. She told her brother to dispose of the house, she had absolutely no interest in it, and couldn't imagine moving back to Savannah.

"Unless you and Allison want to move in."

"It's not big enough for us," he said politely. "Do you want any of her things?" She had some pearls, a diamond watch their father had given her, a few pairs of earrings, most of it was sentimental, but it would have made Paxton feel sick now to start pawing through her jewelry.

"Just send it to me, and take something for Allison."

"Actually," he seemed to clear his throat, "she'd like to have

Mama's clothes, and her fur jacket." It was ten years old and sadly out of fashion, and Paxton looked at him with regret and pity, wanting to suggest he go out and buy his wife a new one, but she didn't.

"That's fine." She'd been a lot taller than her mother, and she would have hated the idea of wearing her clothes. None of it was that important to Paxton.

"What are you going to do now?" he asked the sister he had never really known. He still couldn't understand why she had spent most of the last two years in Viet Nam, even though he had been surprised by how well she wrote, and how good her column was when it was syndicated to the Georgia papers.

"I don't know yet." She looked at him with a sigh, wondering what Tony would have thought of him, and knowing instantly that they would have hated each other. Tony was too blunt and too direct, and too honest to have put up with George's nonsense. "I'm going back to San Francisco tomorrow sometime, and I'll have to talk to them about what they have in mind. I think, for a while anyway, like most of the GIs who come back from Nam, I'll be a misfit. I was last year anyway."

"And you're not going back again?" He looked at her, wondering who she was and if he had ever known her, but she could have told him he hadn't.

"I don't think so. I think I have to stay here now."

"I never really understood why you went . . . except . . . well, that boy dying . . . but that was no reason for you to go to Saigon."

"Maybe not." But somehow that had kept her there for two years. Her sorrow over the war, her need to tell it like it was, her need to be there.

"Anyway, I'll let you know what I'm doing." She said goodnight to him then, and he barely kissed her when he said goodbye. And in the morning when she left, she locked the door, and slipped the key into the mailbox. She wouldn't be needing it anymore, and she had told him to send her things when she let him know where she was staying in San Francisco.

But she felt like a gypsy as she left. She was a person with no home, no roots, and a questionable destination. And if her brother had thought of it, he would have found it strange that someone who had lived under one roof all her life was suddenly so rootless. And others returning from Vietnam were doing the same thing. They came back but they didn't want to go home, they didn't know where to go or what to do, or what would happen when they got there.

She was like that as she flew to San Francisco, and checked into a small hotel. This time there was no suite at the Fairmont Hotel, and the Wilsons didn't invite her to dinner. And after thinking about it for a few days, she decided not to call Gabby. She just didn't know what to tell her. What could you say . . . about France . . . about Ralph . . . about Bill . . . about Tony . . . How did you explain all that to somebody who had been sitting safely at home, going to dinner parties and football games, and movies? You didn't.

She saw Ed Wilson at the paper, and they talked about her plans, and the best he could offer her was a column based on local events. In some ways, it was a small town and a small paper.

"Things are quieter in the country these days. People don't want to hear about the war anymore, Paxton. They're tired of it. They're tired of the noise and the demonstrations, and the complaints. I think this is going to be a quiet time." But he was wrong. He wasn't taking into account the impact of the four students killed and eight wounded by the National Guard at an antiwar demonstration at Kent State University in Ohio. And it proved what Paxton still believed. That some people cared, and the country was still aching over the open wound it had created for itself in Viet Nam and didn't know how to heal now.

But *The New York Times* made it an easier decision. The

*Morning Sun* had been decent to her. And Ed Wilson had given
her a chance in Saigon when she was as green as the countryside
around it. But now she had outgrown them. And out of nowhere, she got an offer from the *Times* to go to Paris and cover
the Paris peace talks. They wanted her to come to New York
and discuss it with them first, but she was very flattered both by
the salary and the offer. They said a lot of very nice things about
the column she'd written for the *Sun,* and they seemed to consider her some kind of expert. It was a little hard to believe, and
she almost giggled like a kid again, as she set the phone down.
She wished she could tell Tony about it, and she thought about
him all that night, silently communing with him wherever he
was. And when she slept, she dreamt of him that night, crawling through bushes and jungle and hiding in tunnels. And when
she awoke, she knew it was only a dream. And yet, she still had
that feeling she had had from the first that he was not dead but
still living. Sometimes she wondered if it was just because she
couldn't stand death anymore. But whatever it was, it was a real
feeling.

Ed Wilson was pleased for her when she told him about the
job with the *Times.* And relieved. He sensed that had she
stayed, she would have become a problem. Like so many of the
boys coming home, she didn't seem to know what to do with
herself, or what she really wanted. It was almost as though Viet
Nam had sapped their strength and their goals and their direction. It had taken their courage and their guts, and taken everything else. Or maybe it was the drugs, he wondered to himself.
Maybe that was it. But whatever it was, he was glad she was
going. She wasn't the same girl anymore, and he knew it. She
was bitter, she was strong, she was sad to her very core, and in a
hidden part of her, he knew she was still angry. He wished her
luck, and she told him to give her love to Mrs. Wilson and
Gabby. She had seen neither of them when she left, and it was a

relief in some ways not to make the pretense that she still cared about the same things they did. The truth was, she didn't.

In New York, she had several meetings at the *Times,* and they put her up at a hotel called the Algonquin. It was filled with journalists and writers and playwrights, and a few businessmen, and they looked like an interesting crowd coming and going, although she didn't talk to anyone. And she liked what the *Times* had to say about what they wanted from her. What they wanted was the truth, and whatever she saw in Paris. They wanted the peace talks, and an interview with Lieutenant Calley before she left, and anything she could think of that related to Viet Nam and what she had seen there. They wanted strong words from her, and the kind of powerful material she had sent back when she was going on missions with Ralph to An Loc and Da Nang, and Long Binh, and Chu Lai, and the other places that had come to mean so much in the past two years she had been there. They wanted it all. The past and the present and the future, until at last the war finally ended. They wanted to consider her their editor-at-large on the subject of Viet Nam, and Paxton knew she couldn't have asked for anything better.

"How soon do I start?" she asked with a look of excitement.

"Tomorrow," the editor in chief answered with a smile of satisfaction. They had been worried that she wouldn't want the job. A lot of people were sick to death of the subject. "Seriously, why don't you tackle the Calley piece next week? We'll go through the appropriate channels to get you in. And you can fly to Paris as soon as you finish. How does that sound?"

"Terrific." If you could call interviewing a man accused of war atrocities "terrific." But she was pleased to have a little time. There was something she wanted to do in New York before she interviewed Lieutenant Calley.

She wandered around New York for a day, feeling the way she had when she first discovered Saigon, investigating new places and smells, watching the people and the action and the traffic. She bought herself a few things to wear, which were much needed by then, particularly if she was going to become an "authority" on Viet Nam for *The New York Times*. And then finally, she went back to her hotel and called him. She sat on the bed and closed her eyes, and then she held her breath, and said a little prayer to Tony, hoping he wouldn't mind. But she didn't think he would, and somehow she knew she had to do it. She called information for Queens, and spelled the name three times, and finally in Great Neck, Long Island, they found him. Thomas Campobello. She prayed it was the right one. But it had to be. There couldn't be too many Thomas Campobellos.

She dialed the phone, and it rang, and for a minute she thought no one would answer, and finally a voice did. It was a woman.

"Mrs. Campobello, please." It was strange now to think that had circumstances been different, this might have been her own name, but she couldn't allow herself to think of that now.

"This is her." A very New York voice answered, but she sounded young, and reasonably pleasant. And unless it was Tony's mother, Paxton knew it had to be Barbara.

"Mrs. Campobello? Barbara Campobello?"

"Yes." She started to sound nervous. "Who is this?" Maybe it was one of those fake surveys where they start talking dirty.

"I . . . I know this is kind of a strange call, but I . . ." Oh, please don't hang up, oh, please . . . "I knew your ex-husband in Viet Nam." There was an endless pause, and both women sat at their respective ends, shaking. "I . . . we were very good friends, and . . . if anything happened to him, he wanted me to call you and Joey." It was a lie, but not completely. Once, very late at night, in bed, he had asked her to look his boy up, if anything ever happened. He just hadn't mentioned the boy's mother. But Paxton thought she had a better chance if she included the double Mrs. Campobello. "I don't mean to intrude at a time like this, but I happened to be in New York and . . ."

"How did you know him?" She was almost whispering at her end, as though his name were forbidden.

"We were . . ." She didn't know what to say. ". . . close friends . . . and . . . he loved Joey very much, I'm sure you know that."

"He hadn't seen him in five years," she said bitterly, but Paxton knew more than she expected.

"He hadn't been back to the States, Mrs. Campobello. After what happened . . . I think he felt he couldn't . . ." A little guilt wouldn't kill her now. It had been almost six years and she had three other kids by Tony's brother. How guilty could she feel, and what difference did it make if it helped Paxton reach out to Joey? "He thought Joey was happy with you and your husband."

"He is," she said defensively, and Paxton could sense that she was losing.

"Does he know what happened to his father in Viet Nam?"

"Only that he's missing in action. He used to write to Joey from time to time, we never kept it a secret from him. I gave him the letters every time," she said, as though trying to clear herself. "I think he was upset when we told him his father died. Any kid would be. But he's kind of a quiet kid, he don't say much." Who would if your mother married your uncle and you never saw your father again? Paxton thought. But she found it interesting that Mrs. Campobello regarded Tony's MIA status as a definite declaration that he had died in Viet Nam.

"Could I talk to him?" There was nothing else to say. "Would you mind that?"

"What do you want to say to him?"

"That his Daddy loved him. That I'm sorry. What he was like at the end. He was one of the bravest men in Viet Nam. He was with a unit unofficially called the tunnel rats, they used to go down in these incredible tunnels the VCs build to circumvent our troops and the South Vietnamese Army. He might find that fascinating and something to be proud of," Paxton said calmly.

"Yeah," Barbara Campobello said. "He might." And then, "I have to ask my husband. What's your name again?"

"Paxton Andrews."

"And you knew him in Viet Nam? Are you a nurse or something?"

"No. I was a correspondent, for a paper in San Francisco. Now I work for *The New York Times,* and I'm leaving for Washington, Georgia and Paris in a few days." She threw it all in to impress her, and she had. Hell, maybe they'd write a story about Tony and his ex-wife and his kid . . . Paxton hadn't missed her mark, she only wondered what the hell Tony had ever done with a bimbo like that, except that he'd been thirteen years old when they fell in love, and eighteen when they married, which made it a little better. "Should I call you back?" Paxton pressed her.

"We'll call you. What's your number?"

"I'm at the Hotel Algonquin in Manhattan."

"I'll call you tonight."

"Thank you," and then, more gently, "I promise I'll try not to upset him . . . I just want to see him . . . for Tony's sake, because I promised." It was true in a way, but she also wanted to see him for herself, because he was a part of Tony. And the boy's mother heard something in her voice and she hesitated for a long moment.

"Were you in love with him?"

Paxton's pause was even longer. "Yes, I was." She was proud of it, but she didn't think it was any of this woman's business. But oddly enough it formed a bond between them.

"So was I, a long time ago. He was a good man . . . and a good father. We had a little girl . . . she died . . . maybe Tony told you about it . . ."

"Yes, he did," Paxton said softly.

"I think that's what finished our marriage. It wasn't anyone's fault, what happened to her, I mean, it was just that every time I looked at him, I thought of it, he was so broken up, I couldn't get away from it. And Tommy . . . well, he made me feel better." Yeah, I'll bet, Paxton thought to herself, but she also suspected that there was some truth to what she was saying. Tony himself had admitted that he was so devoured with grief, and then so obsessed with Joey when he was born, it kind of did something to their marriage. So she wasn't totally wrong. But she had been tasteless in her choice of second husbands. And her lack of tact had driven Tony to Viet Nam, and deprived Joey of his father. But who was she to judge? If Barbara Campobello hadn't married her brother-in-law, Paxton would never have met Tony in Saigon.

"I'm sorry," Paxton said again.

"Yeah . . . I'll call you." And then she was gone, and Paxton spent the rest of the afternoon at the Metropolitan Museum. It was a far cry from Saigon. And when she got back to the hotel there was a message from Joey's mother. Paxton called her right back and to her amusement, she told her to come the next morning. It was Saturday and Joey would be out of school. Tony's mother would even be there, and she wanted to meet Paxton. She didn't tell her that her husband was furious over it, but she had told him they owed it to Tony, and Joey, and that was that, and she was an important correspondent from *The New York Times,* and maybe she'd make a real big stink if they didn't let her see the boy, seeing as it was Tony's last request, that she see Joey. He had agreed, but he was mad as hell. But Barbara didn't care now. She wanted to do it. She gave Paxton the directions on how to come. And the next morning, Paxton rented a car at the hotel, and drove to Great Neck.

And when she got there, they were all waiting for her. Even Mrs. Campobello, Sr., in a black dress, and three little girls in fancy little pink dresses. They looked like bonbons on a cake,

355

and Paxton almost laughed as she looked at them. They were cute, but they were so foreign to her, she didn't know what to say. It was all a little overwhelming.

Barbara and her mother-in-law and the girls were outside when Paxton came, and in the distance she could see a tall, powerful-looking man, but he didn't approach, and she couldn't see from that distance if he looked anything like Tony. And in any case, he didn't seem anxious to meet her. And then Barbara introduced her to her mother-in-law. And when Paxton looked at her, all she could see was Tony. She started to cry almost as soon as Paxton touched her hand, and she had a heavy Italian accent.

"You knew my boy in Viet Nam?" Her voice quavered as she asked, not so much from age, as from emotion.

"Yes, I did." Paxton was fighting back tears, too, as Barbara stepped away with her daughters. "He was a fine man. You can be very proud of him," she said as her voice broke. "He was famous in all of Viet Nam for his courage." The truth was a little stretched there, but not much, and she knew that it would mean a lot to Tony's mother. And then tears stung her eyes and she reached out and took the old lady into her arms.

"It's my fault he wennaway . . . I shouldda stopped what happened, but I didn't."

"You couldn't have," Paxton comforted her, knowing what she meant. They all had so much guilt, all of them. She had told herself for years that it was her fault that Peter had died, and Bill . . . and now Tony? Had she killed them all? Had they? Or had Charlie? "He didn't resent anyone," Paxton reassured her. "He was happy." Mrs. Campobello blew her nose and nodded, and then looked up at Paxton with interest.

"You was his girlfriend?"

Paxton smiled at the term and nodded. "He was a wonderful man, and I loved him very much." And then she wondered why she kept talking in the past tense. Except that for their own sanity, they all kept pretending that they knew he was dead, but they didn't.

"You're a pretty girl," his mother said. "What were you doing over there?" She was torn between curiosity and disapproval.

"I write for a newspaper. That's how I met him." And then she smiled. "We used to fight a lot in the beginning." His mother laughed through her tears at that.

"He used to fight with me too. When he was a kid, he drove me crazy." He wasn't like Tommy, she started to say, and then thought better of it. God had already punished her for that, because Tommy was still there and Tony wasn't.

And then Barbara Campobello came back, and she looked pointedly at Paxton. "Joe's inside if you want to talk to him there."

"That would be nice," Paxton said, and Barbara led her to the front door as Paxton followed. Barbara had obviously had a good figure once, and she had an attractive face, but she seemed hardened, and tough, and somehow disappointed. Paxton followed her inside, and there he was, sitting on the couch, wearing jeans and a clean shirt and a baseball cap, and he looked up at her with exactly the same expression she had come to love so much in his father. "Hi," she said quietly, and much to her surprise, Barbara discreetly disappeared back outside to the others. "My name is Paxton." He looked up at her, and then she sat down slowly in a chair near him. "I knew your Dad in Viet Nam. And he asked me to visit you if I ever came this way. And I happened to be in town, so I thought I'd come by and see you."

He nodded, interested in her, and looking so much like his father that he scared her. "Are you writing a story about my Dad? That's what my Mom said," but Paxton was quick to shake her head.

"No, Joey." She wanted to be honest with him, as honest as

357

she had been with Tony. "I'm here because I loved him. And he loved you very much . . . in fact," she smiled through her tears, "I still love him. I just came back from Viet Nam a couple of weeks ago, and I wanted to come see you."

"What happened?" Joey looked at her almost accusingly. "How did he die?"

"They don't even know for sure that he did die. They just know he's missing in action. That means there was a battle and he got lost, and he never came back. He could be alive, he could be dead, he could be wounded out there somewhere, he could even be a prisoner of the Viet Cong, but no one knows."

"Wow!" He looked excited as he sat up on the couch. "No one told me that!" He was eight years old and she thought he had a right to know, and that was why she had told him.

"No one knows anything. They think he might be dead. And there's a good chance that he could be. But the truth is they're not sure yet."

And then he looked her square in the eye and asked her the hardest question of all. "What do you think?"

"What do I think?" she repeated back to him, wondering if she should tell him. And then she decided to anyway. "I can't tell you why, and I could be wrong, but I think he's still alive. I just feel it in my heart . . . maybe I just loved him so much that I don't want him to die. Maybe that's why I feel like that. But that's how I feel." He nodded, absorbing what she'd said, and moving a little bit closer.

"Do you have any pictures of him?" She could have kicked herself for not bringing them. She hadn't even thought of it.

"I do, back at the hotel. I'll send you copies of them when I get to Paris." He nodded again, satisfied with that.

"Are you going back to Viet Nam again?"

"I don't think so."

"It must have been pretty scary, huh?" He moved closer again, fascinated by her, by how pretty she was, and the fact that she knew his father. There was no one else he could talk to about him. His mom always acted like talking about him was a crime, and whenever he mentioned him, his grandmother cried, and his Dad yelled at him. But Paxton was a direct emissary from his father, and Joey could say anything he wanted.

"It was pretty scary." Paxton smiled at him. "But not all the time. We had some good times too. And he talked about you a lot," she told him, and watched his face light up, and she wanted to reach out and touch him.

"He did?"

"Yeah. All the time. He used to show me your photograph. He wanted to come home and see you." But he never got the chance. Gone at thirty-one, there was a lot he wasn't going to do now.

"Will you come back and see me again?" Joey asked her hopefully, sidling closer to her, and finally reaching out to touch her hair, which was so straight and gold, and so unlike his mother's.

"I'd like that a lot, if your Mom and stepfather don't mind."

Joey made a face and whispered to her, "He's not really my stepdad, he's my uncle!"

And she whispered back, "I know! Your dad told me."

"He told you everything, huh?" And then he laughed. He had a new friend and he really liked her. She stroked his hair then, and touched his face, and she had an arm around him when his mother came back in.

"We had a nice visit," Paxton said, grateful to her for letting her come. "And I'm going to send Joey some pictures of his Dad from Paris."

"Yeah," he said by way of confirmation. And they walked slowly outside, holding hands. It was as though they could communicate now without saying anything. And before she left, she took him in her arms and held him.

"Remember how much he loved you." Joey nodded with

tears in his eyes, and Paxton hugged him to her, remembering how it had felt when her own father died, but she hadn't said any of that to Joey. "I'll call you again."

"Okay."

She saw his stepfather then, lurking nearby, watching her, and he was tall and dark, but he didn't look anything like his brother, and he didn't approach to shake her hand or meet her. He went back to the garage to attend to whatever he was doing. She thanked Barbara Campobello again, and kissed Tony's mother good-bye, and they wished her good luck in Paris, almost as though they knew her.

"I'll send you those photographs," she promised the child again, and he was still waving when she turned slowly around the corner, thinking of him, and how sad it was that he would never know his father.

# CHAPTER 27

∨

She arrived in Paris on a beautiful spring day, a week after she'd gone to Washington to see Pentagon officials and Fort Benning, Georgia, to interview Lieutenant Calley. The interview with him had been brief, and in some ways very painful. He was becoming almost a symbol of the war, and our loss of control, our brutishness and the grief we caused, and as Paxton thought about it later, she was sorry for him, for everyone, for all that had happened.

But Paris healed some of her wounds, and she found a sweet studio near the Seine. And she would walk alone at night, thinking of how different her life was from the life she'd led in Saigon.

Here, her life was solitary and austere, and serious, as she went to the peace talks each day, and interviewed people like Kissinger and Le Duc Tho. And in Saigon, as hard as it was at times, her life had been happier and easier than it was now, filled with only memories of a place she would never see again, and the men she had loved there.

She sent Joey the copies of the photographs, and he wrote her back, in a careful hand, and thanked her. And every now and then, she sent him a postcard from Paris.

She was integrally tied into all the news from Viet Nam, and by October, the American casualties were lower than they had ever been. But still, it would have been nice to know it was all over.

And she spoke frequently to all the connections she had made to find out if there was any news of the MIAs, but there was never any news of Tony. She had stopped expecting it now, and yet there was always that same strange feeling. In some ways, she just thought it was because he would always be alive to her. But by year end, they had almost convinced her it was hopeless.

In November, the *Times* flew her back to Fort Benning, Georgia, for the beginning of the Calley trial, and that was a depressing affair, with hideous photographs, and frightening testimony that, in the end, led to his conviction.

She went to see her brother after the trial, and as usual, had almost nothing to say to him, and she was beyond making the effort with Allison anymore.

She went to Washington after that, for another interview with Kissinger. And then she went to see her editor in New York. And she called and saw Joey again, and this time, she took the boy to lunch. He had just turned nine, and he looked even more like Tony than he had before. She took him to Radio City Music Hall, and before that they had a very grown-up lunch. She had taken him to "21", and he was extremely impressed, as he looked up at the airplanes hanging near the bar. And the head-waiter had recognized her name, as an ardent devotee of *The New York Times,* and they deferred to her every whim, and brought Joey a backpack that said "21".

"This is a terrific place," he said, admiring her taste, and she smiled at him. "Think Dad would have liked it here?" That was the criterion for everything with him.

"I think he would have loved it. We used to talk about coming to New York sometimes. Or going to San Francisco. That's where I used to live. I went to college there." He was enormously impressed and demanded that she tell him all about it, and then as they finished dessert he looked at her with painful seriousness.

"My Dad . . . my other Dad, I mean . . . you know, my uncle." Paxton almost laughed, he was so intense, and somehow it was so grotesque and confusing, and she knew Tony would have laughed too. In fact, he might almost have loved it. "He says that what you said isn't true . . . about my Dad maybe being alive because he's missing in action. He says he's probably dead, and you're crazy."

"He could be right. In fact, he probably is, on both counts." Paxton tried to smile at him. "But the real truth, Joey, is that no one knows. That's what missing in action is. Some of the men who disappeared have been taken prisoners. But we don't even know that about him. I keep pretty close tabs on it, and I call the Pentagon whenever I can, but they haven't heard anything about your dad being on the lists of prisoners. And they haven't found his remains near where he died. So the truth is, no one knows." It was hard for him. It was hard for everyone. It was killing not to know what had happened.

"So that still means he could be alive, doesn't it?" He looked hopeful again, and then as he turned it over in his mind, he looked depressed again.

"But my Dad . . . my uncle . . . he says he's dead. Paxton, do you think he is?"

"No," she said, shaking her head as she looked at him honestly, "Joey, I don't." And with that she took his hand, and held it tightly in her own, thinking again how much he looked like Tony.

# CHAPTER 28

∨

Paxton was busy in 1971, and she spent most of the year in Paris. She still had high hopes for the Paris talks, and conveyed that feeling through much of what she wrote for the paper. But the war still went on. And in Viet Nam, the troops were getting angry. They were getting tired of the war, and there seemed to be more problems with insubordination to the officers than there had been when she was there. And "fragging," GIs using fragmentation grenades to wound their officers "by mistake," was becoming common. Racial issues were tense as well. And in February, the ARVN began operations in Laos, to destroy parts of the Ho Chi Minh Trail. And still, whenever she inquired, in whatever sector, there was never any news of Tony.

And in March, Paxton went back to the States for the rest of the Calley trial, and saw him convicted. And she was in Washington to see the enormous Viet Nam Veterans Against the War demonstration, where some of the men flung their medals on the steps of the Capitol. She wrote about it for the *Times,* and then flew back to Paris.

She was still in Paris when the *Pentagon Papers* were made public by Daniel Ellsberg in June. And in July, when Nixon announced Kissinger's trip to China. And when Thieu was re-elected president of South Vietnam in October 1971, she was still busy covering the peace talks. And finally, in December, she was happy to report that American troops in Viet Nam were down to a hundred and forty thousand, less than a third of what it had been when she was there nineteen months before. And in those nineteen months, there had been not a single bit of news about Tony Campobello. The evidence was overwhelming now. Had he been taken prisoner, or been hiding wounded somewhere, surely by now someone would have heard it. She couldn't offer much hope to Joey anymore, and yet, when he asked her, whenever they talked on the phone, every few months when she called him, she always told him what she felt and that was that his Dad was out there somewhere. He was ten by then and better able to understand it. She had told him about her own father by then, and it gave him a special kinship with her. They had both grown up without their fathers.

And for her, at the end of 1971, life was interesting but strange. She was twenty-five years old, and very beautiful, and greatly admired in Paris. But it was as though a part of her life didn't exist at all, and never had. It was sealed off now. She lived for her work, and a little boy she had come to love in Great Neck. And he was the only love in her life. The rest were memories, and photographs she kept on a table in her living room. Peter . . . Bill . . . Ralph . . . France . . . Pax . . . An . . . and, of course, Tony. It was a strange gallery of people she had loved and lost, in a place she knew she would never go back to, and yet oddly she still missed it. She missed what it had been, and who they were, and what she had been when they all lived there. And yet, she was very successful at what she did, and very respected. And in an odd way, she was content. Not happy, but satisfied, and she still missed him. And his ruby ring was still on her finger.

And in '72, it was painful for her knowing what distress Viet Nam was in. The peace talks had gone nowhere. And in March the North Vietnamese crossed the demilitarized zone with tanks and began moving south down Highway One on a rampage of terror. By May, Route One was filled with refugees and soldiers. The southern ARVN proved no match for the northern troops, and civilians were constantly being killed, children burned and women dying. The photographs she saw, with the rest of the world, particularly in *Time* magazine, were awful.

A second wave of attacks devastated the Central Highlands with similar results in the North. Everywhere people were homeless and starving. The Americans were trying to pull out and turn the war back to the ARVN, the Army of South Viet Nam, and they were losing.

A third attack in April near the Cambodian border, north of Saigon, brought tears to Paxton's eyes as she read the AP reports. Three thousand Vietnamese troops stormed An Loc, and took over the entire province.

It was becoming clear that the "Vietnamization" of Viet Nam was a joke, but a costly one, and no one in Viet Nam was laughing.

By mid April, Nixon authorized the bombing of areas near Haiphong and Hanoi, and for the first time in two years, Paxton was grateful that she hadn't stayed in Viet Nam. It was becoming questionable if anyone would survive it. And wholesale slaughter made no sense. She could do more here in Paris. But what truly worried her, as well, was what would happen to Tony if he were being held prisoner, or hiding somewhere in the countryside. With the constant NVA attacks, American prisoners anywhere in Viet Nam were in great danger. But she still cherished the hope, after two years, that somewhere, out there, he was among them.

And the only thing that distracted her after the fall of Quang Tri in May, was the arrest in June of the five men who had broken into the Watergate complex in Washington. Everyone in the States was talking about it, and although she was still in Paris at the time, she wrote a very amusing editorial, which the

*Times* ran and which won her a lot of favorable comment. She
was slowly becoming something of a star, but it was an aspect of
her life to which she paid little attention. She loved her work,
but cared nothing for the acclaim it brought her. Her mission in
life was to inform, to cut through the lies and brambles with a
sword of truth, as it were, and her journalistic friends teased her
and called her a zealot. But she had no interest whatsoever in
becoming famous. And the fact that Kissinger, Nixon, and important journalists around the world had great regard for her,
pleased her, but to Paxton, it still did not seem of paramount
importance. All that mattered to her was that what she wrote
"made a difference."

The breakthrough in Paris finally came in October 1972, as a
result of meetings between Kissinger and Le Duc Tho, although
few knew it. And on October twenty-first, the North Vietnamese approved the proposed plan for peace, and within five days,
Kissinger himself promised from the White House that "peace
is at hand." But President Thieu of South Viet Nam refused to
sign the agreement, refusing to allow northern troops to remain
in place in the South, for fear of what they would do there.

And less than two weeks later, Nixon was reelected by a
landslide. Two weeks after that, President Thieu demanded
sixty-nine amendments to the agreement that could bring peace
to Viet Nam, and Paxton, along with other knowledgeable journalists, groaned. The situation was, once again, beginning to
look hopeless.

The talks stopped and started all through December. There
were American bombings of military targets, and promises that
fewer civilians would be affected. Hanoi indicated they would
talk if the bombing stopped. The bombs stopped for a single day
at Christmas. Hanoi spoke up again. And at last, on December
thirtieth, the bombing stopped once more, and the talks resumed again. And through it all, Bob Hope had gone to Viet

Nam to put on his Christmas show for the last time. But Paxton wasn't thinking of him this year. She was totally engrossed in the Paris peace talks, and whatever inside information she could get from sources very high up, some of them in Washington. And the high point of her holiday that year was a call from Joey in Great Neck on Christmas Eve. He was fine, and he warmed her heart when he told her in an undertone that he missed her. She was his special ally, special friend, the guardian angel who had been sent by the father he barely knew to love and keep him.

And at last on January 8, 1973, Kissinger and Le Duc Tho resumed serious talks in Paris, the day before President Nixon's sixtieth birthday. And exactly one week after that, Ambassador Ellsworth Bunker, in Saigon, allegedly told President Thieu that if he didn't sign the peace agreement immediately, there would be no further aid from the U.S. forthcoming.

As a result, the cease-fire began less than two weeks later, on the twenty-seventh of January, five days after Lyndon Johnson died. And Nixon demanded that *all* of our POWs be released at once. And he promised to have all American forces out of Viet Nam within sixty days, in March. Paxton heard the news in Paris with disbelief, and silent prayers, that maybe, maybe when the prisoners were released, someone might know something about Tony. And if nothing else, they could lay him to rest at last. It was terrible not knowing. She could hardly stand it her-self anymore, after almost three years. And she had come to realize that not knowing, and always cherishing hope, was too hard on Joey. He always longed for a father who wasn't there, and very probably never would be. Instead of adjusting to the one he had, however lacking he might have been, which by then Paxton knew he was, in spite of the fact that he had been Tony's brother. He resented the boy, she suspected, because he himself felt guilty, and she also suspected that he had gotten more, or perhaps less, than he knew when he got stuck with the first Mrs. Campobello, and by then he knew it.

On February 5, 1973, it was announced that 57,597 men had died in Viet Nam, and just thinking of it tore at her heart, and reminded her of Peter, Bill, and Tony. At times it was hard for her to separate herself as woman and journalist. And when she heard that the first POWs were being released on February twelfth, she lay on her bed and cried, imagining what it must mean to them and their wives to be free at last, from the agony, the loss, the terror.

She was in Paris, writing then, working not only on her articles for the *Times,* but on a book she had promised herself for three years now that she would write about Viet Nam, when her editor called from New York, and asked her to hop a military transport to Manila.

"But why?" Why me? she wanted to ask. It had taken three years for the pain to dim, three years to stop dreaming of the maimed children wandering the streets of Saigon. And the prisoners were coming home, full of their own horror of it. Did she really have to go back there? At long last, she didn't want to go back anymore, didn't long for that incredible green, the smell of smoke at dawn. And now they wanted her to go back and relive it. Back to the memory as she looked into the faces of the men who had been there.

The prisoners of war were flying to Clark Field in the Philippines. And she had two days to get there.

"Is this an order, or a request?" she asked with a tired voice at midnight Paris time. They always called her just before they left the office in New York.

"A little of both," the editor said gently, and Paxton sighed. It was starting again. The hope. The prayers. The wish that someone would have seen him.

"All right," she said after a brief pause. "I'll go."

"Thank you. We appreciate it." But the editor had known

369

she'd go. She couldn't stay away from it. None of them could. Viet Nam had gotten into their very core, their soul. It was a constant pain, even once it grew numb . . . a sorrow . . . a joy . . . an addiction.

# Chapter 29

She flew from Paris to Wiesbaden, West Germany, where she caught a military flight, which got her to Manila eight hours before the POWs arrived. And as she sat among their wives and children, thinking and quietly taking notes, she looked at the faces around her, the children who barely remembered them, and she knew how awful it had been for all of them. She knew it much too well as she watched and listened.

And for some time now, she had begun to accept the loss of Tony. No matter what she felt in her heart, there was no way he could still be alive today, and in her mind, if not her heart, she knew it. And she had said as much to Joey.

But these women were all talking about how they had survived from year to year, with photographs, scraps of news, reports from two men who had gotten out earlier, five who'd escaped two years before. They knew their men were alive, from time to time at least, and they, like their men, had survived it. What remained of them now, was, of course, another question.

And Paxton could feel her stomach turn over as she waited with them, wanting not to increase their pain, their nervousness, or annoy them. She spoke directly to none of them, she just sat there and listened. Later, she would ask for interviews, speak to the men. But now she just wanted to be here and watch and listen. She told herself she was dispassionate, that she was there as a journalist, that she had no right to intrude, but as the men came off the plane that afternoon, she sobbed almost as loud as their wives when she saw them. They were thin, halting, hesitant, battle scarred for the most part, with red-rimmed eyes and fungus in their hair, knuckles swollen to the size of onions from being beaten, legs that seemed wobbly and unstable. On the surface they looked whole, but if you looked beyond that, they looked awful. And as they held each other up, they stood proud, and looked around and cheered as they stood there. It was a victory for freedom and liberty, and love and sheer survival, that touched everyone's heart who saw them.

It was an emotional afternoon, and Paxton spent almost as much time crying as they did. But there was no relief for her, no time off, no incredible embrace they had waited seven years for. How did one survive a time like that? How did one cling to hope? And what did one say to each other when it was over? What if she had been taken prisoner on one of the missions she'd gone on with Ralph! It had been close a couple of times, and she knew it. What if she had been taken prisoner by the Viet Cong? She doubted she could have survived, and marveled that they could.

And the next day, she began her interviews, talking to them after they had been debriefed, talking to their wives, in some cases their children. A photographer joined her eventually, and by the time she was almost through, she herself was overwrought. And then, as she interviewed one of them, she realized he had been a tunnel rat at Cu Chi, and had been taken prisoner not very long before Tony became MIA, and as she attempted to hold her pen, her hand shook so badly she could no longer write what the man was saying. He had been held prisoner for three years, which seemed a long time to him, and to her, but Tony had been gone for just as long and she still didn't know if he was dead or alive now.

"I . . ." Her voice was shaking as much as her hands, "I'd like to ask you something off-the-record." He looked frightened of her suddenly, as though she would ask him something terrible that might disgrace him or his family forever.

"Did you ever know a first sergeant named Tony Campobello when you were at Cu Chi?" He looked at her strangely then and nodded his head, wondering if it was a trick. Maybe Campobello had been an enemy agent.

"Why?"

". . . because I loved him . . . I was in Saigon then," she said in a voice as soft and broken as his own, but he had brought back the past to her and it was much too painful. "He became MIA just after you were taken prisoner . . . and there's been no conclusive report in his case for three years . . . I just thought . . . I wondered . . ." She started to cry and hated herself for it. These people had been through enough without taking on her pain too. But he reached out and touched her hand with his own gnarled, broken fingers. She was his sister now . . . his friend . . . his child . . . And she looked at him through her tears as he answered.

"All I can tell you is that he was alive two years ago. They brought him to one of the prisons I was in. I don't even know what it was called, and I was very sick when I got there," he went on softly, and no one around them could hear them.

"Do you know where it was?" she asked in the same tone of voice.

"No . . . but he was there. I knew him at Cu Chi . . . I hadn't been there long before I was caught by the VC . . . he was tough . . . and he was still alive when they had him. That's all I know. You should ask Jordan. He was there too, and I think he knew him."

But when she finally got to talk to Jordan three days later, he had bad news. Tony was one of three men who had escaped, and Jordan was sure that all three had been killed in the effort.

There had been rumors briefly that only two bodies were brought back, but he was never sure, and he assured her that no one could have escaped their dogs, their weapons, their booby traps, their spears. He would have to have been killed. And in the past two years, their paths had never crossed again, and he had never heard his name. He assured her that Tony was dead. He had to be. And as he told her, he cried, and so did Paxton.

It was a terrible week for her, a brutal time, of facing pain and death and hope and grief and their tales of brutality at the hands of the North Vietnamese. It was endless, and their wives were so brave. By the time it was over, and she went back to France, she felt as though she had been in prison with them. It was the most emotionally exhausting piece she'd ever done, and she swore to herself that if they asked her again, she wouldn't do it. But the piece she wrote as a result was absolutely brilliant, and brought her the praise of her peers, and people began talking about one day Paxton winning the Pulitzer. Ralph used to tease her about it, but that had been years ago, when she was young and green, and so had Tony. And she had her painful answers about him now. There was no hiding from it. And on the first of March, she flew to New York to see his son, and tell him what the two POWs had told her, the first who had seen him briefly two years before, the second who knew he had escaped and was certain he'd been killed by the Viet Cong when they caught him. And from everything she'd heard at Clark Air Force Base, that now seemed certain.

She told Joey as gently as she could before they went to lunch. They went for a long walk in Central Park, and finally she sat him down on a bench and told him. He was eleven now, the same age she had been when her father died, and he was a bright boy, and she knew that he could take it.

"I'm sorry, Joey." Tears filled her eyes again. "I somehow thought that if he'd lived at all, if he hadn't been killed that day, that he'd make it. He was so tough, so strong, so smart . . . so good . . ." But he was gone now, and they both had to face it. Without saying another word, she put her arms around him and held him close to her and they both cried.

"Do you believe it now?" he asked her painfully, and this time she nodded. For his sake as much as her own. At twenty-seven she had loved the man for so long, it was hard to give up hope, but she knew she had to.

"Yes, I do believe it now, Joey. We have to. He's gone." It was like losing him all over again, hearing the words of the man who'd survived the Hanoi Hilton.

"Now what?" the boy asked sadly, as he held her hand.

"I don't know . . ." She felt lost again. Almost as lost as she had three years before. The other women had their men home again and she didn't. "We remember him . . . we think about him and smile, we remember the good stuff, the silly stuff . . . we love him."

"And what about you?" He had always wondered about her, and now he felt he was old enough to ask. He knew she'd been waiting for his Dad, but what would she do now? The same thing she always had done. In Paxton's mind, all that was over. "Think you'll marry someone else?" Joey asked with a worried frown. Maybe someone who wouldn't let her see him anymore.

But she read his thoughts and pulled him closer. "No, I don't. Unless you're willing to grow up real quick. I could wait, you know."

"What are you going to do now? Are you still going to be in Paris?" He missed her when she was there. Between them, they had something very special. It was a little bit of what she had shared with his Dad, but not having children of her own, it was more and less, and different. And she had good news for him in answer to his question.

"It looks like I'll be coming back to New York pretty soon, to work for the *Times* here. Probably at the end of March after the last troops pull out. It won't be long now."

He looked pleased. If he couldn't have his father, at least he had her.

"Maybe your Mom will let us go away for a weekend somewhere when I come back. Think she would?"

"Sure." He would see to it that they'd let him, no matter what. And they were both more peaceful when they went to lunch. Peaceful, but sad. They had finally started to let go of Tony.

# CHAPTER 30

∨

The last American troops left Viet Nam on March 29, 1973, and three days later, on April first, the last American POWs were released in Hanoi. And the day before that, Paxton flew to New York after giving up her apartment in Paris. She was staying at the Algonquin until she found her own place, and when she got to the paper the next day, she couldn't believe it, but they asked her to fly to San Francisco to interview the prisoners of war at the Presidio. And she told them she just couldn't do it. They had to send someone else, she'd just gotten back, she was tired, and she had to look for an apartment. None of which held water, and both she and her editor knew it. And when finally they pressed her, she turned on the editor and told her that she didn't give a damn what they did to her, she wouldn't go, it was just too fucking painful.

They left her alone all that day, and at six o'clock the editor in chief called her in and begged her to go. And finally, tired, jet-lagged, exhausted, and more than a little angry, she relented. She flew out the next day, just in time to meet the plane as it was arriving at Travis Air Force Base. And as she stood looking at the same scene she'd seen in Manila six weeks before, she knew just how draining it was going to be and how painful. But at least this time she was prepared, and she braced herself for what she would hear from the wives, the men, and even their children. And for the next few days, it was every bit as bad as she knew it would be, and worse. But the very worst came when one of the men talked about three men who had escaped, and the story had a familiar ring to it. Part of her wanted not to know, and another part of her told her she had to. And she began asking him the same questions as she had the other men at Clark, but this time, the answers were different. Yes, he was certain three men had escaped. And two others had successfully done it before that. The others who tried it were all killed, he thought, a group of seven once, a foursome, another pair. But some made it through, and of the threesome he referred to, one did. Two were killed, but one of them never came back.

"Who was he?" she asked in a strangled voice, wishing she had never come, not wanting to start the hope again. She was willing to lay him to rest now, why wouldn't they let her? "Do you know who he was, sir?"

"I'm not sure." He racked his memory, which was not what it once had been. They had done everything to him. Electric shock, torture, he had lost both thumbs, and almost lost his leg to gangrene, how the hell did he know who had escaped and lived. How could he do this to her, and yet he was, and she held her breath as she waited. "I know he was from Cu Chi base . . . a tunnel rat . . . but I'm not sure of the name. I might know it if I heard it," he said apologetically, and she was feeling guilty for pumping him, but she had to.

"Tony Campobello?" she whispered.

"That's right." He stared at her. "That's him!" He looked stunned, amazed she knew it. "He escaped, oh . . . I don't know . . . maybe eighteen months ago . . . two years . . . I'm not sure now. And I *know* he made it." She felt faint as she listened to him.

"How do you know, sir?"

"They didn't bring his body back, and . . ." He looked mildly embarrassed. "One of the guards told me."

"Wouldn't he have lied to you?" She almost wanted him to be dead now, wanted not to be tortured with the hope again, but there was no denying what this man said. She couldn't ignore it.

"I don't think so. They hated to admit it when anyone escaped, so if they said it, it was probably true. And they tortured one of the others to teach everyone a lesson."

"Do you know where he might have gone?"

"I'm sorry, I don't. South, I would assume, if he could . . . or he could still be in hiding somewhere in the interior. If he was a tunnel rat, he was probably pretty wily. He could still be alive now." Could . . . and then what? And what was she to tell Joey? That his father "could" be alive somewhere in the interior? Or he could be dead in a tunnel, too, or in a trench, or a hole somewhere, or a tree trunk. She thanked the man, and feeling numb, she finished her interviews and took the red-eye back to New York from San Francisco.

And she spent the next three days locked in her apartment, talking to no one. There was nothing she could do or say. She had to think. She had to go over what they'd said. She read her notes over again and again, but there was nothing she could do. And on Monday, she had made her decision.

She went in to see her editor, and at first she told Paxton she was crazy. But after a little while, Paxton had convinced her. She'd been there before, and she knew the country. There would be others staying now that the military had left. Journalists, medical personnel, a few foreign businessmen, fools, opportunists. Someone was bound to be there. And there was no doubt whatsoever in her mind. She had to go back there, and stay there until she found the answers, no matter how long it took, or what it did to her to be there.

They agreed finally. They had no choice. The choice was to

lose Paxton, or let her go with their blessing, so they let her have everything she wanted.

And that weekend, she went for a long, long walk with Joey. She told him she was going back to Viet Nam to find his father, or his remains, or someone who could tell her for sure what had really happened. She told him about the prisoner of war at the Presidio, and what he had said. He had a right to know, and she had to tell him.

"You know, my Mom and Dad still think you're crazy." He smiled at her, he wondered about it at times himself, but he also knew he loved her.

"Is that what you think?" She smiled at him.

"Sometimes. I don't really care if you are, Pax. It's okay."

"Thanks. To tell you the truth, I think I'm crazy to go back too. But I don't think I'll ever be satisfied until we have the answers. I thought we knew for a while there," after what she'd heard at Clark, from Jordan, "but I guess we didn't. This guy was so sure he made it."

"You really think he could be alive by now? It's been three years since he became MIA." Even Joey sounded skeptical by this time.

"I just don't know anymore, Joey."

He nodded, worried about her now. "How long you think you'll be gone?"

"I don't know. I don't want to promise you anything. I'll write to you, and call you if I can. I don't know what the phone service will be like there now, with the GIs gone. Probably pretty lousy. But I'll do what I can. And I'll come home when I have the answers, and not before."

He grabbed her arm then and held it tightly in his young hand. "Don't get hurt, Pax . . . don't let anything happen to you like it did to Dad."

"It won't," she promised him, as she leaned toward him and kissed his hair, and then stroked it. "I'm not as brave as he was."

# CHAPTER 31

∨

The plane came down at Tan Son Nhut Airport, and from the air it looked the same, but as they flew low, she saw that there were a lot more craters than there had been three years before. And in Saigon, things had changed too. There were more children in the streets, more orphans, more begging Amerasians, abandoned by fathers who had gone home with the military and left them there with mothers who didn't want them. There were more drugs in the streets, more prostitutes, more buildings falling apart. More chaos. And even the Hotel Caravelle seemed somehow less than it had been, although they remembered her, and were very pleasant. And she had a different room this time, which was just as well. She couldn't have borne being in the same room she had once shared with Tony.

The AP office was the same, and she ran into some of the same faces, and in some ways it seemed that nothing had changed, and yet things had. The American soldiers were gone, and subtly that changed things.

She began by establishing her contacts again, and remarkably she still felt at home there. And yet, there were too many memories for her here now, and she had been back in the West for too long. And more often than not, as she lay awake at night, she thought of Joey. Maybe it was different now, too, because she was older. At twenty-seven, she was not quite as anxious to risk her life as she had been five years before. In that sense, she was also different. And thinking of that reminded her of Ralph again, and the missions they'd been on together. Now when she went out into the countryside, she went out alone, with rented cars, or with a driver, or a photographer she got from AP, and everywhere she went, in every town, in every countryside, in every ruin, she asked for Tony. And no one had seen him. But she felt that if she asked enough people for long enough, eventually, if he was still alive, someone would know him. Maybe he was afraid to come out, maybe he was too crippled or too maimed or too injured, and if he was, she would take him home, and heal his wounds and fix them . . . if he was still alive, which was always uncertain. And as she began to see the damage the northern troops had done, and the American bombings before they left, she began to understand how difficult it would have been to survive, and escape unnoticed somewhere. Even knowing he was dead would have been a relief. Something. Some shred of clothing, a bone, some hair . . . anything . . . that had once been Tony.

In April, Graham Martin arrived in Saigon to replace Ellsworth Bunker as ambassador. And in June the Watergate affair exploded in the States, much to Paxton's fascination. Politics seemed to be getting more complicated everywhere these days, and she enjoyed the Teletypes she read in Saigon, while she continued to write articles from there, and search for Tony. And in July, the Senate held hearings on the bombings in Cambodia, which stopped in August. And eight days after that, Nixon appointed Kissinger as Secretary of State to replace Rogers. And that summer, in Viet Nam, things were quiet. It rained constantly, and Paxton continued to drive all over the countryside, showing photographs of him, and asking if they had seen him, but no one had seen him anywhere, and she wound up with pneumonia.

And in September, she was better, and began the search again. And every week, she reported in letters to Joey. It was all beginning to seem more than a little crazy even to her. But everything in Viet Nam always had been. She kept coming across children in the streets who were half American and had been abandoned, and she always gave them what money and food she could, but for them the situation was hopeless. This was the fate France had feared when she had poisoned herself and her children after Ralph was killed. It was hard to believe she was right, but who knew anymore? Who knew anything? Paxton was certain she didn't.

In October, Agnew resigned as Nixon's vice-president, and in November Congress overrode Nixon's veto of the law that would have limited the President's right to wage war. They wanted the same situation never to come again. We had lost in Viet Nam, but they wanted to think twice before we ever got into something like it again. And Congress wanted to maintain their controls on the President forever.

Paxton spent Christmas in Saigon, eight months after she'd gotten there. She told herself she would go home as soon as she found something concrete, or a year after she'd come, if by then she still had no answer. But a year to the day after she arrived, someone recognized Tony's picture and it spurred her on. She was an old peasant woman from the North, and she said she'd found him in a wood and given him food, and then he had been taken away by soldiers. So he had been taken prisoner again, but where and by whom, and then what had happened? She spared Joey the recital of that. There was no point. But she just kept on looking.

And three months later, in August 1974, Nixon resigned, and Ford became president, and the *Times* asked her to come home, and she refused. She was writing beautiful pieces from Viet Nam, and she seemed to have no interest in any other subject.

She spent Christmas in Saigon again that year, her second

since she'd been back. Her brother had given up on her completely by then. And Ed Wilson was intrigued whenever he saw her byline. Her pieces were brilliant, but she seemed obsessed with the country she had gone to as a girl, and which had wounded her, and so many others, so badly. And by then, even Joey was beginning to wonder. Maybe she just liked it there, and maybe she couldn't face the fact that his father was dead, maybe she was more than a little bit crazy, as his parents suggested. He hadn't seen her in almost two years, but the funny thing was, as he secretly told his grandmother sometimes, he still missed her. He wondered if she'd ever come back, but he wasn't sure anymore. He was almost thirteen, and his father had been missing for almost five years, gone from him for ten. It was a hell of a long time to carry a torch for someone. But Paxton didn't seem to want to give up, no matter what, even if it killed her.

And every now and then, someone would recognize a photograph she showed them. But she never really knew if they told the truth, or lied, or wanted a tip, or a reward, or just wanted to please her. It was impossible to tell. But the one thing she could tell, and wrote about in the *Times,* was that South Viet Nam was in big trouble. And she wrote about the Americans secretly promising to get a million people out of South Viet Nam before it fell into Communist hands, which it was becoming obvious that it would soon. And when it did, she knew she'd have to go home and leave Tony there, whether he was alive or not. She would have to go then, and give up. But in the meantime, she just couldn't.

In February 1975 things got tough, and in March they got tougher. Refugees from the North were streaming into Saigon, and farther north, over a million refugees fled the Communists and entered Da Nang, as Hue fell, and North Vietnamese rockets ripped across the city and into the civilians. People were crying and running and falling, and bleeding. Children were lost and trampled by the crowds. And Americans were told to get out, and Paxton with them. The Teletypes into the AP office were going crazy. Everyone had to get out, the Teletypes said, once Hue had fallen. But three days later, people were jamming airports, docks, and beaches trying to get out of Viet Nam by any means they could. And for the last few days, Paxton forgot her futile search and once again turned correspondent.

On Easter Sunday, Da Nang fell to the Communists, and in April the Americans began to pack up, and Paxton with them. It was time to go. It was just a matter of days before it would be all over. The country that had once been so lovely and had cost them so much was about to fall, and secretly everyone knew it.

The Americans still in Saigon were getting anxious about getting out before the Communists arrived, and the Vietnamese who'd been too closely linked to the Americans were panicking that they would be the victims of reprisals. Fifty thousand American and Vietnamese managed to leave during April. But over a million Vietnamese had been promised that they would be able to leave for the States, and in the last weeks of April it became obvious that this was impossible, and very few were going to make it.

Paxton was warned again by the *Times* to get out, but after contacting the ambassador, he promised her a seat in the very last plane, no matter what, and with one bag packed, ready to go, she continued her coverage of the fall of Saigon, with her own camera. She had totally abandoned her search for Tony by then. She had accepted it at last. He was dead, and the people in the countryside who said they had seen him had lied. They had said what they thought she wanted to hear. And as the last days of Saigon came, she knew that he had to be dead now. And she was so exhausted by then, she couldn't think about him anymore. All she wanted was to get back to the States, to a clean bed, a safe town, and see Joey.

On April twenty-fifth, President Thieu left for Taiwan. And

on April twenty-eighth, the Communist troops faced the South Vietnamese Army at the Newport Bridge, at the gates of Saigon. Paxton was staying in the embassy by then, waiting for the very last bulletins. And if she had to go, she wanted to be one of the very last to leave Saigon.

And in a gentle rain on the twenty-ninth, the embassy aides solemnly announced that Option IV was going into effect. It was about to be the largest helicopter evacuation on record. The million Vietnamese that had been promised asylum were being abandoned, and only those the Americans could get out by helicopter would, but it wouldn't be many. All day Paxton watched the operation begin, as helicopters carried refugees and Americans to waiting carriers offshore, and the Communists continued to rocket the Saigon airport.

In eighteen hours on April twenty-ninth, Paxton reported later, seventy U.S. choppers ferried people between the embassy and the waiting carriers. One thousand Americans, and six thousand Vietnamese got out. Not the million that had been promised.

There were buses around the city to bring people to the embassy grounds, but there was so much panic that the buses got bogged down and never got anywhere, and people began running through the streets, screaming and hysterical, and everywhere there were lost and abandoned children. Paxton tried to go out at noon to help some of the people in the streets. She could get nowhere. You couldn't move in the frantic crowd. The embassy gates had been forced open hours since, and crowds of people were on the embassy grounds trying to force their way onto choppers. They were the people of the city, the country, the mountains, some Americans, mostly Vietnamese, desperate to escape the Communists before they took over. She knew she had to go soon, and as she headed back through the embassy compound, she felt her arms and body clawed as she tried to go back the way she had come to where she knew the ambassador was waiting. And then suddenly an arm pulled at her, it was a man, an ancient Vietnamese dragging her with him as he forced his way along, and she saw as she tried to wrestle away from him that he was barely conscious. He smelled terrible and he looked worse, and he was caked with mud as she fought free of him and he lurched forward again into her arms. And then she saw . . . it wasn't possible . . . it couldn't be . . . it was a cruel joke . . . she had finally lost her mind in the midst of the fall of Saigon.

"No . . ." It wasn't. She only wanted it to be.

The man said something to her in Vietnamese as he straightened up again, and instinctively she reached out to him and he started to collapse in her arms, but she knew then without a doubt. It was Tony.

"Oh, my God . . ." People were pressing all around them to get on the helicopters, and most of them weren't going to make it. "How did you get here?" she asked, still confused and stunned as she stared at him, trying to be sure she hadn't dreamt it.

He said something in Vietnamese again, and then listening to her, he knew. He didn't know who she was, but he knew she was American and he was safe now, as she guided him forcefully to one of the buildings.

"First Sergeant Anthony Campobello, Cu Chi Base, Viet Nam," he recited as she dragged him physically toward where they were loading the choppers. They couldn't wait anymore. And she had her story. She wasn't staying there another minute with him. She had to get him out, before someone stopped them.

He had a vicious gash on one arm, and then he looked at her oddly, and tears began to slide down his cheeks as she half carried, half dragged him toward the choppers.

"Come on," she shouted at him over the racket, as someone tried to force a baby into her arms. But she wasn't taking anyone but him. She had fought too hard and long for this. She had looked for him for five years, and so had his son while he waited.

"Tony, come on!" He started to collapse before they reached the chopper, and they had to climb a narrow stair, which she wasn't sure he could still climb, and she couldn't drag him, and there was no one there who would have helped her. "Dammit . . . lift your feet . . . come on, climb . . ." She was screaming at him, and she was crying too. But he was crying with relief. It had taken him two months to come down from his hiding place in the tunnels he had found and used until he reached the outskirts of Saigon, and now he had just made it. And she was there, and he didn't understand how or why he had found her. But it didn't matter anymore. She was there. And they were together, even if they died now.

"This man is a POW!" she shouted at someone who didn't care, and then suddenly a strong pair of arms dragged him up and free of the crowd and pushed him into the chopper, and suddenly with a huge push, she was in it just behind him, and they were pulled to safety as they headed to the open seas, and she was suddenly reminded of the Dustoffs that had saved the wounded men. And now they were free, as Viet Nam shrank slowly behind them. There were people still screaming as they left, people crying, people begging. People who would die and be killed. But she couldn't help them anymore. She had written about them. She had been there off and on for seven years. She had done everything she could for them. And it had been too long. It had cost too much. Too many had died. But at least not Tony. She looked at him in disbelief as he lay in her arms, battered, bruised, scarred, almost unrecognizable. But it was he, and he smiled at her as they began their descent toward the deck of the carrier and safety.

"Where the hell have you been?" he grinned with his dirt-covered face. He had lived in tunnels he had made and found and used for the past two years, and he had survived by wiles and horrors she couldn't have dared to think of. And now, by sheer miracle, by nothing more than chance, or the hand of God, he had found her.

"I've been looking for you," she said softly, gently brushing the dirt from his face. He had hidden in a wagon full of earth and dirt on the way into the city. "I've been looking for you for a long, long time, mister . . ." And so had Joey.

"Welcome home," a voice said, as someone helped them down. "Welcome home!" the voices said as they were welcomed to safety from the chopper, and Tony stood there and cried as she held him in her arms, and their flag soared overhead, and he whispered in the din.

"I love you, Delta Delta . . ."

At eleven o'clock the next day, on April 30, 1975, Saigon fell, and the South Vietnamese surrendered to the North. The battle we had fought for and with them for so long was over.

And on the USS *Blue Ridge*, Paxton and Tony steamed toward home, and their son, and the world they had lost for too long. A world they had all but forgotten. But Nam was gone now. A distant memory . . . a nightmare . . . a dream. For them, and everyone else, now, it was finally over.